SANFORD MEISNER
O N · A C T I N G

SANFORD

MEISNER

ON · ACTING

SANFORD MEISNER

AND

DENNIS LONGWELL

INTRODUCTION BY SYDNEY POLLACK

VINTAGE BOOKS

A DIVISION OF RANDOM HOUSE   NEW YORK

A Vintage Original, August 1987
First Edition

Copyright © 1987 by Sanford Meisner and
Dennis Longwell

Library of Congress Cataloging in Publication Data

Meisner, Sanford.
    Sanford Meisner on acting.
    "A Vintage original"—T.p. verso.
    1. Acting. I. Longwell, Dennis. II. Title.
PN2061.M38 1987   792'.028   86-46187
ISBN 0-394-75059-4 (pbk.)

Book design by Guenet Abraham

Manufactured in the United States of America

Pages 251–252 constitute an extension
of this copyright page.

D987

For James Carville

I wish the stage were as narrow as the wire of a tightrope dancer, so that no incompetent would dare step upon it.
—Johann Wolfgang von Goethe (1749—1832): *Wilhelm Meisters Lehrjahre*, book 4, chapter 2

This quotation Meisner has framed and hung on the wall of his office.

Acknowledgments

I want to thank Kent Paul, who first suggested that I write this book, and whose friendly encouragement helped to keep me going when its end was only dimly in sight. I thank him, too, for lending me his archive on the Group Theatre, material which enriched the biographical sections of this work, and for generous permission to incorporate material drawn from transcripts of the excellent documentary film he produced, *Sanford Meisner: The Theater's Best Kept Secret.*

I am grateful also to Dorothy L. Swerdlove, Curator of the Billy Rose Theater Collection, for swiftly answering tough questions, and to her colleagues on the Staff of the Performing Arts Research Center of the New York Public Library at Lincoln

Center for their unflagging assistance. I received help also from the staff of the John Jermain Memorial Library in Sag Harbor, New York, who secured for me dozens of urgently needed books from libraries throughout the state of New York.

Sanford Meisner joins me in expressing deep appreciation to James Carville for his guidance and discipline in adhering to the clarity with which the technique was expressed. We also admire and thank our tireless agent, Connie Claussen, and our insightful editor, Joseph Fox.

—Dennis Longwell
Sag Harbor, New York
October 1986

Contents

Introduction

We called him Sandy but it felt daring and dangerous, like ordering a martini in a nightclub when you were sixteen and trying to pass for twenty-one. He was too awesome a presence for the familiarity of a first name. It was 1952 and I was eighteen years old and had blundered into his classes at the Neighborhood Playhouse in New York. Nothing had prepared me for the intensity of this experience. It wasn't that he was harsh or mean; it was only that he was so frighteningly accurate. You felt he knew every thought, impulse or feeling in your head, that he had an ability to x-ray your very being and there was absolutely no place to hide. Each time he spoke about acting he crystallized ideas that you somehow knew were true, even though you had no idea that you'd ever sensed them before—like those physicists who discover new particles simply because the theory for their existence is so beautiful. When Sandy spoke it was often difficult to keep from jumping up and shouting, "That's true! That's right! That's absolutely right!" It was stunning to have him hurling those lightning bolts directly to the inside of your brain. One poor guy simply couldn't contain himself and actually *did* blurt out, "My God, that's right!" Sandy simply mumbled, "Thank you, you've just confirmed twenty-five years of my work."

Sanford Meisner's work was, and is, to impart to students an organized approach to the creation of real and truthful behavior within the imaginary circumstances of the theater. Like his contemporaries from the Group Theatre, he has been changing the face of American acting ever since he was first exposed to the ideas of Konstantin Stanislavsky in the nineteen thirties. Harold Clurman, Lee Strasberg, Stella Adler, Bobby Lewis and Sanford Meisner emerged from the Group Theatre as the preeminent teachers of what has come to be known as 'the Method', a kind of lazy label that refers to most of contemporary American acting. Each one of these teachers has really made his own method, honing down and personalizing his approach over the years. Though they all were extraordinary teachers, Sandy's approach has always been for me the simplest, most direct, least pretentious and most effective.

The Neighborhood Playhouse offered a two-year intensive course in all aspects of the theater. It was unequalled anywhere, and even though the faculty boasted such luminaries as Martha Graham, Jane Dudley and Pearl Lang, it was Sandy's daily acting classes that kept our adrenaline pumped up for two years. When I graduated in the spring of 1954, I was invited to return the following fall on a fellowship as his assistant, and so I had the extraordinary opportunity to continue to learn from him for another six years until I moved to California in 1960 to begin directing. I had no aspirations to teach, and certainly none to direct, but the chance to continue to observe and learn from Meisner was impossible to pass up. When truths about one art are deep enough, they become true about all art, and so although Sandy addressed himself only to the art of acting, I was, without knowing it, absorbing the foundation of what would become a very specific approach to directing. The fact is that every area in which I function as a director—writing, production design, costume design, casting, staging, cinematography, even editing—is dominated by, and concerned with, the principles and ideas I've learned from Meisner.

Sandy used to say, "It takes twenty years to become an actor." We thought he was exaggerating. We should have known better; he wasn't. He was referring to that time, if it should come, when all the principles and ideas would be chewed up and digested into a kind of actors' instinct, a technique that functioned almost by itself. He never wanted the work to be *about* technique. If you were his student, you learned technique as a means to an end, never as an end in itself. You'd be surprised by how many acting teachers don't understand that.

In 1981, I went back to New York to film some of Meisner's classes for a documentary. We worked in a small downtown theater given to us by Joe Papp. It had been twenty-one years since I had observed Sandy in action. Of course he had aged. He'd had a laryngectomy (the removal of his vocal cords), had been struck by a van that shattered his hip, had two cataract operations and wore thick glasses with a microphone attached to them to amplify the new way he'd learned to speak by swallowing air. But the same "high" was there in the class, the same intense concentration and the sense of falling forward into new areas of understanding and experience. Some contemporaries of mine, old-timers who had made the pilgrimage back to take the classes again, were present. They were just as nervous in front of him as they had always been—and they were learning just as much as they always had. The only vivid difference to me was that because of the effort involved for Sandy to speak, there were fewer words. When they came, they were like rich, boiled-down broth. (As I write this, I think of a remark made about Chekhov by Maxim Gorky: "In Chekhov's presence everyone felt in himself a desire to be simpler, more truthful, more one's self.")

This is a book about acting. It's also a book about a lot of other things by a man who has spent his life weeding away what is unnecessary, and trying to demystify this process of igniting an actor's imagination and disciplining the truth of his behavior. The first thing that will strike you is that there is no mumbo-jumbo here, no mysterious, elitist attitude about theory. Some of it may appear simple. As with all of Sandy's technique, that appearance is deceptive. It isn't simple; it's just the clarity with which he offers it. Anyone who has ever tried to work truly and privately on a stage or in front of a camera knows that it is anything but simple—at least for the first twenty years.

I believe there are only a few people who can really teach the technique of acting. Most are well-read and intelligent, and confuse their ability to theorize and intellectualize about the subject with an ability to cause real growth in an actor. There are almost no good books about acting. This is one of the best. I envy all of you who may be discovering Sandy for the first time.

—Sydney Pollack

Prologue

When they learn that I teach acting, people who love the theater but are not of the theater often ask me just what one teaches to hopeful aspirants that turns them eventually into trained actors.

"Decent diction, of course," they go on to suppose. "And then voice control and bodily grace. But what else—or is there anything else?"

There is. The other elements in a person's training that will make him or her a distinctive and interesting actor are the most delicate factors that a teacher can impart. One can use standard principles and textbooks in educating people for law, medicine, architecture, chemistry or almost any other profession—but not for the theater. For, in most professions, every practitioner uses the same tools and techniques, while the actor's chief instrument is himself. And since no two persons are alike, no universal rule is applicable to any two actors in exactly the same way.

I once spent four lovely months in Puerto Rico in a little house on the beach where I went specifically to write a book about these matters. I wrote two chapters. Later, when I reread them, I didn't understand them, and I thought that was the end of the book. I decided that a creative textbook about acting was a contradiction in terms, and that it was foolish, even wrong, to attempt to write one.

Still, friends whom I respected convinced me that my experience in teaching young actors their craft was of value, and that perhaps with a collaborator my ideas could be put into the form of a book. A collaborator was found, a book was written, and I was bitterly disappointed at the results. My basic principles were now on paper, but, paradoxically, how I uniquely transmit my ideas wasn't sufficiently apparent. My students weren't in those pages either, nor was the classroom in which we interacted week in and week out. Lastly—and this was the greatest lack—the drama inherent in our interaction, as they struggled to learn what I struggled to teach, was missing. I came to realize that how I teach is determined by the gradual development of each student.

That particular book was never published. My theatrical instinct should have told me why. The confessional mode is impossible to sustain at length in the theater, which is an arena where human personalities interlock in the reality of doing. When we think of the characters in a play, we naturally think of them in active, objective terms. Oedipus, he. Phaedra, she. *Exeunt* Lear and the Fool.

All this past history is related to explain to the reader the form this new collaboration has taken. In it I appear not as "I," but as "he." That is, I appear as I am: a teacher, surrounded by gifted students, of a difficult and ultimately mysterious art, that of acting. Bernard Shaw, who I believe was the greatest theater critic since Aristotle, wrote: "Self-betrayal, magnified to suit the optics of the theatre, is the whole art of acting." By "self-betrayal," Shaw meant the pure, unselfconscious revelation of the gifted actor's most inner and most private being to the people in his audience. In these pages the student actors reveal themselves through the various demands of the exercises in order to achieve the self-knowledge needed to apply the basic principles of my concept of acting. I, too, betray myself in the sense that here, in order to teach what I know, I am forced to reveal much more of myself than any prudent man would confess to his priest.

One final word: if I risk censure for making myself the central character in the chronicle that follows, I do so in the name of the art of theatrical self-revelation, which is exactly the role I play in in my classroom. Stage center!

—Sanford Meisner
New York City
October 1986

Setting the Scene: Duse's Blush

Everything should be as in real life.
—Anton Chekhov to the cast of the first production
of his play, *The Seagull*, St. Petersburg, 1896

At first glance, except for the twin beds, the room resembles any number of small classrooms almost anywhere in the country. Its white plaster ceiling, pale yellow tongue-and-groove wooden walls and waxed, black-asphalt tile floor evoke the campus of a teachers' college somewhere in the Midwest or, in its cloistered quiet, the interior of a one-room schoolhouse at dawn.

To the left of the room's center stands a large, gray wooden desk—clearly the teacher's—set at an angle before a slate blackboard. To its left is a wall of windows, which look out into a courtyard where, through venetian blinds, only the tops of trees can be seen. Below the windows on a simple platform are two rows of folding chairs, about twenty in all, for the students. Two framed exhortatory maxims written in the style of pseudo-illuminated manuscripts hang on either side of the blackboard. Be Specific! says one, and the other, An Ounce of BEHAVIOR is Worth a Pound of WORDS.

The room seems ordinary except for the two beds, which some-one has pushed against the wall opposite the windows. Squat and wide, the beds were specially constructed of two-by-fours bolted together with six-inch steel bolts, and seem sturdy enough to support the combined weight of a soccer team. The striped tick-ing of each mattress is partially covered with a rumpled green cotton bedspread and a pillow without a pillowcase. Like the teacher's desk, the beds have been painted battleship gray. There is something surreal about them. Perhaps it is their exaggerated sturdiness or their utilitarian color that makes them seem more like trampolines than beds or, conjoined as they are now, like the canvas-covered floor of a boxing ring.

Other objects not noticeable at first share the Magritte-like surrealism of the beds: an empty bookcase with a black desk phone and two empty whiskey bottles on its top; a coatrack missing one of its three legs; a console television set with no insides; a mirror propped against the wall, reflecting the sky outside; a long wooden table also painted gray. Together they complete the room's spare furnishings.

In this special New York City classroom in the Neighborhood Playhouse School of the Theatre, as in dozens of similar rooms reaching back in time to the early 1930s, Sanford Meisner has taught acting. After fifty years the number of his students is unknown, but it certainly runs into the thousands. While no individual can speak for all of them, perhaps Joanne Woodward, who studied first as a college student with Sandy (as he is invari-ably called by his students) and later returned to him as an adult, suggests most succinctly what he may mean to the majority of them. "I went back to Sandy because to me he was a teacher," Miss Woodward recalled recently. "To me he was the *only* teacher. This was after I had done *Three Faces of Eve* and had won an Academy Award. It was 1959, and it was a revelation to me. It was a whole turning point in my growth as an actress."

The American playwright David Mamet, who studied acting

with Meisner at the Neighborhood Playhouse, also spoke recently of his importance. "Here was a man who, especially to my generation in the sixties, actually knew something. One of the first authentic people that I, and most of us, had ever met in our lives. Of course he was autocratic about those things he believed in because he knew them to be the truth. And we knew we were being exposed to the truth—that is, to something which was absolutely practicable, which absolutely worked, and which we wanted desperately to learn."*

Sanford Meisner was born on August 31, 1905, in the Greenpoint section of the New York borough of Brooklyn, the firstborn child of Herman and Bertha Meisner. The Meisners, both Jews who had emigrated from Hungary—she as a baby, he as a young man of sixteen—fled the anti-Semitism of the Polish immigrants of Greenpoint and moved to the Bronx a few months after the birth of their son. They settled in an area of the South Bronx in a house on Honeywell Avenue where, two years later, a second son, Jacob, was born. During a trip to the Catskills, made in an effort to improve three-year-old Sanford's health, little Jacob was inadvertently given unpasteurized milk to drink, and the disastrous result was a wasting disease, bovine tuberculosis, from which the second son never recovered.

"I have had considerable experience in psychoanalysis," Meisner recently told an interviewer, "so I know quite clearly that the death of my brother when I was five and he was three was the dominant emotional influence in my life from which I have never, after all these years, escaped. When I went to school —after school, anytime—I lived in a state of isolation as if I was some kind of moral leper, because my parents, who were good people but not too bright, told me that if it hadn't been for me, they wouldn't have had to go to the country, where my younger

---

*The Woodward and Mamet quotes are from transcripts of filmed interviews made for the documentary *Sanford Meisner: The Theater's Best Kept Secret*, produced by Kent Paul and distributed by Columbia Pictures.

brother got ill, and from which illness he died. The guilt that this caused was horrendous. In my childhood I rarely had friends. I lived, as I'm afraid I still do, in a world of fantasy."

A sister, Ruth, to whom Meisner was close—she died in 1983 —and a second brother, Robert, born when Meisner was sixteen and the family had moved to the Flatbush section of Brooklyn, and with whom he has lost contact, completed the household.

Meisner remembers telling his first-grade teacher that he wanted to be "an actor" when he grew up, and, during his teen-age years, directing various cousins in *tableaux vivants* based on themes of death and honor inspired by newsreel views of American soldiers in World War One. But for most of his youth he found an emotional release in playing the family's piano. After graduating from Erasmus Hall High School in 1923, he entered the Damrosch Institute of Music (later absorbed into the Juilliard School) for an additional year's study of the piano and related subjects. But the idea of acting professionally persisted, and at nineteen he began.

"I always wanted to be an actor," Meisner recalls. "I had a friend—I was in Flatbush then—who also wanted to be an actor; his name was Monkey Tobias. He told me that a place called the Theatre Guild was hiring kids, so I went there. Philip Loeb and Theresa Helburn interviewed me, and I remember lying elaborately about my past in the theatre; it may have started with Salvini for all I know. I remember them laughing, but not laughing at me. So I got a job as an extra in Sidney Howard's *They Knew What They Wanted*, and starring in it was the great Pauline Lord. She was a genius, pure and simple. She'd sit backstage and work on her crossword puzzles. 'What's a three-letter word for something a man wears on his head?' she'd ask. 'Hat? Cap?' How could she decide? That's how simple she was. But she was a genius. She had been the original Anna Christie, and I loved to see her play. By that time I was beginning to realize that acting which really dug at me was what I was looking for."

Herman Meisner had become a furrier on his arrival from Hungary, a job he held for over fifty years. His son does a wonderfully funny imitation of Herman in which he is introduced to a young woman wearing a mink coat, suavely kisses her hand and then deftly blows onto the sleeve of the coat to determine the quality and value of the fur. A career in clothing manufacturing was his father's expressed wish for him, and briefly, to please his father, Meisner worked as a stockboy in a pants factory and a lace store. This was before his success at the Theatre Guild. The elder Meisner's response to his son's new career was at first stunned silence. "I told them at dinner," he recalls. "I announced that I had become an actor. Dead silence. No one said a word. My father, my mother, my sister. Then, during dessert, my father asked, 'How much are they paying you?' I said, 'Well, after the first four weeks, if the play is a success, they give you ten dollars a week.' All hell broke loose! The chaos, the eruption at the table when I said ten dollars a week was terrific! But I went right on!"

Meisner received a scholarship to study at the Theatre Guild School of Acting, which was directed by Winifred Lenihan, an American actress who had been the first to perform Bernard Shaw's *Saint Joan* in New York. She was, in Meisner's opinion, "a stock-company technician," and the school was "a very mediocre place." At this time Meisner was introduced through a musician friend to Aaron Copland, a young composer newly returned from studying in Paris, who in turn introduced him to a recent student at the Sorbonne, his friend Harold Clurman, who, Copland realized, was as passionate about the theater as Meisner was. In a short time Clurman became a stage manager, then a play reader, for the Theatre Guild. Through this friendship, Meisner was introduced to another young theater lover, Lee Strasberg. "Strasberg had a great, uplifting influence on me," Meisner recalls. "He introduced me to quality actors and artists of various kinds, and this helped enormously to solidify my emotional needs. I learned from him. I solidified my natural tastes and inclinations with his help. For example, together we went to the Metropolitan Opera and saw the great Russian singer Chaliapin. What made him preeminent was his possession of deep emotional truth and theatricality of form."

Clurman and Strasberg joined with another Theatre Guild worker, Cheryl Crawford, and in 1931, after three years of talks and fund-raising, the triumvirate selected twenty-eight actors to form the legendary Group Theatre. Although it existed as an institution for only ten years, the Group was to exert a profound influence on the developing art of American acting. Meisner, only twenty-five at the time, was a founding member. The result was fortuitous. "Without the Group," Meisner has said, "I would have been in the fur business."

For an insight into the importance of the Group Theatre in the artistic life of the United States in the 1930s, here are the words of playwright Arthur Miller:

"[My] sole sense of connection with theater came when I saw the productions of the Group Theatre," Miller wrote in the introduction to his *Collected Plays* (published in 1957, over three decades after the Group had been disbanded). "It was not only the brilliance of ensemble acting, which in my opinion has never been equalled since in America, but the air of union created between actors and the audience. Here was the promise of prophetic theater which suggested to my mind the Greek situation when religion and belief were the heart of drama. I watched the Group Theatre from fifty-five-cent seats in the balcony, and at intermission time it was possible to feel the heat and the passion of people moved not only in their bellies but in their thoughts. If I say that my own writer's ego found fault with the plays, it does not detract from the fact that the performances were almost all inspiring to me. . . ."

When in 1938 the Group Theatre took to London its most celebrated production, Clifford Odets' *Golden Boy* (in which Meisner played the featured role of the menacing gangster, Eddie Fuseli), the critic for the London *Times*, James Agate, said simply: "The acting attains a level which is something we know nothing at all about."

The source for the quality of the acting in the Group Theatre sprang from the famed Moscow Art Theatre and from the theory and practice of acting, the System, evolved by its co-director, Konstantin Stanislavsky. Stanislavsky was doubly important to the Group. First, he was the teacher of Richard Boleslavski and Maria Ouspenskaya, two noted Moscow Art Theatre actors who emigrated to New York and in 1924 founded the American Laboratory Theatre. In its six years of activity, this school trained several hundred American actors and directors in an early version of the Stanislavsky System. Actresses Stella Adler, Ruth Nelson and Eunice Stoddard were students and members of the Lab's repertory company before joining the Group. Lee Strasberg was a student there in 1924, and he and Harold Clurman also studied in the directors unit.

Clurman was later to write in his history of the Group Theatre, *The Fervent Years:* "The first effect [of the Stanislavsky System] on the actors was that of a miracle. . . . Here at last was a key to that elusive ingredient of the stage, true emotion. And Strasberg [who was the chief director of the Group's productions during its early years] was a fanatic on the subject of true emotion. Everything was secondary to it. He sought it with the patience of an inquisitor, he was outraged by trick substitutes, and when he had succeeded in stimulating it, he husbanded it, fed it, and protected it. Here was something new to most of the actors, something basic, something almost holy. It was revelation in the theatre; and Strasberg was its prophet."

Stanislavsky's second point of contact with the Group was more direct. In the spring of 1934 Harold Clurman and Stella Adler met with the Russian director, who was convalescing in Paris, and for more than five weeks Miss Adler worked with him to clarify those aspects of the System (in the version taught to her by Strasberg) that caused difficulty for her and other members of the Group. The result of her work, which she reported to the Group the following summer, was to deemphasize the importance Strasberg had placed on "affective memory"—which might be defined as the conscious attempt on the part of the actor to remember the circumstances surrounding an emotion-filled event from his real past in order to stimulate an emotion which he could use on the stage. Rather, Miss Adler said, Stanislavsky now thought that the key to true emotion was to be found in a full understanding of the "given circumstances"—the human problems—contained in the play itself. This shift of emphasis was critical, and it led directly to a diminution of Strasberg's hold on the acting company and to his eventual resignation from the Group in 1935. On this issue, Meisner sided with Stella Adler, who was later to become a noted acting teacher and close friend, and affective or emotional memory plays no role in the system Meisner has evolved.

When an interviewer asked, "How were you introduced to the Stanislavsky System?" Meisner's reply was straightforward. "In the Group Theatre, by the pioneer leadership of Harold Clurman and Lee Strasberg; from Stella Adler, who worked with Stanislavsky and to whom I listened attentively and rewardingly; and by the actor Michael Chekhov, who made me realize that truth, as in naturalism, was far from the whole truth. In him I witnessed exciting theatrical form with no loss of inner content, and I knew that I wanted this too. And finally, from the lucid and objective approach of [Ilya] Sudakov and [I.] Rapoport," Russian theorists whose writings stressed the importance of the reality of doing, the foundation of Meisner's system, and were circulated throughout the Group in an English translation in the 1930s.*

On November 30, 1936, the Group Theatre's new production, *Johnny Johnson (A Legend)*, by Paul Green opened. The play is remembered today primarily for its musical score, which was the first work the German expatriate Kurt Weill wrote in the United States. In the program for the play, under "Who's Who in the Cast," Sanford Meisner published a biographical note which is remarkable on two counts. First, it provides an insight into how he felt about his career as an actor; second, the final sentence announces the beginning of a new career: "Sanford Meisner (Captain Valentine) was so long entrusted with the carrying of a spear that it came as a great shock—but a pleasant one—to see him do a full-fledged characterization in 'Gold Eagle Guy.' [This work, by Melvin Levy, was produced in 1934.] He carried the

* Paul Gray, "The Reality of Doing," *Tulane Drama Review* (special edition, "Stanislavsky in America"), Fall 1964, 139.

spear for both the Theatre Guild, whose school he attended, and for the Group. Meisner is a native of the borough of Brooklyn, although he took care to attend school in Manhattan. His schooling included the Damrosch Conservatory, which turned him into a skilled pianist. Since 'Gold Eagle Guy' he has regularly appeared in featured roles for the Group. He teaches acting at the Neighborhood Playhouse."

This shift from spear carrier to teacher is an amusing metaphor. In reality, Meisner's career as an actor had blossomed. In the previous season alone, he had created critically acclaimed roles in two plays by the Group's resident playwright, Clifford Odets: Sam Feinschreiber in *Awake and Sing!* and the young son, Julie, who is afflicted with sleeping sickness in *Paradise Lost*, the part Meisner considers the finest of his career. In addition he had co-directed with Odets the latter's famous one-act play, *Waiting for Lefty*. In the future, Meisner was to play important roles in such Odets works as *Rocket to the Moon* (1938) and *Night Music* (1940), and he continued to act in the theater long after the Group disbanded in 1941. His last stage role was Norbert Mandel in S. N. Behrman's *The Cold Wind and the Warm*, directed by Harold Clurman, which opened in December 1958. The following year, after a rift with the administration of the Neighborhood Playhouse, he became director of the New Talent Division of 20th Century–Fox and moved to Los Angeles, where he began a promising career as a film actor.

But emotionally it was only teaching that fulfilled Meisner in his maturity in the profound way that the piano had fulfilled him as a youth. "The only time I am free and enjoying myself is when I'm teaching," he has repeatedly said. "I love the analysis of technique. I like to work with people who bring a certain seriousness and depth to what they're doing. I feel alive and related when I'm teaching. I get an emotional release from it." The reason why is readily understandable. "All my exercises," he told an interviewer nearly a decade ago, "were designed to strengthen the guiding principle that I learned forcefully in the Group— that art expresses human experience—which principle I have never and will never give up. So now, after about forty years, I am the possessor of a way of working with actors that in practice seems to have worked beneficially."*

In 1962 Meisner returned to New York to direct the acting department of the newly founded American Musical Theatre Academy. Two years later, he returned to the Neighborhood Playhouse, where he remains today. Clearly the Playhouse is a haven to him now, just as it was when he first began to teach there fifty years ago and announced his appointment in the *Playbill* for *Johnny Johnson*—an act perhaps related to announcing his decision to become an actor to his incredulous family at dinner when he was only nineteen.

Today, more than sixty years later, advanced age and accidents have produced awesome physical disabilities in Meisner. He wears thick glasses as a result of multiple operations for cataracts and detached retinas of both eyes. Even more devastating have been the two operations he sustained for cancer of the larynx, the first more than ten years ago, which left him literally without a voice. With great difficulty he subsequently learned to speak again by inhaling air into his esophagus and releasing it in controlled burps. This esophageal speech may be disturbing to those hearing it for the first time, though the listener quickly adapts to it. It is a strangely disembodied wheeze broken by explosive consonant sounds and glottal stops, sometimes fits of coughing. When Meisner teaches now, this "voice" is amplified by a microphone attached to the left temple of his glasses, and connected to a small transmitter, which sends it to a loudspeaker across the room from his desk, thereby emphasizing its eerie, disembodied quality. As if these blows had not been enough, three years ago an out-of-control delivery truck struck him while he was crossing the street, smashing his left femur and hip in twelve places. After surgical reconstruction, he walks stiffly with the help of a cane. Now, during summer and in the dead of winter, he leaves New York for a home he and a close friend,

* Suzanne Shepherd, "Sanford Meisner," *Yale/Theatre*, vol. 8, nos. 2 and 3, 42–43.

James Carville, built twenty years ago on the island of Bequia in
the West Indies. The warm air and water of the tropics are a great
comfort to him.

Still, Meisner continues to teach. In his mind, he once told an
interviewer, he imagines himself to be like "a well-known
painter" (a reference to the French artist Raoul Dufy, probably
as seen at work in the famous Brassaï photograph). "When he was
in his eighties his hands were so crippled with arthritis that he
couldn't hold the brush. Well, he got someone to tape it onto his
hand somehow, and he kept on painting. Now, with all my limitations—I can't talk, my eyes are bad—I come back to this freezing city to teach again! Some people think they've talked me into
it. That's not so. No one can talk me into anything that I don't
want to do. I want to do it. I'm happiest when I'm teaching."[*]

Perhaps the reason why lies in the miracle Harold Clurman
discussed, the "almost holy" miracle of true emotion. Or perhaps
it is rooted in the statement Meisner made, that through the
genius of Pauline Lord "I was beginning to realize that acting
which really dug at me was what I was looking for."

"Did I tell you the story about Eleonora Duse?" Meisner recently
asked a visitor to his office. "I never told you that?" After being
assured that he hadn't, he recounted George Bernard Shaw's
1895 review of the legendary Italian actress in Hermann Suder-
mann's *Heimat* [*Home*] (it was also known as *Magda*, the role Duse
assumed). This is what Shaw wrote:

"Magda is a daughter who has been turned out of doors for
defying her father, one of those outrageous persons who mistake
their desire to have everything their own way in the house for
a sacred principle of home life. She has a hard time of it, but at
last makes a success as an opera singer, though not until her
lonely struggles have thrown her for sympathy on a fellow student, who in due time goes his way, and leaves her to face mother-

hood as best she can. In the fullness of her fame she returns to her native town, and in an attack of homesickness makes advances to her father, who consents to receive her again. No sooner is she installed in the house than she finds that one of the most intimate friends of the family is the father of her child. In the third act of the play she is on the stage when he is announced as a visitor. . . .

"The moment she read the card handed her by the servant, you realized what it was to have to face a meeting with the man. It was interesting to watch how she got through it when he came in, and how, on the whole, she got through it pretty well. He paid his compliments and offered his flowers; they sat down; and she evidently felt that she had got it safely over and might allow herself to think at her ease, and to look at him to see how much he had altered. Then a terrible thing happened to her. She began to blush; and in another moment she was conscious of it, and the blush was slowly spreading and deepening until, after a few vain efforts to avert her face or to obstruct his view of it without seeming to do so, she gave up and hid the blush in her hands. After that feat of acting I did not need to be told why Duse does not paint an inch thick. I could detect no trick in it: it seemed to me a perfectly genuine effect of the dramatic imagination . . . and I must confess to an intense professional curiosity as to whether it always comes spontaneously."

Meisner's paraphrase of this account is brief, but it is correct in its essential details. Moreover, his enthusiasm and genuine wonder at Shaw's story of Duse's blush, a story he has told hundreds of times, is infectious. It is as though time has stopped, and Sanford Meisner can live forever in the miracle of this moment. For a moment, one can understand how this extraordinary man has lived such an extraordinary life.

"Duse played in a play called *Magda*. There's a scene in the last act. When she's a young girl she has an affair with a guy from the same village, and she has a child by him. Twenty-five years later, or thereabouts, she comes back to visit her family who live in this town, and her ex-lover comes to call on her. She accepts his flowers—I got this from Shaw—and they sit and talk. All of a sudden she realizes that she's blushing, and it gets so bad that she drops her head and hides her face in embarrassment. Now that's a piece of realistic acting! And Shaw confesses to a certain professional curiosity as to whether it happens every time she plays that part. It doesn't. But that blush is the epitome of living truthfully under imaginary circumstances, which is my definition of good acting. That blush came out of *her*. She was a genius!"

2 Building a Foundation: The Reality of Doing

MEISNER: What's the first thing that happens when they build the World Trade Center—you know that building?

MALE STUDENT: They dig a hole.

MEISNER: Well, of course they dig a hole. They don't glue it to the sidewalk! [*Laughter.*] What's the first thing they did when they built the Empire State Building?

FEMALE STUDENT: They had to put down a foundation first.

MEISNER: They had to put down a foundation on which . . .

FEMALE STUDENT: . . . they built the building.

MEISNER: . . . they built the building.

September 29

"The foundation of acting is the reality of doing."

It is the first moment of the first class of the semester, and without delay Sanford Meisner states and restates this seemingly simple theme. "Wait a minute, let's say that again. *The foundation of acting is the reality of doing.* The reality of doing. Now, how do you know what that means? I'll clarify it." After a brief pause he asks, "Are you listening to me? Are you really listening to me?"

The students respond in chorus, "Yes, yes."

"You're not pretending that you're listening; you're listening. You're *really* listening. Would you say so?"

"Yes, yes."

"*That's* the reality of doing. Let there be no question about what I'm saying here. If you do something, you really do it! Did you walk up the steps to this classroom this morning? You didn't jump up? You didn't skip up, right? You didn't do a ballet pirouette? You really walked up those steps."

He pauses to adjust the small microphone attached to the left temple of his eyeglasses. "How many of you are listening to me now?" Sixteen hands are raised obediently. "Now, listen to me for a minute. Just for yourselves, listen to the number of cars that you hear outside. Do that."

The students, eight men and eight women in their twenties and early thirties, lean forward, straining to hear the sounds of New York City traffic filtering through the whir of the air-conditioner. After a moment some close their eyes. A minute passes.

"Okay," Meisner says to a young man with a neat brown beard, "how many cars did you hear?"

"None," the student replies. "I heard a plane."

"A plane is not a car. You heard none. Let me ask you this: did you listen as yourself or were you playing some character?"

"As myself."

"What about you?" he asks a thin, dark girl who looks like a model.

"At first I was listening as a student."

"That's a character—"

"And then I was confused because I couldn't hear a car, and the sounds were confusing. Then I heard what I'm pretty sure was a car, and then I got bored, and then I heard another car. So I heard two cars."

"We won't discuss the boredom." The class laughs. "Were you, as you said, listening—what's your name?"

"Anna."

"Were you listening as Anna?"

"At the end."

"So part of your acting was legitimate and two-thirds of it was pretending."

"Yes."

"How many cars did you hear?" The question is directed

to a woman in her late twenties with luxurious dark hair.
"I couldn't be sure which sounds were cars."

"Were you really puzzled, or were you puzzled in character?"

"I don't know. It felt as though I was not quite doing something all the time."

"So you were half an actress." Then, to a young man in a plaid wool shirt and jeans, "How many cars did you hear?"

"None."

"None. Did you listen as—"

"I listened as me, just as John."

"That's what I want to know. It's a nice feeling. Okay, now choose a melody that you like and sing it to yourself—just to yourself, not out loud. Clear? Do it."

Again some students close their eyes, and after a few seconds of concentration heads begin bobbing, marking time to melodies only individually heard.

"How many people were doing it?" Meisner asks. "For yourselves or theatrically? Who can answer that?"

"Half and half." It is the young woman called Anna.

"You have a problem. What's your problem?"

"I was very aware of being in a room filled with people consciously listening to different melodies. About halfway through I got so upset with myself that I was able to forget about it."

"And sing?"

"Yes."

"That's when you were good."

"That's when I enjoyed it, I don't know if I was good."

"It's always enjoyable to be good." He pauses a moment and shifts his gaze to a stocky, blond, boyish young man in the front row. "What about you?"

"I was singing to myself."

"Like Hamlet?"

"I was trying to enjoy the melody."

"You were? For yourself, not as Hamlet?"

"For myself."

Next Meisner asks the class to count the number of light bulbs in the room. The answers range between twelve and sixteen, depending on whether one includes the red bulb over the fire-escape exit sign or excludes the three unlit floodlights angled down from a beam in the middle of the ceiling. The answers are unimportant; what *is* crucial is the doing of the task, the *counting* of the light bulbs, not the results. "Did you count in character —theatrically," Meisner asks, "or did *you* count?

"Nine hundred and thirty-one times eighteen—try to do that in your head," he goes on. "Nine thirty-one times eighteen." The correct answer is 16,758, and no one even comes close to figuring it out. Again, that's not the point. "You may be right, you may be wrong," Meisner says. "That's like life. People come to different conclusions. That's why some are Democrats and some are Republicans. But how many *tried?* You know, it's all right to be wrong, but it's not all right not to *try.*"

"Look," Meisner says, "examine the partner sitting next to you. And give me, when I ask for it, a list of what you observe." Sixteen heads turn to scan the person now called, for the first time, "the partner."

When she is asked, the blond girl in the second row says about the young man seated to her right: "I observed red hair. I observed a soft green shirt which had pink and gray and beige stripes and that was a size medium. I observed a rash on his neck. He has blue eyes and short, thin, lighter-colored eyelashes. Small hands. Kind of burly. Leans over a lot. Stocky. Green pants. Brown shoes—leather, with rubber soles, I think. Clean ears and clean fingernails. Small lips that stay closed and mostly turn under—"

"Okay. Was this observation done by you or by some character out of a play?"

"I don't know the answer. In honesty, I can't quite distinguish which is which."

"Are you talking to me now, or is Lady Macbeth talking?"

"I'm talking to you."

"That's you. That's you in person. Your observation was straight, unadulterated observation. What you observed, *you* observed, not a character in a play." He asks John, the young man in the plaid shirt, "Are you looking at me now?"

"Yes."

"As Othello?"

"No."

"As who?"

"As myself, I guess."

"That's right. Can you hold on to that?"

"I want to ask you a question and I want you, please, for your own sake as well as mine, to tell the truth. How many people in this class can hear very well?" After a moment's confusion, sixteen hands are raised. "Now listen, I'm holding you to something. Everybody says he or she can hear. You can hear? You can hear me?"

They answer, "Yes."

"I want to ask you another question, one a little more difficult. You say you can hear. That's good. Can you *repeat* what you hear absolutely accurately? I'm talking simply. I don't mean the Declaration of Independence. I mean, 'Do you drink coffee?' Can you repeat that?"

"Do you drink coffee?" asks a young woman with short, brown, layered hair.

"You did that, so you can. Now, do you know what you're telling me? First of all, you said you can hear. You also said you can repeat what you hear. You can take it back if you want to! All right, I accept."

"We can repeat the words," says a dark, broad-shouldered young woman.

"That's all I ask—not the spirit, just the words."

"No," says the woman. "I meant we can't repeat *exactly* what we hear. We can only repeat our own representation of the words."

"You can repeat exactly what you hear. Want me to prove it to you?"

"I believe you."

"What's your name?"

"Rose Marie."

"Rose Marie, why should you believe me? 'Your hair is long.' Repeat that."

"Your hair is long."

"So you can do it! You see, I did not recite the first act of *Uncle Vanya*, which perhaps you have never heard before. Now, who's your partner?" John, the young man in the plaid shirt, raises his hand. "Now, look at her. What do you observe about her? Not her spirit, but something about her that has some interest for you."

"She's very . . . I was going to say she's very fresh and open."

"That's an emotional observation. I'm not quite that smart. I see that she has a pink sweater."

"Okay."

"I'm going to tell you something. You're a thinker."

"I know," John says, "that's why I'm here."

"Then stop immediately!" The class laughs. "Do you see that she has a pink sweater? Do you see that her hair needs combing? Do you see the color of her slacks?"

"Yes."

"Now, you told me that you can hear and you told me that you can repeat, which means that, starting with something that exists in her, you should find what interests you and make a comment. Then, Rose Marie, you repeat exactly what he says, and you, John, repeat exactly what *she* says. Do this until I stop you."

"Your hair is shiny," John says.

"Your hair is shiny," Rose Marie repeats.

"Your hair is shiny."

"Your hair is shiny."

"Your *hair* is shiny."

"Your *hair* is shiny."

"Your hair *is* shiny."

"No," says Meisner stopping them, "you're making readings in order to create variety. Don't. Do it again, using another observation."

After a moment John says, "Your earring is small," and Rose Marie says, "Your earring is small." They repeat the sentence five or six times until Meisner stops them.

"Okay, now I believe that you can both hear, and I believe that you can repeat what you hear. It's not the whole story, but it's the beginning of something. You observed her earrings. You commented on them. You repeated what you heard. So far you were listening to each other and were repeating what you heard. That's what I asked you to do."

The students pair off, and the exercise, which Meisner calls the Word Repetition Game, is performed again and again. The boyish, blond young man, whose name is Philip, becomes the partner of the brunette with the layered haircut, whose name is Sarah. They repeat his comment, "Your eyes are blue," over and over until Meisner stops them.

"All right," he says. "This probably seems unbelievably silly, doesn't it? But it's the beginning of something. Are you listening to each other? Are you repeating what you hear? You are."

After another couple repeat "You have bright earrings," he says, "It's mechanical, it's inhuman, but it's the basis for something. It's monotonous, but it's the basis for something."

After Anna and her partner repeat "Your shirt has bright pink lettering on it" a dozen or more times, he says, "Yes, that's correct. It's empty, it's inhuman, right? But it has something in it. It has connection. Aren't they listening to each other? That's the connection. It's a connection which comes from listening to each other, but it has no human quality—yet. If you want to take notes, write down 'This is a Ping-Pong game.' It is the basis of what eventually becomes emotional dialogue."

Meisner pauses for a moment. "Now I'm going to show you where the trouble comes in." He turns to a young woman wearing her brown hair in a thick braid. "You have an embroidered blouse. Is that true?"

"No."

"Then what's the answer?"

"No, I do not have an embroidered blouse."

"That's right!" he says. "That is the repetition from *her* point of view. Immediately it becomes a contact between two human beings." He says to Sarah, "You're carrying a pen."

"Yes, I'm carrying a pen."

"Yes, you are."

"Yes, I am."

"That's right! Already it has become human speech, hasn't it? First, there's the mechanical repetition. Then there's the repetition from your point of view." He looks at the young woman with the luxurious dark hair. "You curl your hair."

"Yes, I curl my hair."

"Yes, you do."

"Yes, I curl my hair."

"I said, 'Yes, you do.' "

"Yes, I do."

"Yes, I can see you do."

"Yes, you can see I do."

"Let it go at that. That's the Word Repetition Game from *your* point of view. That's already human conversation, isn't it?" Then, to the young man whose shirt has bright pink lettering on it, Meisner says, "You're staring at me."

"I'm staring at you."

"You're staring at me."

"I'm staring at you."

"You admit it?"

"I admit it."

"You admit it."

"I admit it."

"I don't like it."

"You don't like it."

"You don't care?"

"I don't care."

"You don't care?"

"I don't care!"

Meisner sticks out his tongue at the young man, and he and the class laugh.

"That's the Word Repetition Game. It mustn't go too far; I won't let it. Now, when you work together at home, do the exercise mechanically, the way you started it. Then practice doing it from your point of view."

. . .

"I started this class by saying that the basis of acting is the reality of doing. How does that definition compare with what we've been doing?"

John says, "If we simply do it, we're not focusing on ourselves."

"You're attached to something outside of yourself," Meisner adds. "What else?"

"If you're really doing it, then you don't have time to *watch* yourself doing it. You only have the time and energy to do it," says Ray, the young man with the neat beard.

"That's very good for your acting. Anything else?"

Sarah says, "They all seem to be very concrete, 'do-able' things."

"Everything I've asked you has been concrete and 'do-able'? What about that word 'concrete'?"

"Well, it's tangible. You can look at somebody and actually count their eyelashes or you can count the light bulbs."

"Something that really, *really* exists specifically," Meisner says. Now, what does 'the reality of doing' mean?"

An intense-looking young man who has not spoken before says, "When you do something you really *do* it rather than pretend that you're doing it."

"And you *don't* do it like a character. When you play the piano, do you open the lid first, or do you just play it closed?" Meisner asks. "Well, musically speaking, the opening of the piano is similar to the reality of doing. Are there any questions here?"

"You gave us things to do that you can really do, like observing another person or listening to cars," says Ray. "And if you're really concentrated on just listening to cars or looking at a person, you don't have to worry about being a character. You have one thing to do and concentrate on."

"That *is* the character."

"That's the character?" Ray asks.

"Yes."

"So you don't have to play at being the character, it's right there in your doing it."

"Right. Do you understand that? Every play, whether it's by that comedy writer—what's his name?"

"Neil Simon?"

"Yeah. Every play is based upon the reality of doing. Even Lear's shaking his fist at the heavens—that's based on the actor thundering against fate. Can you see that?" He pauses. "This will go further in you than you may suspect at the moment. That's all right. It will unveil itself. It will reveal itself gradually. It is the basis, the foundation of acting."

"Another beginning. You'd think I'd quit!" Meisner says to his assistant, Scott Roberts, as they wait for the elevator which will take them to Meisner's paneled office one floor below the classroom. "Somebody should shoot me as they do aged horses."

Scott nods and smiles.

"But, you know, this class is an attractive group, and full of promise. The question is, how many of them will learn to act?"

Scott nods again and pushes the button for the elevator one more time. In the basement an electric motor drones into life.

"I've been teaching for over fifty years and in that near eternity I have attempted to teach literally thousands of young people how to act. And I haven't done too badly. I did well with you, for example."

"Thank you," Scott says.

"But if I chose to dwell on my overall success rate, I'd probably give up, so I don't."

The elevator arrives and they enter it.

"Acting is an art. And teaching acting is an art too, or it can be. Ultimately it's a question of talent—of theirs meshing with mine. So time will tell. But I must say, it's good to begin again!"

3 The Pinch and the Ouch

MEISNER: What does it do for you, Bruce, to imitate the other fellow's movements?
BRUCE: It takes the heat off yourself.
MEISNER: To take the heat off yourself, as Bruce just said, to transfer the point of concentration outside of yourself, is a big battle won.

October 3

"Now," Meisner says, looking at the young man who at the last session wore the shirt with pink lettering, "your name is Vincent and your partner's name is . . . ?"

"Anna," answers the thin, dark woman sitting in front of him.

"Anna. Good. Stand up and turn your backs to each other."

"Touching or not?" Vincent asks.

"Not touching. Now, Vince, come here."

Vincent goes to the gray wooden desk where Meisner is seated, and they confer for a moment. Then Vincent takes his place with his back to Anna in the front of the room. He takes a few coins from the pocket of his jeans and drops them on the floor.

"You dropped some coins?" Anna asks.

"I dropped some coins."

"Yeah, you dropped some coins."

"Yeah, I dropped some coins."

"Yeah, you dropped some coins."

"All right, now listen to me," Meisner says interrupting the repetition. "Vince, I maintain that by this time you should have realized that she has good ears and told her so. It would have been something you said because something she did *made* you do it. And you, Anna, had the right by this time to observe that because he dropped some coins he's careless with his money."

"That would be an assumption," says Vincent defensively.

"It would be an assumption which you could deny. 'I am *not* careless with my money!' Do you follow?"

"Yes."

"All right. Use something new and begin again, slowly."

After a moment, Anna elbows Vincent in the back.

"You poked me in the back!"

"I poked you in the back."

"You poked me in the back."

"Yes, I poked you in the back."

"Yes, you poked me in the back."

"Yes," she says, amused at his displeasure, "I poked you in the back."

"What's funny?" he snaps.

"What's funny?"

"What's funny?" he repeats.

"What's funny?"

"*What's* funny?" Vincent says with unnatural stress on the first word. Meisner interrupts them immediately.

"No! That's a reading! Until then it was very good, but '*What's* funny?' was a way of creating variety. I'll show you something. There is a time when the verbal contact between you changes, and it is based on instinct. *Instinct.* I'll show you what I mean by that. Imagine, Vince, that you walk into a department store with a friend of yours, and you say, 'Do you see that tie? I want it!' Or you go to a party and across the room you see a girl and you say to yourself, 'I'm going to have her!' That comes from your instincts. Do you follow?

"Now, in this exercise there is a change in the words that is dictated by your instinct. I'll show you how it works." He leans toward Vincent and says *sotto voce*, "Vince, whatever I ask you for, the answer is 'No.'" Then, in full voice he says, "Can you lend me twenty dollars?"

"Can I lend you twenty dollars?"

"Can you lend me twenty dollars?"

"No, I can't lend you twenty dollars."

"You can't lend me twenty dollars?"

"I can't lend you twenty dollars."

"You can't?"

"I can't."

"You can't?"

"I can't!"

"You're a big shit!"

"I'm a big shit!"

"That's what *I* said!" The class laughs, and when the laughter ends Meisner adds, "Now, that change was caused by instinct."

After a moment he peers at Anna, comically leering at her from behind his thick lenses. "Will you come to my house tonight?"

"Will I come to your house tonight?"

"Will you come to my house tonight?"

"Will I come to your house tonight?"

"Will you come to my house tonight?"

"No, I will not come to your house tonight."

"You won't come to my house tonight?" He gives her a withering, scornful look. "You're a professional virgin!"

There is another burst of laughter.

"Now let's talk about that. When is something instinctive caused in you? How does it happen?"

"It lives in you," Vincent says. "It hits you a certain way."

"That's right. You wouldn't lend me twenty dollars, so I called you a big shit. She said she wouldn't come to my house in such a way that my instinct tells me that she's a professional virgin. Now, that happens in an exercise, which changes the dialogue. The instinct changes the dialogue. Then it continues and you wait until the instinct changes it again. Any questions here? Ray?"

"What if your partner is doing nothing," asks Ray, "and your instincts tell you that this is aggravating?"

"Use it!"

"Then you can say, 'But you're not doing anything!' "

"Or, 'You're aggravating me!' "

" 'You're aggravating me!' So it's really like there's never *nothing.*"

"There's no such thing," Meisner says, "there's no such thing as nothing. *There's no such thing as nothing. There's no such thing as nothing.*"

"What about silence?" Sarah asks.

"Listen, silence is a moment. A moment of silence is something, too. Let me prove it to you. Ask me whether I think you have talent."

"Mr. Meisner, do you think I have talent?"

His head cocks away from her and he maintains a complete silence. The class begins to laugh.

"That was silent, wasn't it?" Meisner asks when the laughter subsides.

"Well, yes . . ." says Sarah, at a loss for words.

"That's the point, the 'Well, yes . . .' It's the point because my silence was very expressive," Meisner says. "Silence has a myriad of meanings. In the theater silence is an absence of words, but never an absence of meaning."

There is a slight pause.

"Do you mean that I don't have to look at my partner when we're doing the repetition and just say, 'You have a gray shirt on, you have a gray shirt on'?" asks Rose Marie. "If he looks bored I could say, 'You look bored'? I could make a judgment?"

"Of his behavior, yes. There comes a point when one of you has to pick up what the repetition is doing to you. I don't care what it is. Are you bored with the repetition? Then that could be the change. Or maybe your partner sounds a little annoyed at you; from that fact could come the change 'You're angry at me.' In other words, your instinct picks up the change in his behavior and the dialogue changes too. I'm talking about instinct. You walk into a store and see a dress. 'That's for me!' That's instinct. I say that if you take your time, the change in you, which is— I don't like to say 'automatic,' I don't like that word—which is *spontaneous*, will happen. That's what you should work on now. Let your instincts dictate the changes, not just the repetition."

"We began by discussing instinct. Now let's discuss where talent comes from. It is my belief that talent comes from instinct. What does that mean? Can anybody explain?"

Rose Marie holds up her hand. "I think we all really have the same instincts, and if we allow ourselves to be simple and uncluttered, then those instincts or talent will appear. *If* you allow yourself to be open and honest."

"Ah," Meisner says, "but the tendency nowadays is to follow your instincts only when they are socially acceptable. We fear being branded as uncivilized for liking or disliking something. Think of the girl from Miss Finch's School. She was taught to say only what was acceptable socially. A girl from Miss Finch's School goes to see her friend in a play, and her real reaction is that the performance was *terrible*. Yet when she goes backstage she smiles and through gritted teeth says, '*Marvelous!*' "

The class laughs at Meisner's accurate impersonation of a debutante from Westchester.

"You can see the jaw tense to keep the real, instinctive remark from coming out. That's not good for actors. Can you see where that controlling is the opposite of the spontaneous, deeply instinctive behavior we're talking about?"

Wendy and Jim, a pale blond pair in their early twenties, begin to perform the Word Repetition Game. After a few minutes, Meisner interrupts.

"Wait a minute, both of you. Wendy, you're being self-manipulative. Do you know what that means?"

"Yeah, but I don't know why you're saying it."

"I'm saying it because you're doing it. You've got control over what you're saying, and I say *he* has to have the control. What you're doing is self-manipulative. Do you understand?"

"Doesn't he have to *take* that control?"

"What?"

"You said I was controlling us. Isn't he responsible for that too?"

"His responsibility is to repeat, as is yours. You're really working from your head. You're not getting this exercise because you think that you have to manipulate verbal responses, whereas all you really have to do is repeat what you get from him. If you repeat what you get from him, you won't be at a loss for something to say. Your head is figuring out what to say, figuring out what to do next. How do you get away from that?"

"By not thinking about it. I understand that because I'm a dancer, and when I'm good I don't think about my steps any more because I know how to do them. It just happens."

"It has to happen here too, you follow? Jim, you have something of the same problem. Not as much, but something. How do you correct that?"

"As you say, don't think. Just try to take what's there."

"*Listen.* I'd suggest going on with the word repetition, just working off each other, and the more brainless it is the chances are the better off you'll be. It's a question of repeating what you hear. Don't make up anything; you're better off saying, 'I'm stuck, let's quit.' Then begin again from another angle. Thinking has no part in this process."

After a moment Meisner asks, "Wendy, how do you feel?"

"I feel . . . See, I never thought that I thought a lot, but I guess I do. So I guess it's good that I realize this before I get into trouble. It's good. It's easier not to think, I guess."

"Work from your instincts," Meisner says. "That's what we were talking about. Okay?"

October 6

"Joseph, you're doing something that you have to throw away right now. You're compounding the moments, see? If she said,

'You've got a cold,' you'd answer, 'Yes, I have a cold, I got wet.'
That's two moments, one of which is an intellectual explanation
of the first instead of simply repeating what you get from your
partner. If she said, 'Your jaw is tense,' you'd answer, 'Yes, my
jaw is tense. I'm *nervous.*' Those are two moments."

"Are you saying I should leave it as 'Yes, my jaw is
tense'?"

"One moment, one note at a time. Do you understand?"

"Yes."

"Also, you overdo the word repetition. You comment on something you notice about her but if you get no answer, you repeat
it as if it were necessary for her to respond to what you say
instead of using her silence. I'll show you what I mean."

He leans over to Anna, who is seated near his right
hand, and whispers, "Don't answer me." Then, fixing her with
his gaze and pointing to her necklace, he asks, "Is that a gold
chain?"

Anna regards him without moving and in silence.

"Is that a gold chain?" Meisner repeats mechanically. He waits
for her answer, which does not come. "You see, Joseph, that's
what you did. You said the same thing twice. Now, I'll show you
something."

Again he looks at Anna. "Is that a gold chain?" he asks. Again
she regards him silently, but this time Meisner waits for her
response until, out of exasperation, he shouts, "Don't look at me
as if I'm crazy!"

Joseph nods, and Meisner continues. "You should use her silence for a new moment instead of repeating it."

"The moment has changed?"

"The moment has changed because of her silence. Do you get
that?"

"Yes."

"Ask me if we are going to have a class next Thursday."

"Mr. Meisner, are we going to have a class next Thursday?"

He ignores Joseph's question, staring coldly off into space. The
silence becomes painful, and finally Joseph says ruefully, "I guess
we're not."

"Or," Meisner says with a pointed smile, " 'Aren't we on speaking terms?' "

Joseph nods.

"Did you get that?"

"Yes, I understand."

"I thought you did."

"Listen, Philip, you have some kind of cockeyed idea that acting is an imitation of life."

His exercise interrupted, Philip, the stocky, blond, boyish young man, chews his lower lip nervously. Meisner speaks slowly and with great firmness.

"You try to be logical, as in life. You try to be polite, as in life. May I say, as the world's oldest living teacher, *'Fuck* polite!' " Meisner says passionately. "You have one thing to do, and that is to pick up the repetition from your partner. And if he sticks his tongue out, that's not polite. That's not grownup. It's not the way people your age act. But you've got to do it!"

"You mean *go* with it."

"Yes! And if your mother hits you, retaliate!"

"I will. I've got to be around people who aren't so polite."

"You've got to be around people who follow their instincts."

"I know that's my next step, to find a person who follows his instincts."

"No," Meisner says, "it's in *you!* *They* all have it. Can't you see that?" He makes a sweeping gesture indicating the whole class. "Whatever your partner does, you imitate it—right, wrong, polite or whatever. I tell you this: you cannot be a gentleman and be an actor. And you've got the idea that you're a gentleman."

"Yes."

"Forget about it!"

"I'll try."

"Where did you get this delusion that you're a logical gentleman?"

"People just kept saying, 'You're a gentleman, you're a gentleman," and after a while I must have listened to them."

"Philip, do yourself a favor. Kick them in the ass!"

"Today we're going to talk about beginnings. I have an exercise that I'm going to demonstrate to you. It is basic and vital, and it may clarify something. John, stand up. I want to show you where you begin. There are two basic principles involved here, which you can write down if you wish."

He leaves the desk to stand beside John, who is a head taller than he.

" *'Don't do anything unless something happens to make you do it.'* That's one of them. The second is: *'What you do doesn't depend on you; it depends on the other fellow.'* John," he asks, "how are you on learning a script? Are you pretty good? You're fast? Here's your text: 'Mr. Meisner.' Can you learn that? Can I hear that?"

" 'Mr. Meisner,' " John says simply.

"Not bad." The class laughs. "Now, I said don't do anything until something happens to make you do it, and I said that what you do doesn't depend on you but on the other fellow, didn't I? Now, you've got a script. Do you remember it?"

"Yes."

"What is it, please?"

" 'Mr. Meisner.' "

"Perfect. Would you mind turning around?"

Sensing what is to come, the class begins to titter.

"What are you laughing at? I haven't done it yet!"

Then he reaches up and gives John's back a big pinch.

" *'Mr. Meisner!'* " John shouts, jumping away from him. There is laughter and scattered applause.

"That," Meisner says, "is the illustration of what I just told you. 'Don't do anything until something happens to make you do it. And what you do doesn't depend upon you; it depends on the other fellow!' Did I force that screech out of you?"

"Yes, in a manner of speaking."

"That's justification. Okay, John, sit down. You were very

good. Now we go into more dangerous territory. Rose Marie, come here."

She rises and joins him in the center of the room.

"How are you on texts?"

"Great."

" 'Mr. Meisner.' "

" 'Mr. Meisner,' that's my text."

"That's your text. Shall we rehearse it? What's your text?"

" 'Mr. Meisner,' " Rose Marie says.

"And what's the principle?"

"Not to do or say anything until something happens to make you do it."

"Don't *do* anything, never mind about saying, until something happens to make you do it! What's the text?"

" 'Mr. Meisner.' "

"Good. Turn around with your back to me, please. Concentrate on the text. Don't do anything until something happens. . . ." Casually he reaches around her shoulder and slips his hand into her blouse.

" *'Mr. Meisner!'* " she giggles, drawing away from his touch.

"You see how true that acting is, how full emotionally," Meisner says. "I didn't know you were ticklish."

The classroom resounds with laughter.

"Now, look. I'm talking and illustrating something which is basic, which is organic to the technique. What did you see here?"

"I saw truthful responses," says Joseph, the serious young man with the deep voice.

"To what?"

"To your grabbing or pinching them."

"In short, my pinch justified their ouch, isn't that true?"

"True."

"And their ouch was the direct result of my pinch?"

"Yes."

"What's the principle involved in this?"

"Not to do anything until—"

"Something happens. Didn't something happen to him? Didn't

something happen to her? Spontaneity is involved in this, right?
What else?"

"Truthfulness," Joseph replies. "It is the basis of being truthful."

"Yes," Meisner says, "it is."

"You know, in the early days of the Group Theatre, the actors
used to do what they called 'improvisations.'"

Meisner leans back in a comfortable armchair angled before
the unlit fireplace in his paneled office. The class was a long one,
and outside a red sun is about to set. Scott Roberts, a large leather
briefcase across his knees, sits on the daybed against the wall.

"These were general verbalizations of what we thought was an
approximation of our situation in the play. We were retelling
what we remembered of the story of the play using our own
words. I came to the realization that this was all intellectual
nonsense. A composer doesn't write down what he *thinks* would
be effective; he works from his heart.

"I decided I wanted an exercise for actors where there is no
intellectuality. I wanted to eliminate all that 'head' work, to take
away all the mental manipulation and get to where the impulses
come from. And I began with the premise that if I repeat what
I hear you saying, my head is not working. I'm listening, and
there is an absolute elimination of the brain. If you say, 'Your
glasses are dirty,' and I say, 'My glasses are dirty,' and you say,
'Yes, your glasses are dirty,' there is no intellectuality in that."

Meisner glances for a moment at the framed black-and-white
photograph of Eleonora Duse which stands on his small mahogany desk.

"Then I came to the next stage. Let's say I say to you, 'Lend
me ten dollars.' And you say, 'Lend you ten dollars?' 'Yes, lend
me ten dollars.' And that goes on for five or six times until—and
this is vital—your refusal sets up an impulse in me which comes
directly out of the repetition and it makes me say to you, 'You're
a stinker!' That's repetition which leads to impulses. It is not

intellectual. It is emotional and impulsive, and *gradually* when the actors I train improvise, what they say—like what the composer writes—comes not from the head but truthfully from the impulses."

"I know," Scott says. "But the problem is that on a superficial level all this repetitive back-and-forth can seem boring. Vincent, for example, the guy who's Anna's partner, told me before class that the repetition exercise drives him nuts."

"Ah, please," Meisner says with a dismissive wave of his hand, "Vincent comes from California, for God's sake, where he claims to have studied with one of the legion of teachers who *claim* to have studied with me! Look, I'll tell you why the repetition exercise, in essence, is *not* boring: it plays on the source of all organic creativity, which is the inner impulses. I wish I could make that clear!"

He pauses for a moment. "Of course, if I were a pianist and sat for an hour just making each finger move in a certain way, the onlooker could very well say, 'That's boring!' And it would be —to the onlooker. But the practitioner is somebody who is learning to funnel his instincts, not give performances. The mistake we made in the Group was that our early improvisations were performances of how we remembered the original play.

"You know, a friend of mine who owns the house in which Joan Sutherland has an apartment says, 'Sometimes she drives me crazy with the repetition of the scales, but then I hear the purity of the tones and all is forgiven.' I'm a very nonintellectual teacher of acting. My approach is based on bringing the actor back to his emotional impulses and to acting that is firmly rooted in the instinctive. It is based on the fact that all good acting comes from the heart, as it were, and that there's no mentality in it."

4 The Knock on the Door

Class Motto: "Repeat"
—from a brass plaque on the side of a steel-gray Puro
water cooler, "Gift of the Class of 1971," which stands
outside the door of Meisner's third-floor classroom.

October 9

"Let's see now. I want to start something new today. Vince, go
across the hall to the teachers' room, where you will find a telephone book. Bring it in, *presto, presto.*"

Vince returns in a moment with a thick Manhattan telephone
directory. He sits at the long table in the center of the room, the
book open before him.

"Last week, Vince, you met a beautiful girl at a party and she
said, 'I'm having a party next Saturday night, and if you want to
come to it, my family is in Europe, so you can stay all night.' Do
you like that?"

"Yes."

"Good. Now, you wrote her name and address down on a slip

of paper but you lost it. Fortunately, you remember her name.
It's K. Z. Smith, and she lives in Manhattan on the East Side in
the upper Seventies. Now, do you have a good reason to look up
her address?"

"Yes, I want to spend the night."

"Let me call your attention to something. I deliberately made
this difficult. A *Smith* in Manhattan? There are fourteen pages of
Smiths in Manhattan! Another difficulty is the reason why you
have to find her, or else . . ."

"I'll spend Saturday night alone."

"That's difficult. Anna, give him a little time to get into it and
then play the Word Repetition Game just as you've been doing
it."

Vincent begins to search the Smith section of the Manhattan
telephone directory. He quickly becomes absorbed in the task.
Then Anna says quietly, "Looking for something?" "I'm looking
for something," he responds, and the repetition exercise begins.
It is essentially unchanged, except that Vince's attention is fixed
on solving the problem of locating K. Z. Smith, a task made more
difficult by Anna's insistent pursuit of playing the word game.
The result is that the dialogue is more focused, and there are
more impulsive shifts in its direction, more surprises.

"That's pretty good," Meisner says after a few minutes. "I
invented something for you to do with that telephone book. That
story about the girl with the obliging parents is sheer invention,
but finding her has a virtue. It is *difficult* to do. It takes all your
concentration, and out of that some emotion will come." He
pauses for a moment. "We're moving forward. Putting the repetition exercise together with an independent activity is a new step.
I want all of you to choose something to do which is above
all *difficult, if not almost impossible.* This is very important. You
have to have a reason why you want to do it. You *must* have a
reason why you want to do it, because that's the source of your
concentration and eventually of your emotion, which comes by
itself."

Meisner pauses to adjust the microphone attached to his eyeglasses. "Let's talk about this. To be inventive, to have ideas, is
an organic part of being talented. You're all very imaginative,

aren't you? The answer is 'Positively.' Go to Woolworth's. Buy a plate for ten cents and break it. Steal your brother's glue and put that plate together as though it had never been broken. Now, consider: why should you do that?"

"Perhaps you will get into a lot of trouble if it's broken," says Rose Marie.

"That has validity. Suppose it's the best plate in a fabulous collection that your mother owns."

"And it has great sentimental value for her," says Rose Marie.

"And her anger means a big headache for you. Would that propel you? Remember this; the independent activity must be difficult, truly difficult, and the reason why you do it has to have a consuming reality for you."

October 13

"Let's go very slowly," Meisner says to Joseph and Beth, the young woman with the luxurious hair. "This is so vital; it's at the core of the way you handle yourself. Joseph, do what you have chosen to do. Beth, give him plenty of time to get immersed in what he's doing. Let's not rush. Take your time. Make a mistake. I don't care—just make the first step."

"May I ask you a question?" asks Beth. "During this exercise when I come in and Joseph has a task, I feel that I don't want to keep interrupting because he's concentrating. If it were me, I'd just leave."

"No, it's not you in real life," Meisner says. "It's you practicing an exercise."

"That's what I mean. My conflict . . . There's a tension—"

"Then wait!"

"Wait for something to happen?"

"Yes. Where could it come from?"

"Something that he does . . . ?"

"Something that he does. Do you follow? Otherwise what you're saying is that acting is talking, and what I'm saying is don't do anything until something happens to make you do it.

Otherwise you will create an untruthful thing. Let me try to make this clearer."

Meisner pauses to light a cigarette. "Now, wait. I said we're going to go slowly." He regards Joseph. "What are you going to do?"

"You want an explanation of my independent activity? My nephew is sick and is going into the hospital. I'm making a cartoon for him to try to explain to him that he shouldn't be afraid."

"Fine. Do that as if your life depended on it. When I knock, you and I will begin the word repetition."

Joseph carefully sharpens a drawing pencil on a small sheet of sandpaper and begins to work on his cartoon. When Meisner sees that Joseph is engrossed, he knocks on his desk top.

"You want my attention?" Joseph asks, looking up from his work.

"But you have to continue to do that!" Meisner exclaims, referring to the independent activity.

"I know," says Joseph.

"So do it!"

Joseph hunches over his work. Meisner regards him intently. "What are you doing?"

"What am I doing?" Joseph repeats, looking over at him.

"Why did you look over at me?"

"Why, to see what you were doing."

He begins to draw again. A minute passes. Meisner, his curiosity aroused, stands up and walks slowly to the table where Joseph works. "You're busy?" he asks casually.

"I'm busy."

"You're busy."

"I'm busy."

There is another pause. Meisner edges another step closer to Joseph. "You're very busy," he says admiringly.

"I'm very busy," Joseph admits.

"Busy."

"Yeah, busy."

"Yeah."

"Yeah."

Again there is a moment of silence; then Meisner takes a step that brings him looming over the seated Joseph. "I'm busy too," he announces.

"Are you?" says Joseph, hunching over his drawing board.

"Yeah, I'm very busy," Meisner replies, leaning over Joseph's shoulder.

"You're very busy," Joseph says, and then in exasperation he stands up and says, "You know, you're preventing me from doing this!"

"That's what I'm busy at!" Meisner exclaims proudly, and the class laughs. "Now, what point am I making?"

"To really do what you're doing," Joseph says. "You're busy bothering me and I have to do this activity *and* respond to you too."

"Am I adjusting to you?"

"I think you are. You're working off me, if that's what you mean."

"Falsely or truthfully?"

"I'd say truthfully."

"What did I say to Sarah last week? What did I say to you, Sarah?"

"A moment of silence isn't nothing," she replies. "It's a moment as well."

"It means something, right? Acting is not talking. It is living off the other fellow. What's that mean?"

"Acting isn't chatter," Beth says; "it's responding truthfully to the other person."

"That's right. Joseph, sum this up for me."

"The meaning is in the behavior. You don't do anything until that behavior makes you do something."

"And then you do it in what way?"

"You do it truthfully and fully. You really do it."

"You try!"

"You do what it makes you do."

"You do what it makes you do. Now, Joseph, you had a certain merit in what you were doing, in the sense that your independent activity was specific and it had some kind of meaning to you. The error here, which you will gradually overcome, is to think that you have to keep on talking. What's the opposite of that?"

"The opposite of talking?" Joseph asks. "Silence."

"Silence. *Until something happens to make you do something!*"

October 17

Bruce, a tall man in his late thirties with thinning gray hair, has been casually moving bits and pieces of a wooden puzzle in and out of a cardboard box. Meisner motions for Lila, a student new to the class, to sit down and then interrupts the exercise.

"Whenever you do what you *have* to do, which is that puzzle, and let whatever comes from your partner come as an accident which you repeat, this exercise works for you. But while she was up there you were more conscious of her than you were absorbed in solving the puzzle."

"The reason was that this independent activity didn't work for me."

"Why were you doing it?"

"There was a million dollars at stake. If I put this puzzle together I would get a million dollars."

"Don't you think that's a little exaggerated?"

"Maybe. I wanted to see if money would make it any more real for me."

"What about a thousand dollars?" Meisner asks. "That doesn't mean anything?"

"I thought a million was better."

"Then ten million is ten times better still, but that's not the point I want to make. I'm having a tough time with you, Bruce, and one of the reasons is because you are audience-conscious. What makes you audience-conscious? I can understand Milton Berle being audience-conscious, but what makes *you* audience-conscious? Stanislavsky, no slouch, had a phrase which he called 'public solitude.' He said that when you're alone in your room and nobody's watching you—you're just standing in front of the mirror combing your hair—the relaxation, the completeness with which you do it is poetic. He calls this relaxed behavior on the stage 'public solitude.' On the stage 'public solitude' is what we want. You have only one element to give up to get to the area where your real acting personality is, and that is yourself."

"That has to do with the motive for my independent activity, doesn't it?"

"The silly million dollars?"

"It didn't work."

"It never will. It's not imaginative to say a million dollars. It's exaggerated and false. What would honestly work for you?"

"A hundred dollars," Bruce says simply.

"So why be theatrical? And theatrical in a false way? You see, only you know what's truthful for you. A couple of years ago I was hit by a goddamned truck, and now there's a lawsuit going on. People say to me, 'You're going to get three million dollars.' Do you know what my reaction is? I laugh. It's ridiculous. But when somebody says, 'You might get a hundred thousand dollars,' I say, 'Really?' That I can believe; otherwise it's ridiculous."

Meisner takes a puff on his cigarette. "Since I don't walk well I take taxis frequently. Do you know who was driving my taxi today? *Mrs. Ronald Reagan!*"

Someone chuckles quietly.

"Did you get it? Joseph, what are you laughing at?"

"That's ridiculous," Joseph says.

"Of course. But if I'd said, 'Her son, the ex–ballet dancer—' "

The class laughs.

"Truth and public solitude. Believe me, Bruce, you should have 'Public Solitude' engraved on your stationery, because that's what you need. Not public exhibitionism, but public solitude. When you are at home, when you have a job to do, you do it. You comb your hair, and you don't watch to make sure your pinky's out. You exhaust me. Have a seat."

October 20

Wendy holds up her hand. "I feel a little unclear about the independent activity. I mean, I find it very difficult to do this.

THE KNOCK ON THE DOOR

It could be as simple as doing the alphabet backwards, right?"

"But there would be no point to it."

"If there's a reason, there will be a point to it."

"What's the reason?" Meisner asks and waits for her response.

"I can't think of anything except—"

"That's right, you can't. You'd have to go to Bellevue to get a reason. Everything in acting is a kind of heightened, intensified reality—but it's based on justified reality. To recite the alphabet backwards is not reality. You'd have to invent some weird reason to justify it, and I don't know what that could be."

Wendy nods in agreement.

"If you're a good caricaturist like, to take a minor one, that fellow who does all those theatrical caricatures for the Sunday *Times*—"

"Al Hirschfeld," Wendy says.

"Al Hirschfeld, yeah. You always recognize the real source of his caricatures. What I'm saying is that everything is based on life, on reality. My mind goes back to Ed Wynn, who was Keenan Wynn's father and a truly great clown. He had an act which consisted, among other things, of inventions. He was trying to sell the audience a very complicated machine that was designed to let you eat watermelon without getting your ears wet. Now that's ridiculous, right? But the feeling of desperation, the feeling of fear that he wouldn't succeed made it first-class clowning."

Meisner pauses. The moment is clearly meaningful to him. "I brought this up because of what you said about how difficult it would be reciting the alphabet backwards. It would be even more difficult to walk from here to L.A. on your hands, but it would also be crazy, which means abnormal. The greatest piece of acting or music or sculpture or what-have-you always has its roots in the truth of human emotion. Beethoven was a bastard in real life, you know. He was a real bastard. But his music is pure and based in his real feeling. That is why he was great. Not because he fired his servant, which he did, because a sock was missing out of the laundry. What I'm saying is that the truth of ourselves is the root of our acting."

. . .

"I'm going to show you a brand-new thing. Years ago, before you were born, there was a show called *Florodora*, and there was a song in it entitled 'Every Little Movement Has a Meaning All Its Own.' Now, I changed that a bit to say, 'Every Little *Moment* Has a Meaning All Its Own.' You sort of know that already, don't you? All right, now. A knock . . . a knock has a meaning. Follow this carefully. *A knock has a meaning.* John, go outside and knock —truthfully—and then wait ten seconds and knock a second time with a second meaning. Then knock a third time."

"Three different meanings?"

"Right. Ralph, you tell me what each knock means to you."

There is a quiet rap on the door.

"Is anybody there?" Ralph says.

"No, it was timid. Call it timid."

Then there is an emphatic, rapid knock.

"Nervous," Ralph says. "He sounds nervous."

"All right."

Finally there is a huge, booming knock.

"Angry, really loud—"

"All right, call him in."

John reappears.

"John—everybody—knock so that it has some resemblance to life. Don't knock theatrically. Your last knock was on the verge of being theatrical. Do you understand?"

John nods his head.

"Now here's the catch. The first moment of the exercise is the knock. The exercise begins with the knock. The second moment is the opening of the door, and the third moment is your interpretation of the knock. The third moment is the meaning the knock has for you, verbalized by you as you open the door. Right? Then you go back to what you're doing. Do whatever the third moment permits you to do and then go back to your independent activity and let the exercise continue."

Ralph seems puzzled.

"Let's go over the knocking," Meisner says. "After the first two, tell me what they mean to you. After the third one, open the door. And use—verbally—what the third knock meant to you. Then go back to your independent activity and the exercise. Any questions?"

"I understand the order of it," Ralph says, "but if you were doing the activity and didn't want to be interrupted—"

"Then don't interrupt—"

"No, you're doing the activity and you *have* to open the door, right?"

"*No!*" Meisner exclaims.

"Okay, that makes it clear."

"*No!* You understand?"

"Yeah—"

"*No!* You understand?"

"I understand. Yes."

"Yes? Tell me why."

" 'You don't do something until—' "

"Okay. You understand."

"Lila, the thing that we have to correct here is to take away the logic, because the repetition will induce real emotion and the logic stays mental. Do you understand that?"

"Yes," Lila says. A hennaed blond in her late forties, she is the oldest student in the class.

"Now, look. You've had plenty of experience, and when you picked up a script in the past, I imagine, your tendency was to read it according to what you thought was the right feeling or mood—call it what you will. Now I'm pulling you away from that habit and I'm saying a simple thing. Be foolish but be repetitive. Keep up the repetition until something happens to you, something that will come right out of you. Right?"

"Right."

"But to ask your partner questions continuously, as you did, is using your head, and what I'm trying to do is get you out of your head. Do you follow?"

"Get me out of my head," Lila says.

"Into what?"

"My emotional life."

"Point to it."

Lila points at her heart.

"That's right. That's my first step in getting you away from indicating. Repeat to me what I just told you."

"You're trying to get me away from using my logic to using my . . ."

"Your impulses—"

"My impulses, my instincts. Gee, if I could only do that!"

"If you try to do it for two minutes today, you'll do it for four minutes next time. Do you follow?"

"Right. I'll try."

"Of course you will. Repeat. Repeat."

"What was your difficulty, John, do you know?"

"I felt like, just get through it. She was very emotional and I didn't want to make it worse so I started saying to myself, 'Get away.' "

"Isn't that in your head?"

"Yes, exactly."

"Isn't that where you've been doing most of your acting—out of a mental desire to keep the exercise going in a helpful way?"

"Yes."

"Is that good or bad for your acting?"

"Bad, very bad."

"That's stock-company stuff, what you're doing. You're writing a logical text. The opposite of that is to work off her. Why did you do it?"

"In my past it's usually not trusting directors. It's just standing outside of myself whenever I got cast in something and feeling that this guy doesn't know what he's talking about, so I keep my sense of what's going on outside the work."

"Are you saying that I don't know what I'm talking about?"

"God, no! I'm paying too much for this to walk away with that attitude."

"Then why don't you do what I tell you?"

"Well, I'd like to. I just don't know if it's too ingrained a habit."

"Well, next time you'll have the independent activity. Make it something which is quite difficult and quite meaningful, and don't open your mouth unless you repeat. And if you are doing an experiment on cancer and your partner says, 'I feel like having some spaghetti,' you've got to repeat it! You're quite right, I suppose, when you say that some directors don't know what the hell they're talking about, but you've got to trust your instincts and not your head. The playwright gives you what to say. Your job as an actor is to fill the role with life. That's the point of this exercise. I've been wary of your intelligence right from the beginning. I spotted that you worked up here," Meisner says, pointing to his head. "I can fix it, but you've got to help me. What do I mean when I say you're doing the cancer experiment and she comes in and says, 'I love spaghetti'?"

"Whatever she does, work off it."

"Repeat! Repeat!"

"Repeat!"

October 27

"Now, what about this independent activity?" Meisner asks. "What are some of its characteristics?"

"It has to be urgent, truthful and difficult to do," says Vincent.

"For the moment I would concentrate on the difficulty," Meisner says. "What else?"

John raises his hand. "You brought up the example from Stanislavsky, what he said about 'public solitude,' and you said that if you really involved yourself in the activity—just as if you're at home combing your hair in the mirror—it would be poetic if you were totally involved in it."

" 'Public solitude.' What else?"

Sarah leans forward in her seat. "That the activity and the reason you choose to do it can't be too exaggerated or too far fetched. It has to be something realistic, not like Mrs. Ronald Reagan driving a taxi."

"Because she's a terrible driver!" Meisner exclaims, and the class laughs. "What else? What did I say was the essence of the independent activity? The most important element in it?"

"The reason *why*," John says, "the specific reason you're doing it."

"That's important, but it's not the *most* important element."

"The difficulty?" John asks.

"Yes, the difficulty."

"It strengthens your concentration," Sarah adds.

"Indeed it does," Meisner says. "That's common sense." He pauses for a moment before asking, "How many of you have some kind of reasonably familiar knowledge of another creative art?" Bruce raises his hand. "You do? Music?"

"Singing," Bruce says, "but I'm not an accomplished musician."

"Suppose you wanted to be. What's the first thing you have to know essentially, besides knowing you have a good voice? What do you have to know if you want to play the Emperor Concerto with the Philharmonic?" Bruce has no answer. "Anybody?" Meisner asks.

"You have to know the music," Vince suggests.

"Of course."

"You have to open the piano," Wendy says.

"No! To become an accomplished musician you have to realize that it takes *twenty years* to be a master at it! *A master!*" Meisner's use of the word is thrilling. He pauses before adding, "And the same is true of acting." The students regard him soberly. "Well, does anybody want to say anything?" After a moment he adds, "I do. Why do you think this is vital? Why should you be doing that independent activity? Why did I *choose* to have you do it? Anna?"

"Because you learn to use your instincts based on what somebody else does to you," she says.

"As opposed to what you have to achieve by yourself. What else?"

"It helps us in our concentration because it takes us out of the classroom," Anna continues. "We're *doing* something that we have to do which is unrelated to anybody else, and it doesn't matter where we are. We could be at home or on the street or even on stage—it's of its own world. Also, it's good to have something else going on in the exercise, bouncing off somebody else."

"That's true."

"That's very hard," Anna says.

"What?" Meisner asks in surprise.

"I think that's very hard," Anna says in a firm but quiet voice.

"Time," Meisner says. "Give yourself time. In only nineteen years and eleven months you'll be amazed at how simple it all was." The class laughs.

"It seems to be quiet here today. Nobody seems to want to be dramatic, but that's all right, provided we follow the basic rules."

Meisner has just interrupted a repetition exercise between Ralph, whom Wendy described on the first day of class as stocky, burly and stooped—he was a wrestler in high school—and Dave, a dark, slightly imperious young man who was a first-rate collegiate swimmer and who currently teaches the sport in a New Jersey health club.

"Now, for the most part, this was spotty. The weakness in it was the way you kept letting it drop all the time. In terms of continuity, the contact between you broke too often. You let it stop. When the thing logically seemed to end, you let it. 'Can I help you?' 'No, you can't help me.' Period. 'Can I pick that up?' 'No, you can't pick that up.' Finished. I didn't mind because basically, like the others today, it was relaxed, easy and unforced. These are all significant values, but the continuity was missing."

"I understand that," Dave says defensively, "but I'm uncomfortable with its application to what I was doing. I didn't want to force it or push it—just to let it happen."

"You were absolutely right."

"In terms of the repetition—"

"It was up to Ralph," Meisner adds.

"That's right," Dave agrees and begins to gather up the deck of playing cards scattered over the table. His independent activity was to make a house of cards.

"I'm sorry," Ralph says, "It seems that I was waiting for something to happen, and when it didn't happen I—"

Meisner interrupts. "My dear fellow, I have illustrated that there is no such thing as nothing, right? And I have also illustrated that what you do doesn't depend on you, it depends on the other fellow. He was concentrating very intently. You could have noted that, but you let it slide without comment. Let me tell you something. I am, in a way, delighted with what I have seen so far today because it represents an understanding of the problem on its smoothest, least excited level. I like it! It's like a vacation! And the reason you behaved as you did was valuable. It wasn't producing any clichés; it was true."

He regards Ralph intently for a moment and then asks, "Are you afraid of him?"

"Yeah," Ralph says quietly, "sometimes."

"You should use that. It will do something for him *and* for you. Why are you afraid of him?"

"He's a big guy, he's very willful, very tempestuous, and I feel I have to get on his good side."

"That's not theatrical," Meisner replies. "It's bad for you, and it's unfair to him. You're putting him in the position of having a hundred dollars in his pocket, and all he is allowed to buy is jelly beans. Do you understand that?" Ralph nods. "But in a real way, I liked what you did. There was progress in it. There was knowledge in it. The thing that's going to bring it to a different level has yet to come. The reason behind the knock, the reason *why* you come in and engage him in human conversation—you follow?—has yet to come."

The exercise between Bruce and Lila proves tedious and painful to watch. Bruce has chosen to play the harmonica as his independent activity, but he does so for no compelling reason; it is merely unskilled noodling. Lila knocks timidly on the door and enters when Bruce opens it for her. Rose Marie, who is sitting in the front row next to Meisner's desk, gasps. Lila has chosen to costume herself in a flaming-red woolen bathrobe with matching slippers. She is affecting a generalized emotional state. On seeing her, Bruce says, "I thought you'd never get here."

Meisner is visibly distressed, and after a few minutes removes his glasses and covers his eyes with his hands, his head bent over his desk. In another minute, he interrupts the exercise.

"There is so much to talk about here," he says, lifting his head and repositioning his glasses. "First of all, Lila, you are playing a part, the part of some unhappy woman."

"True," Lila says, sitting beside Bruce on the bed.

"Where did you get that red—that costume?"

"The robe? It was given to me years ago."

"You brought it in because it fit the part?" Meisner asks.

"Maybe. I didn't think of it that way, but that could be behind it and I didn't realize it."

"What did you wear when you came to class?"

"Black sweater and pants."

"That's what you should have done the exercise in."

"Right," Lila says simply.

"In other words, if you don't give up acting out your clichés, I can't help you to learn how to act. I'm trying to get you to do an exercise, not to play a part."

"I understand. I knew I was way off base—"

"No talking!" Meisner exclaims, and the extent of his distress is evident in the sharpness of his tone. "Yes, you were way off base. You were way off base. You were like somebody—I'll say this and then won't say any more—you were like somebody who's been playing the piano for years *by ear,* who decides to study the instrument and finds a teacher—this is not meant unkindly—who says, 'Okay, learn to do that.' " Meisner holds his right hand before him as if he were seated at the keyboard of a piano. " 'Learn to raise a finger without tensing and then drop it. Then learn to raise another.' And he takes you back to the absolute beginning of learning how to play. And if I were that teacher, I wouldn't say to you that when you come to take your first lesson you should be sure to dress like Wanda Landowska, a great harpsichordist who's been dead for about forty years! Wear gold lamé with a train thirty feet long! I don't tell you to dress for the exercise. If you've got slacks on, that's what you do it in!"

"Right."

"Now, you," Meisner says, looking at Bruce. "An independent activity has to have two things. It must be *difficult* and there must be a compelling reason *why* you are doing it. If you had picked a piece of music you had never played before in your life, that unfamiliarity would be part of the difficulty in learning how to play it. You follow?"

"Yeah."

"I say, 'You follow?' and you say, 'Yeah!' "

"I can't play a Chopin étude on this harmonica because I don't know how it goes in my head," Bruce says.

"Then pick a piece that fits that instrument, one you know but have never played, and practice it with all the difficulties that involves. I don't care if you choose to learn 'Deutschland über alles,' as long as you learn to play it like a virtuoso! And the next thing is, why is it absolutely imperative that you learn to play 'Deutschland über alles' on the harmonica? If you decide why, you are exercising your imagination. If it is difficult, it will intensify your concentration. When something is difficult to do, it forces you to use your concentration. Have I made myself clear?"

Bruce nods, and Meisner shifts his gaze back to Lila. He is profoundly disturbed.

"God almighty, woman, stop acting! I can't stand it! Give the problems here your attention, your concentration and your time. Don't behave as if acting were something that any amateur can turn on! It's not true! I can understand why, after a good many years of acting, it's hard for you to throw off your habits. I can understand where you got the idea to dress for the part. But it's nonsense!"

"I agree."

"All right, you agree. You both are making me be very sharp and determined because you don't put enough work into what you're doing! And don't tell me that you do! I'm a past master at knowing what has been thought out! I will not let you take this any more lightly than I do! Now, I beg you, work the way a real actor works, bring in the result of your efforts, and I will be the first to recognize it. But don't throw something at me as if I were an amateur that didn't know the difference! I repeat. Lila, don't act. Bruce, an independent activity has to be difficult because that strengthens your concentration, and it has to be justified because everything must have a reason for being. I don't care if it's only because there's a part you want to play and in order to play it you have to learn to play that German song *like a master!* Have I made myself clear?"

"Yes, extremely," Lila says.

"Well, okay, my friends," Meisner says. The episode has drained him, and his voice, though amplified, is no more than a whisper. "I have all the sympathy that you need, but please give me back a percentage of what I give you instead of kicking me in the ass and thinking you're going to get away with it. I won't have it. This country is full of actors who have been trained beautifully—by me! But they worked! I say, 'Don't act, don't fake, don't pretend—work!' That will train your concentration, your actor's faith and, maybe, your emotion. Then you can hold up your head and say you're learning how to act, and I can hold up mine and say I'm teaching you."

■|

"Oh my God, that Lila! After a scene like that I feel so discouraged and old!"

Meisner unlocks the door of his office. "It's brutal, you know, on me as well as on them. But they provoked me and I couldn't help myself. It's not something to be proud of, but scenes like this do happen and they are nothing to be ashamed of either. Besides, I'm too old to worry about it."

He enters and Scott Roberts follows. "Sandy," he says, "I got the job. They asked me to direct the Cocteau play next season at Circle Rep."

"That's terrific," Meisner says. "I'm proud of you."

"I hope you'll come to see it," Scott says.

"Yes," Meisner says, "if I'm still alive—and that's a big 'if'— I'll come to see it."

"Good. I just wanted you to know. I'll see you on Monday."

"Good-night," Meisner says.

"You know," Meisner says, picking up his black wool coat with a mink collar from the office daybed, "twenty or more years ago, Lila was a star—musical comedies mostly, but light straight plays, too. She was beautiful and she could belt out a song. Scott tells me she does television commercials now. I wouldn't know; I don't see well enough to watch television anymore."

He turns off the light and locks the office door. "I was surprised and touched when she called me last spring and asked to become a student. It must be very humbling to return to square one. She realized, she said, that if she wanted to go on working in the theater, she would have to grow, to deepen herself as an actress. And she's right, I think. Well, we'll see. Maybe after a class like this she'll quit."

Meisner walks slowly to the elevator. "I am heartened, though, by the progress of most of the others. Do you remember the exercise Joseph did with me several classes ago? 'You're busy.' 'Yes, I'm busy.' Simple, unforced and clear. He held his own. John, and also Anna, strike me as very talented. Well, we'll see. Right now, I'm delighted to go home. After a day like this, I need a good, stiff drink!"

5 Beyond Repetition

STUDENT: I'm getting the feeling: Don't think—do!
MEISNER: That's a very good feeling to have. That's an actor thinking. How does an actor think? He doesn't think—he does.
STUDENT: Right.
MEISNER: That's a good feeling.

October 31

"Listen, everybody. Next time, the person who comes in has to have a reason for coming in. And the reason has to be *simple* and *specific* and not death-defying in its urgency. In other words, come in for a can of soup, not because your brother is pinned under a truck on the street and they can't get him out. Suppose you're having a party and your neighbor, your partner, has a rare collection of Sinatra. So you want to borrow it. But no more dramatic than that. It gives you a reason for knocking at the door and then you'll forget it anyway. You're making a spaghetti sauce and you have no oregano. See?"

"So that influences the knock," says Ray. "The knock isn't arbitrary, right?"

"The knock is just as it is, one knock. But if you come in for a pinch of oregano, what the hell kind of knock does that indicate?"

John raises his hand.

"I have a question. When I was outside, before knocking on the door I made up a little story for myself because you said that the person who came in should have something he needs from the partner. About halfway through I was going to bring it into the exercise, but I didn't because I was unsure if you wanted it brought up or if you just wanted it to root us."

"Just to root you. Never bring it up, because the script will bring it up anyway. Hamlet doesn't keep secret what's making him feel so lousy. You follow?"

November 3

"The question for today is what, if anything, are you getting from this procedure? What, and in what way, if any, are you being helped by this process? Based on the fact that none of you are kids and all of you have had experience, what's been going on with you in this class?"

Rose Marie raises her hand. "What I am trying to concentrate on is forgetting everything I've done before and just listening to what's going on and not applying it to anything else. I'm a little confused, but that's okay."

"Why are you confused?"

"Because I don't know how I'm going to listen and answer truthfully, moment to moment, when I get a script."

"That's the way you are going to *begin* with a script. Be patient, you'll soon see. Who else has something to say? Curiously enough —just a minute, Lila—for a class who has had considerable experience, there are not many problems involved. Lila, what's your question?"

"I had no question. I thought I would try to answer what this class means to me so far."

"The answer to what it means to you is one word."

"Truth?"

"Reality. The truth of your instincts is the root of your foundation. Right?"

"Right."

"You see, you've all had experience. That's not only my problem, it's your problem, too. Ray?"

"I was going to say in answer to your question about what this class means is that it seems to me that usually when I have acted well, it has been by accident. And finding a way to act well on a regular basis is maybe what this class is doing for me, I think."

"That's great."

"The other way," Ray adds, "the way that Lee Strasberg and the Actors Studio people use, seems to do the opposite. They make you go inside, and you can get stuck in there."

"That's right. I told Lee that when he was alive. I said to him, 'You introvert the already introverted. All actors,' I said, 'like all artists, are introverted because they live on what's going on in their instincts, and to attempt to make that conscious is to confuse the actor.' Needless to say, he didn't pay any attention to me, but that's the reason I'm a better teacher than he was."

"Listen, Philip, how do you feel?"

"Up-tight," the fair-haired young man replies instantly. Then he stammers nervously, "I—how do I feel? Now?"

"That's what I said."

"I feel nervous," Philip says, sitting dejectedly on the bed. Sarah, his partner, sits beside him.

"Don't you know that you're always going to feel nervous? You're the nervous type. What makes you feel nervous?"

"Thinking that other people will see me nervous."

"How do you want other people to see you?"

"Relaxed."

"Well, they'll think you're relaxed if you don't tell them you're nervous, because you don't *look* nervous. It comes out, though, in a certain indecision about just repeating. How are you going to fix that?"

"I'm going to deal more with my partner."

"And less with . . . ?"

"Me?"

"Your nervousness. How did you get so nervous?"

"I'm not so sure. Maybe a lot of sugar, a lot of coffee—"

"A lot of parents!"

"Parents?" Philip asks. "Yeah, they did it." The class laughs.

"I told you what to do to your mother."

"Kick her? Just kick her?"

"I didn't say kick her, I said retaliate."

"Punch her out?"

"I'll tell you what. Don't punch her out, just lay all your attention on Sarah and stop announcing to the world how nervous you are. *Everybody's* nervous! Aren't you?" The class responds with a chorus of "Yes."

"You know, you get better all the time. You don't have real freedom yet, as you well know, because you're always afraid you'll be wrong. I think that's where your mother comes in."

"And father."

"Him too?"

"Yeah."

"Stay away from them."

"I do that as much as I can."

"Then put all your attention on Sarah." Meisner regards Philip and adds, "It gets better. You had long passages in there that were pure without your announcing how you felt. Nobody gives a damn how you feel, you know? Nobody cares. We *care* when your concern about how you feel hurts your exercise. What do you want? For us to burst into tears because you're nervous? To hell with us! Put your attention on Sarah and repeat what you hear, okay?" As Philip and Sarah return to their seats Meisner removes his microphone and whispers to Scott Roberts, "You know, he gets better all the time."

"Now, I'm not talking about anybody in particular; I'm talking in general. Where is the performance born in good actors? What makes a Maureen Stapleton? Where does her performance come from?"

"Herself," Ray says.

"In her ability to believe in the given circumstances of the script," John adds.

"She has great actor's faith," Meisner says. "What is actor's faith?"

"She believes that the imaginary circumstances are truer than true," Joseph says.

"Let's just say that she believes they are true. What else? Ralph?"

"You're willing to believe it even though you may doubt that it's true."

"A real actor finds a way of eliminating the doubt."

Vince holds up his hand. "You do it for its own sake without having to understand it intellectually."

"What does intellect have to do with acting?" Meisner asks.

"Nothing," Vince says. Meisner nods, and for a moment seems lost in thought.

"Next week I'm going to start you with scripts, which we will treat as if they were exercises. They're usually better parts than you normally get to play, even though they're very old-fashioned. They all have a human problem. Scott, it's up to you when I give them out."

"I'll have them on Monday," Scott Roberts says.

"I'd like to start on the problem of preparation before Christmas," Meisner says with a sly grin. "I hope it doesn't ruin your holiday."

November 7

"Joseph, for the most part you were all right. But there's occasionally a tendency to be logical and mental. Now, when you get to a text—which is coming up—you don't have to worry about being logical because the text does it for you. If the script has your partner announce that he is going to get drunk, the playwright will give you an appropriate response. But in this exercise if you stick to the repetition, which is illogical and comes purely from what you hear, you'll overcome a tendency to use your head logically. Do you understand?"

"Yes."

"Beethoven had a landlady who reported that after he had been working for a certain period of time, he took a pail of cold water and poured it over his head. He was a nut, but that need for water wouldn't have happened if he was working logically from his head. He needed it because he was working from his intestines. That's why he was so emotionally overheated." Meisner pauses to put out a cigarette. "Joseph, you were right to go when you did. The impulse to go was genuine. She provoked it and you got the message, right? Acting is all a give-and-take of those impulses affecting each person. Am I making myself clear?"

"Yes," Joseph says.

"Am I to you?" He asks Joseph's partner, Beth, whose hair has been pulled back from her face with a black ribbon. She nods. "What were you doing?"

"I was filling out some forms in order to get an important project approved, and I didn't realize that there was a deadline. They have to be in the mail by midnight."

"If that activity were as significant as your words tell me it was, Beth, this would have been a different exercise because you would have been totally involved, and Joseph would have been in an upheaval. You follow? Beth could have driven Joseph *crazy* with that exercise if she'd made this activity more important than the repetition."

"Well, this was absolutely real to me in the sense that it was more important than anything else," Beth says defensively.

"I can only accept that if it's in your behavior. Beethoven couldn't pour a pail of water over his head to cool off unless what he was doing was a very strong, inner experience. Try to tighten the repetition. Try to let it move in its organic rhythm. Don't be torn between 'sense' and the emotional impact of so-called 'senseless' repetition."

"Would you say that again?" Beth asks.

"What did I say?"

"You said don't be caught between 'sense,' " replies Joseph, "and the impact of the . . . the *emotional* impact . . . of the so-called 'senseless' repetition."

"Why did you come into the room, or have you forgotten?"

"I came in to invite her to go to a party with me."

"Had she lived truthfully under the imaginary circumstances imposed by her independent activity, this could easily have ended with your giving her the old heave-ho and going to the party with some other girl. How I would have loved that! That would have been marvelous!"

November 10

Before John and Rose Marie begin their exercise, she helps him move the long table to the center of the room and push the bed against the back wall. Then she leaves the room, closing the door behind her. John sits at the table, takes a sheaf of typed pages from a manila envelope and begins to read them intently, marking them occasionally with a red pencil. Suddenly there is a sharp rap at the door, then another, and finally a third. Reluctantly John leaves the table and opens the door.

"Persistent," he says.

"Yeah, persistent," Rose Marie says, framed in the open doorway.

"Persistent," John repeats.

"Yeah, something wrong with that?" Rose Marie inquires.

"Something wrong with that?"

"Something wrong with that?"

"Nothing wrong with that," John says, and for a moment hesitates.

"Are you inviting me in?" Rose Marie asks.

"Am I inviting you in?"

"Yeah, are you inviting me in?"

"Am I inviting—"

"Yeah," Rose Marie snaps, "some big question?"

"Well, it's not a big question," John says with annoyance. "In or out?"

"In or out!"

"In or out?"

"What is this, an interrogation?" Rose Marie asks.

"No, it's not an interrogation," John says. Rose Marie glares at him defiantly. "In or out!" he exclaims.

"Don't treat me like a baby," she warns.

"I'm not treating you like a baby."

"You're treating me like a baby."

"In or out," John says with great finality. After a moment, Rose Marie walks into the room. John closes the door, then moves quickly to the table and resumes editing his papers.

"That's pretty stupid," Rose Marie remarks, looking at his seated figure. "So I'm not here now!" John glances in annoyance at her for a moment, then returns to work. "You have such a mean look!" she exclaims; yet she continues to watch him working with fascination.

After a pause Rose Marie says, "That must be pretty hard."

"Yeah, it's hard," John says, and begins to chew his upper lip.

"Ah ha!" Rose Marie exclaims. "You're chewing your mouth!"

"Yeah, I'm chewing my mouth."

"Oh, sorry. You're so *business* like."

"I'm so businesslike."

"Right," Rose Marie says, and pauses for a few seconds before taking a step toward the table.

"What do you want?" John asks sharply.

"What do I want?" Rose Marie repeats.

"What do you want?"

"Are you pissed off at me?"

"Am I pissed off at you?"

"*Yeah*, are you pissed off at me?"

"Yes," John says firmly, "I'm pissed off at you."

"All right, I'll go."

"You'll go."

"Yeah, I'll go."

"You'll go?"

"That's what you want, right?"

"That's what I want, right!"

"You're being mean."

"Mean?"

"Yeah, don't you think you are?" she says. He glares at her. "Nice look!" After a moment she adds quietly, "You're just being a jerk." She regards him intently and then walks firmly to the door and closes it behind her.

"Scott," Meisner says to his assistant, "we'd better get to those scenes quickly because they're playing them! That was a scene, you know. It was a *scene.*"

"It was?" Rose Marie asks, coming back in.

"Oh, sure. It was not a repetition exercise, but I'll tell you this; if you were the right type for a part, if you looked like, as they say, 'the girl,' and if you, John, fit the playwright's description of 'the man' and you played your scene with this much unforced, simple, unpushed reality, you'd be good! But it wasn't repetition, except *occasionally.* It was really a scene. What point am I making?"

Ray leans forward in his seat. "Instead of sticking to the rule of the exercise where you repeat and repeat and repeat until something changes what it is that you are repeating, they left all that unsaid and emotionally went from one thing to another. And it had its own sort of logic about how long she was going to be allowed to stay in the room, how angry he was—"

"Were they relaxed?"

"Very," Ray says.

"Were they emotionally true?"

"Yes," Joseph says.

"Was their dialogue acceptable as simple, truthful dialogue?" Heads nod in agreement. "That's what you had; you had a *scene.* Occasionally you went back to the exercise, but this kind of relaxation, plus working off each other, is what makes a scene." Meisner looks at John and Rose Marie, who stand opposite him behind the table. "In a way I'm paying you a compliment, while at the same time I'm not really crazy about the fact that you're already playing a scene."

November 14

"John, take her by the left arm and throw her out! Right now!"

John grabs Wendy's arm, coolly pushes her out the door and slams it shut.

"Now, you should have done that without my suggesting it. Why didn't you?"

"Because it didn't seem valid in terms of doing the exercise. I know what you're saying—that my impulse should have been to throw her out because she really was bothering me."

"So why didn't you?"

"Because I didn't."

"So why didn't you?"

"Because I was working out of my head. I was doing what I *thought* I *should* be doing."

"If you threw her out, there wouldn't be any exercise?"

"Right."

"But the point is that you do exercises in order to train yourself to follow the truth!"

"I know. I just missed it, that's all."

"Look, let me tell you something seriously. In life . . . life is terrible, I think. But on the stage you have a wonderful opportunity to tell the truth, and all that can come of it is praise. That's true, do you understand?" John nods. "Your work is all right, but the quality is more important than the quantity. What does that mean?"

"It means that even if the exercise had gone on only a quarter as long, if I had followed my impulse to throw her out, it would have been much more truthful."

"And to your ultimate advantage as an actor. Do you see?"

"Yes."

November 17

"I have a surprise for you all today—scripts! They are all old-hat scenes, antiques, but they're perfect for our immediate needs.

These scenes are old-fashioned only in the sense that they were
written before you were born. But every one of them has a
compelling human problem; that's why I picked them. I want
you to take your script and learn it *without* meaning, *without*
readings, *without* interpretation, without *anything*. Just learn the
lines by rote, mechanically. I want that to be very clear. 'To/
be/or/not/to/be/that/is/the/question.' " As Meisner coldly recites the famous line, his hand taps his desk mechanically on each
syllable. "No *tsuris*—that's French for trouble—no iambic pen-
tameter, nothing but the cold text. Then, when you know the
words mechanically, with ease, take a walk with your partner—
any street will do—and go over the text so that you know yours
and she knows hers. If you want to stop off and get a cup of coffee,
it's okay with me. Do the lines then. Shock the busboy who's
studying at the American Academy. 'They don't know what
they're saying! They speak like robots!' Shock the pants off him!"

November 21

With cold, mechanical precision, John and Ralph have just re-
cited a scene from *Mister Roberts*.

"Okay," Meisner begins, "they said those lines in a way that
must be terribly alien to you, right? No meaning, no readings.
Nothing that rote permits anybody to see as a human experience.
Now, does anyone have any suspicion of what I'm getting at
here? Bette, what's your suspicion?"

Bette, the daughter of a famous comedienne recently married
to a producer of television commercials, looks relaxed, but there
is an edge of nervous energy contained just beneath the surface.
"I had a glimmer when Bruce and I were practicing. I felt that
it's so raw and so untouched when we do it by rote that what we
can add to it emotionally is unlimited because we are free of
immediately insisting that it be read one way or another."

"I like what you said. 'Raw.' You follow? *'Raw.'* I'm insisting
on this mechanical approach in order to avoid calculated results.
John?"

"I think it's tough," John says.

"You think it's tough?"

"You know, on the way over here we were doing it and there were times Ralph said to me, 'You're reading, you're doing a reading.' I guess I fell into that old pattern I've done all my life."

"That's right," Meisner replies. "I'm trying to eliminate a habit that, as you said, you've done all your acting life. In order to build up performances which are coming out of you, which are coming out of your emotional grasp of the material, I choose to reduce you to a neutral, meaningless, inhuman object—a robot, call it what you like. In order to fill those words with the truth of your emotional life you're first going to learn the text coldly, without expression, in a completely neutral way."

"I want to show you something. John, come over here."

John leaves his seat and stands next to the desk. Meisner moves around it to stand next to him.

"Now turn around," he says. "Make your position as firm and as rigid as you can. If necessary, hold on to the desk but make yourself absolutely steadfast."

"Okay."

"I don't think you're solid enough. Are you?"

"Yeah."

Meisner places the palms of both hands on John's shoulders and attempts to budge him. "I don't make any impression on him!" he says. "I'll try again. John, do the same thing."

Again John holds on to the edge of the desk, so tightly that the knuckles of his hands turn white.

"He's stiff!" Meisner says, and then spells the word "S-t-i-f!" The class laughs. "Now, John, relax."

John lets go of the desk, turns and shakes the tension from his arms and shoulders. Meisner gives him a firm but gentle shove and John takes two long, loose steps forward.

"He's responsive! Do you see that? Relax." Meisner pushes him again, and again John ambles forward. "He's responsive to what I do. Thank you, John. Sit down.

"Now, if you are neutral . . . Neutral—what's that mean? Open

to any influence, right? If you are neutral, you will achieve a kind
of emotional flexibility, won't you? If you're tense, if you're
unrelaxed, like John was at the beginning, you're not responsive
to the influence of my push. Consequently I say a logical thing:
I say, 'Learn that text in as unmeaningful and yet in as relaxed
a way as you can, so that you'll be open to any influence that
comes to you.' Do you follow the logic of that? If you don't,
say so."

"Neutral and relaxed," Philip says. "Not firm and tense."

"Not set, not fixed. I'm saying to you as actors who work
constantly with texts, with words, 'Learn those words as empty,
as unfixed, as relaxed as John was when I pushed him.' Is there
any question about this? That's why I'm asking you to learn these
lines with the precision of a machine. Mechanical precision.
Then we'll go on from there."

"If you find yourself reading the words, putting something
into them, do you slow down or stop or what?" Philip asks.

"You stop. Look, I'm going to give you a line. 'Oh, God, my
soul is bleeding.' Let me hear you say that."

"Oh, God," Philip says, "my soul is bleeding."

"Now say it expressively."

"Oh, God, my soul is bleeding," Philip says with added volume.

"More!" Meisner says. "Don't you believe in God? And in
pain?"

"Oh *God*," Philip bellows, "my *soul* is bleeding!"

"That's what I *don't* want you to do. You follow?" Meisner
recites the line quietly, mechanically. " 'Oh/God/my/soul/is/
bleed/ing.' Eventually that line will come right out of the heart
of you."

Meisner interrupts Dave, who has been reading his scene in a
spooky, mechanical way, with the objection that, as is his tendency, Dave has gone too far; the work is too mechanical.

"Dave, explain to me what I said to you."

"You want it repeated mechanically and neutrally."

"That's right."

"I'm putting too much into it."

"In what way are you putting too much into it?"

"Overemphasizing the mechanicalness of it, the syllable by syllable."

"That's right," Meisner says. "What did I say to you about your repetition?"

"That I wasn't picking up on the behavior. I was simply repeating for the sake of repeating."

"Isn't that somewhat like this? That you're overdoing the machine part of it a little too much?"

"I was doing the exercise in an academic way. You kept saying, 'Repeat, repeat, repeat,' and basically that's all I was concentrating on. I was doing the exercise in an academic way instead of just letting it happen, moment to moment."

"The word 'academic' is well chosen."

"I find this very tough to do," Dave's partner, Joseph, says.

"You do? Why?"

"We learn words by associating them with the way we say them—like, 'Oh, how *nice* to see you.' If you eliminate all that, you've lost your footing."

"That's right," Meisner says, "until you are mechanically, absolutely secure in this text, with no interpretation."

"But we all memorize by using an emotion to give the words some sort of significance so that we can remember them," Joseph says. "So it's usual to have a cadence attached to the way we're doing it."

"Which you have in your ear, right?" Meisner asks. "This way of working eliminates all that. What might be the value of this to you?"

"Well," Joseph says, "it deprives you of any preconceived emotional associations, so that once you learn the text this way, the emotion will come out of what your partner is giving you."

"To *begin* with," Meisner adds. "So that you don't have the habit of saying, 'Go to the store and get me a salami sandwich because I *love* salami!' " His eerie voice through the microphone seems to slide up and then down an octave on the word "love," and the class laughs.

"The 'love' is a cliché," Meisner says. "What other reactions are there? John?"

"It seems that whatever we do get out of this exercise is going to be full and honest—"

Meisner interrupts. "And improvisational. It's going to be an improvisation. Fundamentally that's a very healthy thing to do. It strips you of your past habits."

"I like that," Bette says. "I like that a lot."

"I don't blame you in the least."

November 28

Anna and Vincent, whose partners are absent, get ready to perform an exercise. Vincent has an independent activity (attempting to memorize a script in preparation for an audition), and Anna is to knock and enter the room. Before she leaves, Meisner calls her over and whispers a brief instruction in her ear.

The effect on the exercise is galvanizing. Anna enters enraged. Though the exact reason for her anger is never discussed, her behavior makes it clear that she believes that Vincent has slandered her. She is livid, and Vincent is rendered almost speechless. Meisner is pleased.

"Okay," he says when Anna slams out of the room, "that was very good. Now, look," he says to the class, "that was the basic exercise, but it had something added to it. What?"

"She came in furious," Bette says.

"An emotional circumstance. I, as the director, added an emotional circumstance to the exercise, and that made it into a scene. In an exercise there is no learned text. All of you are now in the process of learning a text. What's absent from that learning is what we just witnessed—an emotional circumstance."

"Sandy, would you say again what's missing?" Joseph asks.

"What's missing from what you're doing now with these texts is anything that has to do with an emotional circumstance."

"You're talking about our learning the lines mechanically?"

"Yes. In the future . . . But that brings up the thorny subject of preparation, which I'm saving for your Christmas present.

Anna, that was very good. Vince taught you some naughty words."

"I know."

"That's all right," Meisner says, "you taught him some too."

"Let's talk about this."

Meisner interrupts a scene between Rose Marie and John. They have memorized the lines and are saying them quietly, but with the sound of human conversation.

"What we're looking for is the picking up not of cues but of impulses. One doesn't pick up cues, one picks up impulses. I'll show you. Rose Marie, say something to me."

"You have very smooth skin."

"Yes, but keep going."

"You have very smooth skin. It looks like you spend a lot of time in the sun."

"Yes, I have smooth skin," Meisner says. "Now, when did the impulse for my speech come? The impulse for my speech came early! At the *beginning* of the speech. I'll show it to you in another way. It's very simple, very improvisational. John, ask me if I want a drink, and then tell me that you have scotch, vodka, bourbon, gin and a lot of soft drinks."

"Sandy, would you like a drink? I have scotch, vodka, bourbon, gin and—"

Meisner, whose eyes lit up and whose right hand waved politely in the air on hearing the word "scotch," interrupts John's litany with the line "Scotch, please."

The class laughs.

"Now, when did the impulse for that happen?"

"Scotch," says Rose Marie.

"At the beginning! That's very different, picking up the impulse instead of picking up the cue."

"So you're saying that if the impulse is at the beginning, you must sustain it until he stops and you can say, 'Scotch'?"

"Until the cue comes. You don't pick up cues, you pick up *impulses.*"

"I guess it's a matter of my knowing the script a lot better in order to be able to tune in to the impulses," John says.

"Absolutely right," Meisner says. "But that's not bad for the first time. That's the way a script initially resolves itself. Rose Marie, why did you knock on the door?"

"I thought I was supposed to for the exercise."

"You live here!"

"I know. I'm still a little unclear about what exactly we're doing. Is this an exercise or is it a scene?"

"It's a scene which is being handled improvisationally—that is, impulse to impulse."

"I'm supposed to work off his behavior and not the text, right?"

"Both. Look, I'll do it for you. Your speech to me is, 'You're weak. You promised that you'd never take another drink again if you lived to be a hundred, but you've broken your word.' And my answer is, 'I'm not weak.' Now, where does the impulse for that happen? Right at the beginning! *Don't pick up cues, pick up impulses.* Say your text to me again."

" 'You're weak. You said you'd never take a drink again as long as you lived and you didn't even keep your word.' "

" 'I'm *not* weak.' I was acting all through that! Did you see that?"

"You're not necessarily asking us to start our line before the partner finishes his line?" Bette asks.

"No! I said wait for the cue, but the impulse, the emotion, comes whenever it's felt. You'll get used to it once you have a command over the script. I'm saying two things to you: learn the lines; pick up the impulses."

"I liked it very much."

Joseph and Beth have just completed their scene.

"Joseph, you know your wife's betraying you, right? I don't care what you do or how you do it, but you, Joseph, get into a certain condition when you find out your girl's betraying you. I'd like to see that next time.

"Beth, you're going to be free of that creep of a husband pretty soon. Doesn't that make you feel good? Let's see what happens when Beth feels in good spirits. Now, one of these days—I hope it will be before we quit for Christmas—I'll begin to show you the elements of that agonizing problem, preparation, which is the self-stimulation of your emotion. It's the most subtle problem in acting, believe me. And we'll get to it, but not yet. Next time finish the scene with these two additions: Joe in a lousy mood—I don't care what you do—and Beth in a wonderful mood—I don't care what you do. I'm anticipating emotional preparation."

" 'There goes your mother after her darling David,' " Meisner says, quoting Sarah's line from a scene from Sidney Howard's *The Silver Cord,* which she and Philip have just completed. "Now, that line is spoken while you're looking through the window and seeing his mother walking, right? But you're never going to see his mother walking. If you look out the window onstage, you're going to see scenery stacked up against the wall. You're going to see the stage manager trying to make the ingenue. You're going to see everything but what you're supposed to see. Suppose I'm reading from my script in rehearsal while we're still sitting around the table, and I read, 'If it doesn't stop snowing, I'll never get back to New York and I'll lose my job!' " His reading of the line is quiet, yet the sense of panic is palpable. "So how you *feel* about what you see is already in you when you're sitting there reading the script. Don't try to see snow, because if you look you're going to see the stage manager and the ingenue."

The class laughs.

"Finally, at the end of the road, they bring in the scenery, and on one side is a wall with a window. So as a convention, you get up and walk to the window to make the audience believe that you're looking out. It's for the *audience,* not for you! And what it means to you is something emotional: *'I'll lose my job!'* You follow? If you went to the Actors Studio you'd spend six months seeing the snow before you could say, 'Look at the snow.' This takes a terrible burden away from the actor, who thinks he's got to see the woods and the snow. 'Give me my gun! I see a rabbit! Give me my gun!' " Meisner sounds thrilled at the possibility of a hunt. "That happens when you're still sitting there reading.

Then when they put in the scenery you move to the window. Isn't that simple? How simple it is to solve the problem of seeing things when you know that it's all in you emotionally, and that walking to the window is only a convention."

"Dave, what would you do if you were suddenly given a hundred thousand dollars? By the way, I once said that to a class—no one older than twenty-two—and a girl sitting right there said, 'But I *have* a hundred thousand dollars!' "

The class laughs.

"What would you do, Dave, if you had a hundred thousand dollars?"

"Buy myself a home."

"That's too general and prosaic. Besides, what kind of a home can you get for a hundred thousand dollars?"

"Not in New York City."

"In Uganda? What would you do?"

Dave pauses, his face rapt in thought. "That's what I'd do. I'd—"

"That's all?" Meisner asks. Dave looks straight ahead in silence. "It's interesting that you can't or won't—the chances are you won't—answer that question." He looks at Bette. "What would you do if I gave you a hundred thousand dollars?"

"I'd thank you and thank you and thank you."

"That's not activity, that's politeness."

Vince raises his hand. "The first thing I'd do is call my accountant."

"What?" Meisner says incredulously.

"The first thing I'd do is call my accountant," Vince repeats, "and make sure that I'd covered all the taxes and shelters, and then I'd probably buy some art I want, some Miró aquatints."

"What are you saying?"

"I'm saying I'd make sure to protect myself so that I wouldn't have to pay taxes, and then get some Mirós I really want to buy."

"You know," Meisner says, "the trouble with your answer, Vince, and with yours, Dave, is that they're prosaic and worldly and commonplace. Any garbage collector would think of them. I like you both, so I'm not recommending you to the Department of Sanitation."

"What are you saying?" Rose Marie demands with great seriousness. "That if somebody's dreams are ordinary, then they're not talented? If they say something like that, they're not worthy?"

"I'm saying that wishful thinking is a product of the imagination. On the one hand, if someone said, 'I'd pay my rent for the next five years,' I'd say, 'Bullshit. That's too realistic, it's too unimaginative, it's too practical.' On the other hand, what if a girl said, 'I'd like to go to the White House in a dress that's made of solid emeralds. Gorgeous! Solid emeralds! On some kind of cloth which can only be made by one nun in India!' That's extravagant, but it's the essence of wishful thinking."

Meisner pauses to adjust the microphone on his glasses. "I'm talking about imagination. Wishful thinking is based on imagination. Stimulating imagination—do you see that? If I say, 'I'll give you a hundred thousand dollars. What will you do with it?,' and you say, 'I'll buy a house, furnish it and pay the taxes on it for the next twenty years!,' that's practical. It's not out of your imaginative soul; it's out of your wish to be secure. But the dress made of emeralds is pure, untouched imagination. That's what wishful thinking is. Am I making the difference clear? One is the product of imagination and the other is based on prosaic reality. I want to make that point very clear because it is a prelude to preparation. That's all I'm going to say now; it's a prelude to the imaginative use of yourself. As I said—to repeat—it's a prelude, a remark which is a prelude to preparation."

"Sandy?" says Bette. "I have a suggestion."

"Yeah?"

"I think that the next time you should ask us what we would do with a million. A hundred thousand doesn't go as far as it used to."

"That's true," Meisner says. "I've found that out."

The class laughs.

The menu is the usual: tuna on a seeded roll and black coffee.

"Scott," Meisner says, "remind me this afternoon of the actress I once heard of who, when she got a role, wrote it out as if it were one continuous sentence, so that the other fellow always came in like an unpremeditated, spontaneous interruption. That would be good for all of them."

Scott Roberts nods and makes a note on his yellow legal pad.

6 Preparation: "In the Harem of My Head"

BEN: [*enters*]. Let's go.
LIBBY: Where to?
BEN: Empire. We'll see Marlene Dietrich.
GUS: Marlene—she's the intellect and artistic type. . . .
Marlene, I got her in the harem of my head.
—Clifford Odets, *Paradise Lost*

December 1

"Today is going to be devoted to preparation," Meisner says. "Preparation is that device which permits you to start your scene or play in a condition of emotional aliveness. The purpose of preparation is so that you do not come in emotionally empty. I want to be very simple about this whole subject. If you sign the contract in the Shubert offices for a wonderful part in a wonderful play, the obvious implication is that you are bursting with joy when you write your name on the document. Even if you live in Riverdale, forty-five minutes away by subway, the pleasure and pride that was instilled in you in the Shubert office is still there in some form by the time you get home. Ask me questions if I don't make it clear."

He pauses, but the class understands what he is saying.

"Now, preparation is going to present you with certain problems. One is the temptation to show it. 'Look, Ma, how happy I am—or miserable.' 'Look, audience, how overjoyed I am.' So you project your state of being. You do things to make people sense your emotional condition. Another thing, which cannot be repeated too often, is that preparation lasts only for the first moment of the scene, and then you never know what's going to happen. I'll illustrate that. Rose Marie, don't let me forget to illustrate that.

"In the early days of the Stanislavsky System, Mr. S. was looking for true behavior, and if what he wanted was great pleasure, he asked where you look for the reality of great pleasure. His answer was simple: you *remember* a time when you were under the influence of great pleasure. That's called 'emotion memory.' I don't use it, and neither did he after thirty years of experimentation. The reason? If you are twenty and work in a delicatessen, the chances are very slim that you can remember that glorious night you had with Sophia Loren. The chances are slight that you know the full pleasure of that kind of glorified sex. Am I making myself clear?"

The class nods.

"In other words, what I am saying is that what you're looking for is not necessarily confined to the reality of your life. It can be in your imagination. If you allow it freedom—with no inhibitions, no proprieties—to *imagine* what would happen between you and Sophia Loren, your imagination is, in all likelihood, deeper and more persuasive than the real experience. Is that clear? Can anybody tell me what I'm saying?"

John raises his hand. "You're saying that our imaginations are every bit as strong, if not stronger, than the experiences we can recall from our past."

"Right. Rose Marie?"

"So if I needed to feel that some great burden had been taken off my back, could I use something like, 'I'll never have to work for the next ten years—I won the lottery'? Is it better to use the circumstances from my real life, like how much I hate serving bacon cheeseburgers, and how sudden freedom from doing that kind of work would make me cry with joy?"

"It's better to use what moves *you*, what affects *you*."

"So I don't have to pretend that I'm Cinderella—"

"No!"

"Or that I live in a hut and have always wanted to have a pair of glass shoes—"

"No, you don't have to, but if living in a hut and finally getting a pair of shoes does it for you, use it. All I'm saying—don't complicate it—is don't come in empty. Get your inner life from what given circumstances suggest. This has to do with the self-stimulation of your emotion. The reason I asked you about wishful thinking was because I want you to find in yourself that element which belongs only to *you* and to no one else, which is stimulating for *you* and for no one else. Now, the source of where you find that inner life is not necessarily related to the needs of the scene. In the last century, the English actor William Charles Macready, before playing a certain scene in *The Merchant of Venice*, used to try to shake the iron ladder backstage that was embedded in the brick. He'd try and try, and would get furious because he couldn't budge it. *Then* he went on and played the scene. Am I being clear?"

"You say that your preparation is not necessarily related to the scene," Ray says. "In the case of Macready, could it be that he got furious at the ladder and then went on to play a love scene?"

"It could be that he got furious at the ladder and then went on to play the fact that his girl had kept him waiting in front of Radio City for an hour and a half. That's possible. Look, I'm presenting you with the premise, 'Don't come in empty.' Yes?"

"I find the things that stimulate me," Bette says, "are physical things more than thinking about serving hamburgers or Cinderella or something intellectual, which doesn't move me."

"You've got to find the things that stimulate *you*. If I want to come in feeling romantically sad because my girl left me for an older man—"

The class laughs.

"I might be able to get it from singing that schmaltzy theme from Tchaikovsky's Sixth Symphony. Are you getting the general idea? The dress embroidered with emeralds is pure imagination. You don't even know what there is about emeralds that titillates you, but you do know that two big emeralds on your finger make you feel like royalty!"

"I thought about that all week," Rose Marie says, "and maybe I should see a psychiatrist, but I have never even given myself the option of thinking of dressing in emeralds like that. Maybe I should stop thinking of mundane things and start to dream more."

"It's not true that you only think about mundane things," Meisner says. "I'll tell you what I mean about that. First of all, Dr. Freud—Ziggy, his friends call him—maintains that all fantasy comes either from ambition or sex. For example, if I gave you a million dollars—I've gotten more charitable since last week—and you told me that you'd use it to build yourself a glorious house in Hollywood, that would be ambition. And for sex? I'm reminded of a joke. Two guys go to the movies. They get on line, and one of them says, 'You know, Sophia Loren was marvelous in bed the night I had her.' The other guy doesn't reply, and the first guy says, 'I had a fine time with Liz Taylor, too. She has great *élan*.' The other fellow still doesn't say anything, but finally he smiles and says, 'You know Greta Garbo? I'm having her now.'"

The class laughs.

"That's preparation! Right now! 'The beast with two backs.'"

Again more laughter.

"Did I tell you about the guy on a bus who hated David Merrick? Well, this guy—a would-be playwright who was desperate to get away from his father's zipper factory—spent the day sitting in David Merrick's outer office, and Merrick wouldn't see him. Going home on the bus, he sees an advertisement with an elegant man smoking a cigar and, though the guy doesn't realize it, the man looks a little bit like Merrick. Suddenly his mind begins churning. 'That fool! Just because he's got a desk sixty feet long filled with plays, he thinks he's a producer. Well, he's had more flops than the Shuberts and the Nederlanders put together!' Well, he continues to fume about the incompetence and crass stupidity of David Merrick until the bus comes to his stop. An old lady has her feet in the aisle, but he's not looking because he's so furious, so he trips over the poor old lady's feet. He says, 'Go fuck yourself!' "

The class laughs.

"See, the accident of the advertisement led to free association, which led in turn to the rage that the poor old lady bore the brunt of. That's an example of how free association can induce a preparation. Macready shook a ladder, somebody else sings a song, somebody else wears a dress made of emeralds, somebody else wins the lottery and has ten years with nothing to do but to become the best actress she can be. But these approaches can be repeated only as long as they're effective. When I was sixteen, I was mad for the Tchaikovsky symphonies, but if I hear one now, my reaction is, 'It's so corny!' In other words, what stimulates you changes."

Meisner pauses to let the class absorb his point.

"When I was thirteen—excuse my using these personal examples—I always talked through the regular Monday morning assembly in public school. I was a very nervous kid. I even talked while they were playing "The Star-Spangled Banner." Finally the principal, Julius Bloom, called me out from the audience and said, 'Go to my office and wait for me,' which I did. Well, I had to bring my mother. I had to bring my father. My punishment was that I had to sit in the corner in the last row and nobody was allowed to talk to me. This was during the First World War and, since I was unpatriotic, I must be a German sympathizer. That went on and on, and it's not fun to be ostracized that way. Then they had a big contest: write an essay on why we should all buy Liberty Bonds. I won first prize. What could they do with me? Here I'm not patriotic and I write the prize-winning composition! So I was reinstated."

Meisner lights a cigarette.

"The point I'm making is that when I think back on that experience, I think it's both amusing and stupid, but that's not what I'm supposed to be feeling when somebody says, 'Remember how hysterical you were when they threw you out of school?' Over time the meaning of the past changes. That's one of the reasons I don't like 'emotion memory,' and that's one of the reasons Stanislavsky gave it up." For a moment, Meisner seems lost in thought.

Rose Marie holds up her hand.

"Sandy, you asked me to remind you to illustrate something."

"Oh, yes. Do you want to do it?" She stands up. "Then pick someone to be your partner, your boyfriend." She chooses John. "Look, I'm going to tell her what the precircumstances are— what you, Rose Marie, bring onstage with you. The two of you live here together. Scott Roberts?" he says to his assistant, who sits next to the amplifier that supplies his voice. "Turn that off so I can whisper."

He whispers to Rose Marie for a few moments and then she leaves the room, closing the door behind her.

"Now, John, I want you to lie on that bed." When projected, Meisner's unamplified voice can easily be heard. "You've just had a fatal heart attack, and now, and for the rest of this scene, you're dead. Can you manage that?"

"Sure," John says, and he sprawls on the bed. Minutes pass before Rose Marie, looking radiantly happy, bursts into the room. In a moment she sees John's lifeless body and lets out a cry of surprise. She goes to him, takes his hand, and with her other hand pats him on the cheek. She is panic-stricken, and after another minute turns to Meisner and says, "This is where I would call a doctor."

"Okay," Meisner says. "Now this illustrates my point: preparation lasts only for the first moment. Do you see my point? I'll tell you something, Rose Marie. No criticism. It's a comment. Your preparation was too thin. Suppose you'd decided to come up to the third floor singing at the top of your voice? I told her that she'd just signed a tremendous Hollywood contract and that her boyfriend was included in it. They were going to California. That's why she came in, and that's why I said, 'Your preparation was too thin.' And I told him what I told him. He's dead; he had a heart attack. Very extreme, but that's the point. Any questions?"

"You said my preparation was too thin," Rose Marie says. "If I was home I probably would have been screaming with joy. A few weeks ago I got a phone call—"

"Then *that's* what you should have done!"

"I was afraid I'd be 'showing' what I felt."

"No! You wouldn't be showing it. Do you know what 'showing it' means? Let's say an idiot director tells me that one of my precircumstances comes from the fact that I saw a cute little dog run over, and I go to a dark corner to prepare. So I prepare and I prepare and I prepare, and nothing happens, perhaps because I don't like dogs. Then my cue comes up so I come onstage and say, "Agh, agh, agh!" You follow? I've *indicated* the preparation. I've *indicated* the emotion I don't have. That's no good."

Meisner pauses to put out his cigarette.

"Just one more thought and then I'll shut up for a minute. Some years ago I owned a car. In winter when I got into my car, what's the first thing I did when I started the car? I pulled out the choke to give the cold motor some extra gas. It's a warming-up process, right? Well, for an actor, preparation is a warming-up process."

He looks around the classroom. "Let's take a break."

"The purpose of preparation is simple: it has to do with self-stimulation. Rose Marie, you said that the idea of winning the lottery was stimulating to you because it meant you wouldn't have to serve cheeseburgers and could devote yourself to your acting. You said that this made you feel so good that the tears came to your eyes, remember? So before you began to think about what you would do with the money, you were one kind of person. Then, when the idea of the prize money began to play on you, you were not the same person. You were Rose Marie in a full state of happiness, right?"

Rose Marie nods.

"So preparation is a kind of daydreaming. It *is* daydreaming. It's daydreaming which causes a transformation in your inner life, so that you are not what you actually were five minutes ago, because your fantasy is working on you. But the *character* of our daydream is taken from the play. Let's take Joseph Morgan as an example. What is the precircumstance of his scene with Beth? He knows that his wife is being unfaithful to him. Freud says that fantasies come from either sex or ambition. He also says that as we get older we become ashamed of having fantasies, that they don't belong with adulthood, that they're for children."

Meisner looks at Joseph. "Suppose—and don't follow this, Joe Morgan; I'm simply using your scene because it's relatively easy. Let's assume that you decide that knowing your wife is unfaithful to you is an abject humiliation. Therefore you have a certain amount of work to do on your innards in order to propel Joe Morgan into an acute condition of self-humiliation. Now, where does he get that? Suppose he thinks of an incident where a director, after three days of working with him, stops the rehearsal. This might have happened in his real life or, more importantly, he could invent it. He has a choice! The director says in front of the entire company, 'Morgan, you're fired. You have about as much talent as a dead chicken!' Do you see? You can build that up any way you personally like. Then the director, who is a real bastard, says to you, 'I know a girl who knows you and she told me that you're sexually inept, and the description she gave to me of your trying to be Rudolph Valentino was positively hilarious!' Every word of that fantasy cuts like a knife, so that you'd like to crawl under the table and disappear. That's how ashamed you've become!"

Joseph shifts uneasily in his chair.

"Can you see the process here? Let's continue with our imagination. Suppose that this preparation induces in Joe a need to go into a corner and try to disappear. Then in comes the wife, and the scene is between the wife and the worm! Now, that worm, that pathetic man, ashamed, humiliated—call it what you like—has been induced by imagination! You're prepared. You're ready. *Then* the scene begins. Am I conveying a logical process to you?"

The class nods.

"The fantasy of the daydream is the most personal, most secret of the acting values. What it means in ordinary language is that we use our imagination in order to fulfill in ourselves what we have more or less determined is our emotional condition *before* we begin the scene. I've quoted Freud. I've said that preparation is a product of your ambitious or sexual imagination. The guy on the bus who's imagining how wretchedly he'll treat David Merrick when he begs for the right to produce his next play is using his ambitious imagination. Feeling that you want to die of shame because of your sexual incapacities is obviously sexual. But you may get all this from a piece of music. It can come from anywhere. It is self-inducement coming from the imagination, which is the product of inventiveness."

Meisner pauses. "Did I tell you about Charlie Laughton in a picture from years ago called *If I Had a Million?* In it he played a bookkeeper—berated, persecuted, miserable. One day he inherits a million dollars. In those days, that meant something. Suddenly he has a scene with the awful boss who's mistreated him so badly. He has to enter and say, 'I'm finished here. Take your job!' Laughton's interpretation was that he was walking on the top of the world. He was triumphant! So before he knocked on the door and entered the boss's office, he had to have a sense of triumph. If he were Vince, he might get that feeling of being on top of the world from his experience with girls. That usually gives you a feeling of being unconquerable. But suppose Laughton got that feeling from boys? He's not going to reveal his preparation, but he's going to have it! And if anybody says to him, 'Where did you get that feeling of being a conqueror when you knocked at the door?,' his only answer is, 'None of your business.' That's how private and personal preparation is. Suppose there were an actor—now I'm being ridiculous, or maybe not so ridiculous—who comes from South Dakota, and the nearest farmhouse is a hundred and seventy-five miles away, but between those two houses are thousands of available sheep?"

"Poor sheep," Anna says.

"Not to the actor," Meisner says. "I'm talking about the personal, secret, intimate knowledge of preparation. So if somebody says to you, 'Where do you get that marvelous emotion you bring on in the third act?' The answer is simple: 'Talent.' "

The class laughs.

"I'll tell you something else about preparation. Be prepared to let it go astray; be prepared to make mistakes. There's more I could tell you, but I think I've said enough for today. As I talk about it, I tend to make it seem dramatically significant, but it needn't be. Sometimes you don't need any preparation."

Again Meisner pauses. "I'm open to a few legitimate questions."

John raises his hand. "When we're working on the stage," he asks, "is the idea to make our preparation as full as possible because we're in a theater, as opposed to being in a film, where acting is much more contained?"

"I'll tell you this: you cannot escape the impact of emotion, whether it's in a big theater or a tiny one. If you have it, it inflates you—correction, 'inflates' is not a good word. If you have it, it infects you *and* the audience. If you don't have it—like Helen Hayes—don't bother; just say the lines as truthfully as you are capable of doing. You can't fake emotion. It immediately exposes the fact that you ain't got it.

"Maureen Stapleton has it all the time. Kim Stanley sometimes has too much. Geraldine Page is lovely. There are many good actors. If you're an actor and are working off your partner the way you've been doing here, something's going to happen."

Bruce holds up his hand. "When you told Joseph a couple of classes ago just to go out and *think* about his wife's unfaithfulness—that was a form of preparation, wasn't it?"

"All I meant is that actors are responsive, just as butchers are, to the idea of a faithless woman. What I said was, 'You're no child. If you think about your girl being unfaithful to you something emotional happens to you.' I depended entirely on his normal reaction to that. I did not say, 'Prepare.' *Today* I said, 'Prepare,' didn't I? Today, for the first time, I said, 'Prepare.' It's simple. Don't come in empty. What do you bring with you because of where you've just been and why? That's all I said to you. Did I say more? I don't think so. I will. I told you about Duse's blush. Who's going to explain that?"

"A good preparation?" Vincent suggests.

"No. It came from living truthfully under imaginary circumstances. Preparation could never have induced that. It came from her genius, her completeness in living truthfully under imaginary circumstances."

December 5

"Next class I'm going to see all of your scenes with a preparation. Be prepared!"

"Scenes or exercises?" Ray asks.

"You each have a scene, don't you?"

"Are we supposed to rehearse it at home with a preparation?" Anna asks. "I mean not save it until Monday?"

"Save it? No, do it. Change it if necessary."

"Do you want the independent activities to be the same?" Bette asks. "Like Anna was putting on her makeup and I was reading a magazine?"

"But each one adds a preparation."

"On top of it?" Bette asks.

"No, underneath it."

"Underneath it," Bette repeats and the class laughs.

"The person who comes in does the preparation," says Rose Marie. "What about the person who's sitting there?"

"He has the preparation that comes from the independent activity. One comes from what you're doing, and the other comes entirely from the way you bring the emotion to the surface."

"So in Joseph's case, where he's just sitting there stewing, waiting for his wife to show up—"

"There's preparation in that case. When you prepare, go into a dark corner if you can find one. What were we talking about today?"

"We were talking about what you do imaginatively inside yourself to put you in an emotional state that carries you through the first moment of the scene," Bruce says.

John raises his hand. "Sandy, you said it would be best to find a dark corner or something—"

"To be alone. It helps. Look, the fact that you're sitting here in relative quiet does not mean that what I said isn't penetrating into you, because it is. Now, tell me your interpretation of what I said."

"What I got out of it," Ray says, "is that before the scene begins, through your imagination—maybe by daydreaming, or however you go about it—you get yourself ticking emotionally, so that when you enter the scene you have an emotional fullness which lasts as long as the first moment. It may or may not come up again in the course of the scene, but it brings you on alive and full. And you can't necessarily relate it to the scene because it has to be something deeply personal to you, that only you know about, that only stimulates you."

"That's right," Meisner says.

"Sandy?" John asks. "Is there a technique of talking out loud that somehow could pull preparation out of us rather than thinking about it?"

"I'll tell you something in answer to your question. There's nothing as personal as what makes an actor act, and of all the personal, secret things, preparation is the most. That's why I'm not saying anything more today."

Ray raises his hand. "In other words, you're saying you can't tell us how to do it—just that we have to do it. I don't mean that to sound glib. You're saying it's a totally personal thing, and there's no technique for it. Preparation is simply something that must take place, and we just have to learn to do it."

"It is something that should take place," Meisner says, "and I'm pointing out as far as is possible a conscious way of starting the process. You follow?"

December 8

Lila and Dave are about to perform a scene from William Inge's *The Dark at the Top of the Stairs*.

"What are the circumstances preceding the actual scene, Lila?" Meisner asks.

"Reenie comes in. I tell her that I think it would be good for her to go to the party, and she gets upset and goes out to practice the piano."

"That's the story of the play, right? I say that what precedes that scene is that you're altering a dress which is going to make your daughter the belle of the ball. How do you feel about that?"

"Oh, I'm elated. It's a beautiful dress."

"So Lila King is in a condition of elation, right? Now, I don't know how you're going to induce elation. You may get it from remembering a good notice you had some years ago. You may get it from the fact that tomorrow they're going to take down Ethel Barrymore's name and put up Lila King's. I don't know where your imagination is going to lead you, but when you're ready, sit down with that dress and do anything you want—sing to yourself, maybe—while you're altering it. Then we'll have not Lila King, the actress, but Lila King, the elated woman. Who's to stop you—except the dumb director—from waltzing around the room with the dress? Who's going to stop you? Not me!"

Meisner turns to Dave. "Now we have the husband. '$19.95.' What does that mean?"

"Murder," Dave says. "She's gone out behind my back and spent this huge amount of money."

"Go into the fact that you can't afford it."

"We barely have enough money to pay the rent and the electric bill. We can hardly make ends meet, let alone have any money for extras like party dresses."

"That's the foundation for building in you an emotional attitude which has to do with financial destruction. We won't go too far into this scene, but set yourself up in here, then go outside. When you're ready, come inside and act. Right? Has what I've said to you been clear?"

They both nod.

"You should go out to different corners. Dave, make sure that she's in here before you enter."

Lila and Dave leave the room, closing the door.

"It's really very simple, isn't it?" Meisner says. "It just takes a few years to learn."

After a few minutes Lila enters, takes the dress from the table and, holding it before her, admires her reflection in the full-length mirror against the wall. She begins to hum contentedly, then sits at the table to thread a needle. Dave enters suddenly and the scene begins. Three or four minutes pass before Meisner stops them.

"Let's talk about this. It's all right, nothing wrong with it, but it's a question of quantity, not quality. What does that mean?

Quantity instead of quality. The quality of your behavior is good. I'm talking only about the beginning. It's not full enough. I'll show you what I mean. Dave, when you came in and saw her dancing around with the dress, had it made you want to tear yourself to pieces, because here's the proof that she's ruining you, I would have loved it. You follow? And Lila, if before he came in we saw you dancing like a fifteen-year-old girl, like your daughter, I would have loved that. Dave, unless I'm quite wrong —which is possible—to be disgusted, revolted and furious at somebody's unreasonable behavior should not be difficult for you. Right or wrong?"

"You're right," Dave says.

"That's what I was looking for, you follow? And Lila, to be like a fifteen-year-old girl dancing around with the dress as if you were the belle of the ball would, I think, come easily to you." She nods in agreement. "That's what I was looking for. But we're at the beginning, and to begin with a full emotional inner life is difficult at best. I just want to show you the possibilities that are open to you. Both of you have always had reality in this scene. It never achieved the fullness it might have, but you always had emotions of the right quality. I'm talking about *fullness* at the beginning, that's all. What I'm trying to establish today are the qualities of preparations that are fuller than simply knowing that you, Dave, are angry at her because she's extravagant, or that you, Lila, are elated. That's what I'm talking about."

December 12

Ray and Rachael, a thin and pretty blond young woman who, like Anna, works as a model, are about to begin their scene.

"Why do you come in?" Meisner asks Rachael.

"I'm coming in to tell him—"

"You don't have to worry about that. The scene will take care of that. Where are you coming from?"

"From my new lover's place."

"How new?"

"Seven months."

"Almost a record," Meisner says, and the class laughs. "Okay, you're coming from your lover of seven months. What can you invent, what can your imagination invent, that happened tonight to put you on cloud seven? You've got something?"

Rachael nods.

"Personal to you? Right?"

She blushes and continues to nod.

"Now, Ray, let's take what I said to Joseph before. You're deeply humiliated, like a child who has been publicly embarrassed and scorned by all the other children, right? When you're both ready, come in."

When they leave the room, Meisner says, "There's been no problem in their being able to handle their script in an alive way, but now we're talking about a different level. What's the level?"

"The level of preparation," Vince says.

"Preparation brings you to it," Meisner says.

"The personal level," Rose Marie says.

"Emotional honesty," John adds.

"Fullness!" Meisner exclaims. "Where are we moving?"

"To a fuller emotional plane," Beth says.

After a few minutes the door opens, Ray enters and sits on the bed. Rachael comes in, the scene begins and they play it through to the end.

"All right," Meisner says, "that helped. The behavior was more meaningful than last time. Now, I want to try something. Rachael, I want you to go outside, and when you feel as if finally all your dreams are coming true, *dance* in! I don't care what you do. Go outside and prepare for that."

"Okay," Rachael says. "With or without the text?"

"With the text," Meisner says. "But Rachael, I want to see you at your most ecstatic. I don't care if you get it from buckwheat cakes! And Ray, I want you to sit on that bed with your back to the door and cry and keep on crying until your heart breaks. I don't care if you get it from the fact that your dog died. If you want to be private, go outside and then come back in."

Both leave in order to prepare. In a few minutes, they return and perform the scene again.

"This didn't change as much with you, Ray, as it did with you" —he looks at Rachael—"though it was rather slight. Look, Ray, are you sensitive to tears?"

"Do you mean, am I sensitive to somebody else crying?"

"Why didn't you cry?"

"I don't know. . . ."

"Were you self-conscious?"

"Somewhat. I think I was trying too hard. I think I felt I needed to succeed, and that was what was in my mind."

"You don't need to succeed; you need to learn. Right?"

Ray nods in agreement.

"I said, 'Cry.' That's a result. I don't care if it's because the waiter brought you fried eggs instead of scrambled. I wanted to see you break down, that's all. And Rachael, I wanted to see you come in like Carmen. That's what I was looking for."

"A dramatic change in the way the scene was going," Ray says.

"Something entirely different," Meisner says. "Work on it. We'll see what you do with it next time."

December 15

"Let's have *Mister Roberts,*" Meisner says, and John and Ralph come forward and sit on two gray metal folding chairs in the middle of the classroom. "John, we know from the play that Ralph's character is a pain in the ass, right? We know that you would do anything to squash him, right, and finally you've got something on him. What is it?"

"I have a letter," John says, "that proves to me that he fucked up."

" *'No leave for the men.'* How do you feel about that?"

"How do I feel? Ecstatic!"

"So sit behind your desk and enjoy your power," Meisner says. "This is a scene about a cruel bastard whose greatest pleasure is to watch somebody electrocuted, and who's getting his wish."

John moves his chair behind the long table and begins to arrange into a neat pile some papers he has brought with him.

"Now, Ralph. Did I ever tell you about the 'Magic If'? This scene is 'as if' you've just come from the funeral of your three-year-old brother. In other words, a tragedy is occurring. Never mind that this scene is about the navy. Emotionally, a tragedy is occurring, you follow?"

Ralph nods.

"Go out and prepare. Johnny, you just sit there and tickle yourself with pleasure. That's all. But go outside if you want to."

John starts to leave, and Meisner begins to speak again. "Haven't you all had marvelous dreams in which you killed somebody? Dreams where you've taken revenge and killed somebody you hate?"

John says, "No."

"Well, you'll have to find a substitution for it."

John nods and leaves the room.

Meisner looks at Rose Marie.

"Suppose your best friend once said, 'Rose Marie, give up acting. You haven't got it.' Now, you've just opened in a play in which you got all the notices and she got fired. Isn't that a wonderful feeling?"

Rose Marie grins.

"Are you beginning to see how this works?" Meisner asks, looking around the class. "Yes? But not unanimously. You wouldn't give me that satisfaction, would you?"

In a few minutes, John returns to his table and begins to read with pleasure a typed letter on top of his stack of papers. Ralph knocks on the door and John tells him to enter and take a chair. Ralph sits before John's desk like a small boy brought up before the principal. His preparation is very full, and as the scene progresses, he becomes increasingly desperate before the obdurate cruelty of his superior. With tears in his eyes, he pleads for the order canceling the leave of his men to be rescinded. At the end, when, through a twist of the plot, the captain is forced to rescind the order, Ralph heaves a sigh of relief and cries openly with joy.

"That was good," Meisner says. "You see what preparation does for you? Ralph, your emotion was lovely."

"Thank you," Ralph says. He is clearly pleased and smiles even as he blows his nose and wipes his eyes with his handkerchief.

"How's that for a Christmas present?" Meisner asks.
Ralph nods and the class laughs.

Meisner stands on the corner of Fifty-fourth Street and First
Avenue looking for a cab to take him to his apartment.

"Dave concerns me," he says. "There's a level of emotional
reserve in his work that isn't productive in an actor. It's as though
he searches for reasons for *not* becoming involved, for *not* acting
fully. Restraint is a virtue, but reticence in an actor isn't. This
is a problem he's going to have to grapple with. Of course I love
Sturm und Drang. If I go to a restaurant and there's no salt on the
table, they have to carry me to my bed. I wish a bit of that could
rub off onto Dave."

A fine mist begins to fall, and there are no cabs in sight.

"Ray, though, is developing nicely," he says. "So is Rachael.
They tell me that he was studying to become a Jesuit but was
defrocked for drinking the communion wine. That's probably
not true. He's intelligent. I can always count on him to summa-
rize accurately whatever point I'm struggling to make. Of all of
them, he would make the best teacher, I think."

A cab turns onto the avenue and Meisner raises his cane to
hail it.

"So he couldn't break down. That's not important at this early
stage. As I said, preparation is really very simple. It just takes a
few years to learn."

The cab pulls up and Meisner gets in.

7 Improvisation

Let us try to learn some of the characteristics of day-dreaming. We can begin by saying that happy people never make fantasies, only unsatisfied ones. Unsatisfied wishes are the driving power behind fantasies; every separate fantasy contains the fulfillment of a wish, and improves on unsatisfactory reality. The impelling wishes vary according to the sex, character and circumstances of the creator; they may be easily divided, however, into two principal groups. Either they are ambitious wishes, serving to exalt the person creating them, or they are erotic. In young women erotic wishes dominate the fantasies almost exclusively, for their ambition is generally comprised in their erotic longings; in young men egoistic and ambitious wishes assert themselves plainly enough alongside their erotic desires. But we will not lay stress on the distinction between those two trends; we prefer to emphasize the fact that they are often united. In many altar-pieces the portrait of the donor is to be found in one corner of the picture; and in the greater number of ambitious day-dreams, too, we can discover a woman in some corner, for whom the dreamer performs all his heroic deeds and at whose feet all his triumphs are to be laid. . . .
—Sigmund Freud, "The Relation of the Poet to Day-dreaming"*

February 6

"Vincent just asked me a peculiar question: 'When do we begin on character work?' Well, in one way you never begin on character work. In another way, you've already begun to do characters because character comes from how you feel about something. So every time you got up and did an exercise, you were playing a character, though the word wasn't mentioned. For the most part, character is an emotional thing. The *internal* part of character is

*Collected in *On Creativity and the Unconscious: Papers on the Psychology of Art, Literature, Love, Religion,* selected by Benjamin Nelson (New York, Evanston, and London: Harper & Row, 1958), 47–48.

defined by how you feel about something. If you go into a clothing store, for example, and see a suit that you like very much but can't afford, and you buy it anyway—what kind of person are you?"

"Impulsive," Joseph says.

"Impulsive," Meisner repeats. "Or foolhardy. That would be the essence of one internal component of the character. Let's take a difficult Strindberg character like Miss Julie. Her wish to destroy men because of her hatred of them also makes her want to look beautiful so that she can entice them into a trap and destroy their egos. Here are *two* components of character: the inner component, which determines the kind of person she is, a destroyer of men, which is dictated by Strindberg and which the actress intuitively extracts from the written text; and an outer component, the external portrait epitomizing her wish to be beautiful."

"What about accents?" Joseph asks. "Are they inner or outer components of character?"

"The man who recently arrived in America from France might have a heavy, distinctly French accent. But if the author tells us that he has spoken English for most of his life, he might have only a trace of an accent. But neither circumstance would mitigate the fact that at heart he is *French*: cosmopolitan, witty, cynical in love —whatever the idea of being French might instinctively mean to you. At this early stage of our work, you must rely on your instinctive reaction to the playwright's text. At this point character is justified by your inner response to what you read in the text. But remember, an accent is not basic and organic to the character. It is an external attribute, like red hair or a gold tooth. The basic thing is an emotional essence—'cosmopolitan,' 'cynical.' That's the source of character."

He looks at Vincent for a moment. "You look like a disappointed character to me, Vince, because you're not hearing what you want to hear."

Vince starts to speak but stops.

"Look," Meisner says, "if somebody says to two other people, 'Do you want to drink some unbelievably strong Japanese *sake?*' And the first guy says emphatically, 'Yeah! I do!' And the other guy says, 'Yes.' Pause. Pause. 'I do.' Their words are the same but are *they* the same, or do they have two different characters?

Vince? You started me on this, so I'm asking you. One character you can define as being what?"

"Impulsive," Vince says.

"Impulsive. And the other?"

"Cautious."

"Well, that's how you establish character. This will become clearer when we begin to work with the material from Edgar Lee Masters' *Spoon River Anthology*. Vince, I'm glad you asked me that question. I didn't mean to start this way, but I guess I'm an adjustable character."

"Here's the outline of an exercise that everybody is going to do. Two people are living together, not necessarily sexually. One person has an independent activity, and the other one comes in from some situation which requires a vivid preparation. I said that you're living together, so there's no question of knocking on the door, but you can live separately if you want to. That's your choice. That's the exercise. Two people, one of whom has an independent activity and the other of whom comes home from some situation which he has created and for which he has prepared. The process is one of working off each other, moment to moment. That's essentially the improvisation. Ray, who's your partner?"

"Rose Marie."

"All right, come up here, both of you. You're living together, and Ray, you're at home. That means you must have a genuine independent activity. It doesn't have anything to do with her—it's entirely yours—and that's what you'll be doing. Have you something you can do?"

"I have a script here which I could memorize for an audition," Ray says.

"Good. Now, Rose Marie, you have just come from a situation of your own invention, out of which you get a preparation. Preparation is self-stimulation. Your nature, your instinct, dictates the kind of preparation you want. If you'd just gotten a great part in a wonderful show, the self-stimulation that is your preparation could be that you're divinely happy. It could also be that you're mystified by how this wonderful situation came about. Aren't you lucky?"

Rose Marie nods.

"So to begin with, we have Ray at home immersed in his independent activity, and then Rose Marie comes home from some invented situation out of which she has extracted a preparation. Then you work off each other's behavior moment to moment. Are there any questions?"

"Sandy," John asks, "are you saying that when we come up with a make-believe situation for ourselves, we should try to make it so real that it can move us emotionally?"

"You must."

"Okay."

"Let's start. Rose Marie, where's your hat and coat?"

Rose Marie takes her coat and purse from a chair and starts to leave the room.

"Ray, where are you going to do your independent activity?"

"Here," Ray says, "in my house."

"It's her house, too."

"Yeah," Rose Marie says. "I don't have to knock."

"Who are you to each other?"

"Should we decide that together?" Ray asks. "Is it necessary for me to know what she thinks our relationship is?"

"It's necessary for *you* to know if you're living together as man and wife or brother and sister or whatever."

Rose Marie asks, "In an exercise like this, is it better to come in with a feeling or to come in with a purpose?"

"If you were just fired from your dream part and came in fully prepared and determined to write that director a letter, you could do that. Or you could come in just riding your preparation."

"Just because we live together," Rose Marie says, "doesn't mean that when I come home I'll find the other person at home too. I mean, I could come in and find an empty apartment."

"That is correct."

"Along this line," Ray says, "I wanted to ask if the preparation that the person who's entering uses to self-stimulate himself emotionally can be connected to the person who's in the room?"

"It's much better at first if it's not," Meisner says. "Come on, let's see what you do."

Ray and Rose Marie whisper together briefly, and when she leaves the room he sits at the long table with his script and begins to memorize it. After a few minutes she enters and they perform the exercise as Meisner has outlined it.

"Okay, how was that?" Meisner asks. "No one wants to offer their opinion?"

"Pretty good."

"You'd say that, Joseph? Pretty good? Why?"

"Because her emotion was truthful and he was aware and working off it."

"What was her character?"

"Angry."

"Tempestuous, I think. What was his character?"

"Helpful?"

"Right. Let's have another. Who wants to go?"

Ray and Rose Marie return to their chairs.

"Incidentally, Ray, your independent activity wasn't interesting enough."

"I just made it up when you called on us because I hadn't come prepared with one."

"How could you have made it more interesting?"

"I could have learned the speech with a particular accent out loud, or I could have done it in a particular rhythm and I had to walk in that rhythm—"

"If that's not too bizarre, you could have done that, I suppose. Otherwise, you were just a plain memorizer—a little too plain. You must learn to make your independent activity more involving and interesting to you. Who can tell me what this exercise is all about?"

John raises his hand. "It's being totally involved in an activity or coming in with a full preparation, and then reacting honestly to an outside source and going along from moment to moment."

"Who's the outside source?"

"Well, the activity could be, but also your partner."

"Yes, it's your partner. What does it mean to use what exists? Joseph?"

"To allow what exists to affect you rather than working out of your head—what you think *should* exist—so that you're working from an actual moment."

"That's about right," Meisner says reflectively. "That's about right." He adjusts the microphone attached to his eyeglasses. "You see, this exercise adds another dimension. The actor doing the independent activity is now not just being interrupted. Rather, he is confronted by his partner, whose inner life, because of his preparation, is compelling and persuasive. The partner enters the room with a full emotion, and the two of them react to each other moment to moment."

"Let's talk about this. It's nearer to what's wanted," Meisner says.

John and Rachael stop improvising and sit down together on the bed against the wall.

"John, where did you come from?"

"I came from seeing someone on the street."

"Seeing who?"

"A writer whose play I want to produce, and he's very particular. It's almost impossible to get his permission, but he agreed to give me thirty minutes of his time to tell him my ideas to see if we agree."

"Okay. Listen, everybody. It's *because* you met a playwright, and it's *because* he has a play you'd like to produce, and it's *because* he said he'd come and talk to you: *How do you feel?*"

"I feel excited."

"Then you could have had more excitement, you see? The more you have, the more she would be stopped from doing her independent activity. Because you didn't pick a situation which is provocative enough to you, you didn't bring in a full enough emotion. What's that mean?"

"It means that I didn't generate a real, honest, strong feeling that overwhelmed me," John says.

"And what would you need to get that?"

"A better situation that moves me."

"And *then* you improvise."

Ray raises his hand. "When you say 'improvise,' do you mean

that we should be doing less repetition and more . . . talking, so that it sounds more like dialogue? I know what you mean by improvisation, but what I'm asking is does it lead to something that sounds more like dialogue and less like repetition?"

"Yes."

"Okay. The other question I have is that the relationship between the two people doesn't seem to matter at this point, except that it removes the knock and spontaneously affects the attitude they have toward each other."

"Yes."

"Other than that, it's just like what we've been doing?"

"Yes. This improvisation is the same thing as the exercises you have been doing all along, except that it adds a stronger, fuller preparation. What have I added to the exercise that you did before Christmas?"

"You've added that we know who we are to each other when we enter," Bette says.

"And I've added that you come from a strong situation which gives you a springboard for a full preparation."

"You have to have a story, as well as your emotional preparation, right?" Ray asks. "Earlier, emotional preparation was anything you imagined to set yourself off emotionally, but now we have to give it . . ."

"Justification," Meisner says.

"Yeah. So that I'm able to say that the emotion I came into the room with is the result of something that just happened to me."

"Yes."

"That strengthens it," Rose Marie says, "doesn't it?"

"Sure."

"It makes it more like a play," Ray adds.

"No, it makes you fuller. You must give your self-stimulation more of a chance to be deeper and bigger. What's that mean?"

"Don't put limitations on your emotional behavior," Rose Marie says.

"Certainly not. That's right."

"It's difficult to do because we've been trained since we were children to be restrained emotionally—at least some of us have —and every day we're constantly aware of what our proper limitations are. We always know what our boundaries are and it's difficult to break them, even in an acting class. But emotional freedom gets easier when you try to go along the path your inner life is sending you."

"I'm glad you said that," Meisner says and the class laughs.

February 9

"Let's talk about this. I liked it."

Joseph sighs in relief.

"I could wish that it were fuller on your part, Joseph. What would have made it fuller?"

"A preparation that was fuller."

"But what preparation would make it more provocative to you?"

"Something that was more specific and meaningful to me."

"What were those two words?"

"Specific and meaningful."

"That's right."

"I had it, but then I lost it."

"That's very possible, but I don't criticize you for that. You're well on your way towards preparation, and now it needs to be genuinely fuller, more forceful. Do you understand?"

"Yes."

"In *Hamlet*, in the beginning . . . I'm talking badly today. Can you understand me?"

"Yes," say the students.

"In the beginning of the play, Hamlet is in a deep depression. What causes it?"

"The death of his father," Joseph says in his quiet, deep voice.

"His father was murdered, right?"

"By his uncle."

"That adds to it. If somebody had swatted a fly on his desk and left it there, would that cause a deep depression?"

"No."

"I don't think so either."

"Let me ask you a question about Hamlet specifically," Joseph says. "In the beginning of the play he has that speech about his mother, the one that starts, 'O! that this too too solid flesh would melt, / Thaw and resolve itself into a dew. . . .' It's about his mother marrying his uncle, his father's murderer. What would one use for a preparation?"

"I don't know," Meisner says. "I don't know who's playing it."

After a pause Joseph says, "It's just what works for you, then?"

"That's right. Work for a fuller preparation. You know, one thing that's constant in a brick wall is that a brick is a brick is a brick. What's that mean?"

"It means that it's never anything other than a brick," Bette, Joseph's partner, says.

"It's that the basis of the performance is the fundamental reality that you had today. But instead of a pint of acting, I'm looking for a legitimate gallon." He looks at Bette, who still sits at the long table. Cards with printing on them are spread before her. "Why were you playing with those cards? How much were you going to win?"

Bette says, "I don't know whether I do this right. I have a whole scenario planned which is very specific and personal to me, and I'm afraid it might sound corny to anybody else."

"Twenty-five dollars is enough."

"Oh, no, it was—"

"More complicated?"

"Maybe I should tell you, because maybe it isn't the right kind of thing."

"Tell me."

"Okay. In my imaginary situation I'm doing volunteer work at Sloan-Kettering, the cancer hospital. I work with older kids, and I befriended a fourteen-year-old boy who said that his dream was to be an actor. But a lot of kids there aren't going anywhere. But there was some hope for him, and I've just found out that he's not going anywhere either. I promised him that when I came in on Monday we were going to recite Shakespeare—these cards have passages from Shakespeare on them—"

"It's too complicated."

Bette pauses to think for a moment. "What if I used these cards to make a house?"

"At Sloan-Kettering? Learning how to do it to distract them?"

"Do you think that's stupid?" Bette says.

"No! I was at Sloan-Kettering!"

"But you think my earlier reasons were too complicated?"

"Yes."

"Because they get too jumbled up?"

"You've got to get a reaction from inside yourself, and the more complicated it is, the more difficult it is to get involved emotionally."

"So I can get more self-stimulation by just showing the child how to build a house of cards?"

"Involvement. You can get more *involvement* for yourself by knowing that you're doing it to entertain a dying child. Simplicity is essential. Don't clutter yourself. All I have to say to myself is 'Hitler,' and something is there. Do you understand that? It's because I'm Spanish."

"Bruce, do you remember hearing Ray ask if in this form of the improvisation the repetition becomes less mindless and more reasonable, so that the result is more like human dialogue?"

In frustration, Bruce runs both hands through his thinning hair. "Yes, but I couldn't seem to do it."

"You couldn't seem to do it? Wait a minute. What color is your shirt?"

"It's maroon."

"That wasn't repetition. I asked you what color the shirt was and you told me. You didn't repeat, did you?"

"No, I didn't repeat. I just answered the question."

"What color are your socks?"

"Black."

"Do you have a name other than Bruce?"

"Sure."

"What is it?"

"Patrick."

"Did you repeat? Why do you say that you can't answer a question? You just did it!"

"I don't know. I just felt stuck."

"It's all right. What's the color of these walls?"

"Yellow."

"Do you like that color?"

"It's okay."

"What color would you prefer?"

Bruce pauses a moment to reflect. "Gray."

"Did you think about that?"

"For a second."

"And then when you'd thought about it, you answered, right? So when somebody asks you a question you can answer it, can't you?"

"Yes. But when Lila kept asking me in the exercise what was wrong, the answer should have been, 'I'm upset.' But I thought I wasn't supposed to reveal what my preparation was."

"Look, you're going to ask me a question, and I'm going to show you a way of answering by not using the direct truth. How old am I? How old do you think I am?"

Bruce bursts into laughter.

"What's so funny?"

"About fifty?" Bruce asks.

"Right!" Meisner replies, and the class laughs. "Bruce, how old are you? Lie to me."

"Twenty-eight."

"You don't look it," Meisner says and Bruce laughs again. "What's funny about that?"

"It's such a lie!"

"What's a lie?"

"Twenty-eight."

"That's a lie?"

"Yeah."

"You see, we're having a conversation, aren't we? That's the direction in which the improvisation exercise is going. Do you understand?"

Bruce nods.

"Lila," Meisner says to Bruce's partner, "the same problem exists with you. What does it mean to respond reasonably?"

"To respond reasonably?"

"What time is it? What's the logical response?"

"I don't know."

"Why don't you know? You're wearing a watch. Why don't you look at it?"

"It's about five-ten."

"That kind of indecision is no good for this exercise. What should you have said?"

"Five-ten."

"Right. Now, if I say, 'What time is it?,' what's your repetitive, theatrical answer?"

"My theatrical answer?"

"In this exercise."

"I'm confused," Lila says, and her large blue eyes scan his face anxiously.

"Your repetitive, theatrical answer to my saying, 'What time is it?' is for you to say, 'What time is it?' Then I say, 'What time is it?' and you say, 'What time is it?' and I say, 'You're getting annoyed,' and you say, 'I'm getting annoyed,' and I say, 'Yes, you're getting annoyed,' and you say, 'Yes, I'm getting annoyed,' and I say, 'Yes, that's right, you're annoyed,' and you say, 'Yes, that's right, I'm annoyed!' Now, is that dialogue reasonable, or is it repetitive and, in the sense of this exercise, theatrical?"

"Theatrical."

"Yes. In the beginning the mindless repetition of the basic exercise had value. It eliminated a need for you to think and to write dialogue out of your head in order to keep talking—as if acting were talking, which it is not. And the illogical nature of the dialogue opened you up to the impulsive shifts in your instinctual behavior caused by what was being done to you by your partner, which can lead to real emotion. This is fundamental to good acting. Now I'm saying we have moved beyond the fundamental. Now it's possible to respond reasonably. So if your partner asks you what time it is, for God's sake look at your watch and tell him! And if he has the temerity to ask you how old you are, you have my permission to lie to him through your teeth!"

February 13

Sarah sits on the bed against the wall, intently reading a book. Suddenly, with an explosive burst, the door slams open and Vincent hurtles into the room. Under an open gray cardigan he wears the same T-shirt with bright pink lettering on it which he wore on the first day of class. He stands breathing heavily for a moment and then quickly closes the door and begins to barricade it with a chest of drawers. "Good God," Sarah exclaims, "what's going on?" Vincent ignores her question and begins to stack first one chair and then another onto the chest.

Meisner whispers to Ralph for a moment. Ralph nods, and leaves the room quietly by the back door. Vincent is now attempting to hide, and crouches between the head of the bed on which Sarah sits and the wall. He continues to breathe in an exaggerated, theatrical way. Suddenly there is a sharp rap on the door, then another, then a third.

Meisner raises his hand and stops the exercise. "How come, Vince, when there was a knock at the door, nothing happened to you? But you came in like gangbusters. How come? Who was chasing you?"

"I have no idea who he was. Some guy on the subway."

"Why was he chasing you?"

"I don't know. He was crazy. I stepped on his foot and he ran after me all the way saying, 'I'm going to kill your mother-fuckin' ass.' "

"Too general," Meisner says firmly. "Not specific. And meaningless. You were playing a melodrama. If you had come in here because a cop was on your tail, the knock would have meant something."

"You mean not wanting to get cut up wasn't enough," Vince says defensively.

"But what happened to you? Nothing happened to you except an assumed fear. You were playing a drama, being chased by a guy with a knife. Was that it? That would be acceptable if it were more specific and you had an emotion. But when the knock on the door came, nothing happened to you. So it had no reality, did it?"

"I see what you're saying," Vince says quietly.

"What about you, Sarah?"

"I didn't know what was going on."

"Did it ever occur to you that maybe he was crazy?"

"Yes, because when I asked him what was wrong, he wouldn't answer me. He just hid."

"You see, the truth wasn't in this. A melodramatic situation was being indicated, but nothing happened to you, do you follow?"

"Yeah," says Vince.

"What did I say?"

"You said that what I was doing was not real. It was an indication of what I thought being frightened and being afraid should be."

"Why are you angry?" Meisner asks.

"Because I told you that I knew!"

"How can I take that for granted unless you're more explicit?" Meisner asks.

Vincent shrugs his shoulders as if he wants to drop the subject.

"I should have used that, right?" Sarah asks.

"You should have used the fact that there was something illogical or untruthful in his behavior, yes."

Vincent shifts his weight from his right leg to his left.

"Let's assume that Sarah is your sister and you share an apartment. Why would it have been better, Vince, if you'd come home after finding out that your girl was going to marry some guy with a lot of money? Why would that be better?"

"Because . . . I don't know."

"Is it human? Is it in you? The disappointment, the humiliation, whatever it is, would that be in you? One can imagine that if you had that, you'd come in and go sit in the corner because she'd just made a jackass out of you. Do you see?"

"Are you saying that in a circumstance like that you say to yourself, 'How does that affect me? It affects me like this.'" He puckers his face into a pout. "And then you come in doing that?"

"No. It affects you, and *then* you come in and do whatever your impulses let you do."

"I understand exactly what you said. I'll try to do that."

"Do you understand what I mean when I say that this was a general, melodramatic situation and that you were indicating?"

"Yeah."

"Sarah, you didn't get anything specific from him except curiosity?"

"Actually, I did, but I didn't—"

"What?"

"Well, I didn't feel that it was real."

"That's what I'm telling you!"

"And I didn't comment on it."

"You're too polite, and in acting politeness will get you nowhere! Look, find in yourselves those human things which are universal. Don't act out what you see on television! All we needed here was a posse coming through the door!" He pauses for a moment. "What if you were a kid and you came home from school much earlier than usual, and you told your mother that the school was closed because there was a big fire and you almost got burned? Now, that's a lie! What makes your mother believe it? What makes her believe that you're telling the truth?"

"Specifics?" Bette asks. "You tell her specific things that happened."

Meisner says, "The playwright would give you that. What would make you a convincing liar?"

"Your behavior," says Joseph.

"What part of your behavior?"

"If you believe it—"

"Your *emotional* behavior. If you go like this," and he puffs lightly on his fingers, "that's not going to do it."

"If you walk in sobbing it might," Bette says.

"It's the reality of the emotion which makes the lie convincing," Meisner says. "I could say more about that, but I don't want to now."

"Joseph, what you had was very good, clear and sensitive. It needed to be fuller. It needed to be more personal, which would have made it fuller. Why were you writing that letter?"

"I just learned that someone I loved, my aunt, had died. I thought it was pretty personal."

"But you didn't let go. You started out well, but then it began to wane, until it had the reflection of a mood. How could you have made it fuller? I'll tell you: if it had something personal to you which had rocked you."

"There were moments when it got away from me, yes. But it came back as well. It came and went, is what I'm saying."

"It should have started on a more driving level." Meisner turns to Bette, Joseph's partner. "That was nice: sensitive to him, simple, true, with content. Where did you come from?"

"I'd just spoken to my agent, who told me that the other girl who's up for the same part is going to take another job. The part I want is ninety percent in the bag for me."

"Then that should have made you ecstatic!"

"I was ecstatic, But I was also afraid. I didn't want to blow it by being too excited. I'm very superstitious that way."

"You should try it anyway. Otherwise you're saying, 'I want to be proper.' Don't be proper! Joseph was proper. It was very nice, it was sensitive and true, but it wasn't full enough."

"I don't quite understand," Ray says. "You use the word full a lot. Sometimes it sounds to me that you mean it as a synonym for deeper, and sometimes for larger."

"Not larger, deeper."

"Which doesn't necessarily mean that the actor is going to be any bigger than he already is?"

Meisner nods.

"So Joseph could use the fact of his aunt's dying," Rose Marie says, "but he should have made it more personal to him, like she was the one who raised him since he was two years old, or—"

"Or," Meisner says, "that he was responsible for her death. If he'd been a medical student and given her a pill which was experimental and it killed her, that would make it fuller."

He pauses a moment while the class absorbs his point.

"Originally my preparation was going to be that I got the job," Bette says finally. "I was going to come in crazy, wild and happy! But I have trouble getting there."

"Take your time," Meisner says. "Take your time."

"But I don't know if I'll ever get there."

"Try it!" And after a pause, *"Try it!"*

February 16

"I'm in a terrible mood today and I'm going to take it out on you. Why should I be masochistic? You know, most of you have studied with other teachers—I should say 'mis-studied' with other teachers—and that doesn't make our problem any easier." He looks at Scott Roberts. "Who isn't here?"

"I believe everybody is here."

"What?"

"I believe everybody is here. I was just going over the list."

"Your diction is awful!"

"I'm sorry," Scott says. "I believe everybody is here. Yes, everybody is here."

Meisner adjusts the microphone before continuing. "Do you honestly think—and I mean honestly like what exists in the Bible and no place else—that you're learning?"

There is a chorus of yesses from the students.

"Don't flatter me!" Meisner exclaims.

"I'm not," Anna says.

"How many people think they're not learning?" He looks around the room.

"What was the original question, Sandy?" Joseph asks. "I didn't understand it."

"Repeat it!" he says to Rose Marie.

"Do you think—honestly as in the Bible—that you're learning . . . something here in class, I guess he means."

"That's the question."

"Raise your hand if you're not," Rose Marie says.

"I don't see any hands," Meisner says, his eyes scanning the two rows of seated students. Slowly, but with sureness, Vincent raises his right hand into the air. After a moment, Meisner says to the class, "Do you think this technique is for everyone?" There is a pause. "I don't, and that's right, Vince, you're not learning. I suggest you pack it in here and go find another teacher more to your liking."

Vincent's hand drops to his side. "Okay," he says quietly and shrugs his shoulders.

"I think you should leave right now!" Meisner exclaims. Vince nods stiffly, as if in shock, and then proceeds to collect his coat from under his seat and stand up. There is a pause while he works his way to the aisle and begins to cross the acting area, moving toward the door. At midpoint Meisner asks, "Who was your partner?"

"Sarah," Vince says.

"Sarah? Who can take on two partners?"

Ray raises his hand.

"Ray, you'll give it a try?" Meisner asks.

Ray nods.

"Then work with Sarah."

Vincent stands frozen in the middle of the room. He slowly raises his right hand again, this time in a kind of salute. "Thank you."

"Okay," Meisner says with a wave of his right hand. "So long and good luck."

Vincent turns, walks through the open door and is gone.

"Okay, Lila and Bruce, let's go!"

The two students stand and move onto the acting area and the class resumes.

▌▌

"It kills me when I have to ask a student to leave my class," Meisner says as he opens the door to his small, one-bedroom apartment. "But when I see that he cannot learn what I have to teach, and that his presence has become detrimental to other students who *are* learning, then, as a responsible teacher, I must do it. I usually write to say that I regret that in my opinion I am not the right teacher for him or I have Scott call him to explain the same thing—whichever is less painful for both of us. The theatrics of this afternoon are not the norm."

Meisner stiffly removes the heavy wool coat with a fur collar, his protection against the icy New York winter. "I've decided to ask Philip and Bruce to leave too."

He walks slowly with the aid of his cane into the living room of the apartment and perches stiffly on a special high-backed chair with long legs that he had built for his use after his hip operation.

"Philip is a sweet kid—too sweet perhaps to survive as an actor —although he wants to be one desperately. Scott told me that he works in some kind of a cafeteria that stays open all night. He works then so that his afternoons are free to take classes and go to auditions. It's clear to me that he wants to act but that his inhibitions—I blame it on his parents—have crippled him. I seriously doubt that he will ever become a successful actor.

"In a funny way, Bruce is quite similar. Although he's been in this business for twenty years, like Lila—who God knows I should get rid of too—he has no technique. Instead, he has accumulated an awesome number of superficial tricks in an attempt, I suppose, to make himself feel more secure. But the result is an intense self-consciousness that cuts him off from his partner and the possibility of transcending his own scared self.

"Acting is a scary, paradoxical business. One of its central paradoxes is that in order to succeed as an actor you have to lose consciousness of your own self in order to transform yourself into the character in the play. It's not easy, but it can be done. I'm only sorry that I cannot teach Bruce, Philip and Vincent— and so many others—how to do it."

8 More on Preparation: "Quick As Flame"

. . . In the great scene of the third act of the "Merchant of
Venice," Shylock has to come on in a state of intense rage
and grief at the flight of his daughter. Now it is obviously
a great trial for the actor to "strike twelve at once." He is
one moment calm in the green-room, and the next he has
to appear on the stage with his whole nature in an uproar.
Unless he has a very mobile temperament, quick as flame,
he cannot begin this scene at the proper state of white
heat. Accordingly, we see actors in general come bawling
and gesticulating, but leaving us unmoved because they are
not moved themselves. Macready it is said, used to spend
some minutes behind the scenes, lashing himself into an
imaginative rage by cursing *sotto voce*, and shaking
violently a ladder fixed against the wall. To by-standers the
effect must have been ludicrous. But to the audience the
actor presented himself as one really agitated. He had
worked himself up to the proper pitch of excitement which
would enable him to express the rage of Shylock.
—George Henry Lewes, *On Actors and the Art of Acting**

February 20

"The text is like a canoe," Meisner says, "and the river on
which it sits is the emotion. The text floats on the river. If the
water of the river is turbulent, the words will come out like a
canoe on a rough river. It all depends on the flow of the river
which is your emotion. The text takes on the character of your
emotion. That's what this exercise is for: how to let the river of
your emotion flow untrammeled, with the words floating on
top of it."
Bruce runs his hands nervously through his thinning hair.

*London: Smith, Elder & Co., 1875, 44.

When told he was dropped from the class, Bruce asked for another chance and Meisner reluctantly agreed.

"This is a very significant exercise for you because your tendency, Bruce, is to sit on your emotion and hide it. You had a moment before you began, before Lila came in, when I thought you were going to sob. But then you squelched it!"

"It's hard to let go," Bruce says.

Meisner waves his hand impatiently. "Begin working on this problem by allowing yourself to overdo it. You should do what I do when I practice diving in the Caribbean. I just go! I *know* it's not easy. It's formidable. Just go! And don't give yourself a reason why you shouldn't! If you want to throw yourself on the floor and chew a leg of that table, it's fine with me. It's undignified, it's unmanly, it's ungentlemanly—but it's very good for your acting!"

"I'll try," Bruce says.

"I don't care when you learn the lines," Meisner says. "And don't try to learn them in relation to the emotion you think you should have. First build a canoe and then put it on the water, and whatever the water does, the canoe follows. The text is the canoe, but you must begin by putting the emphasis on the stormy river. I can't be any clearer than that." He turns toward the seated class and continues. "We're not talking about a finished performance; we're talking about an exercise. When Horowitz plays scales he isn't concerned either with Beethoven *or* an audience. To change the metaphor, I cannot train baseball players who only know how to bunt!"

Bruce and Lila return to their seats, and Meisner waits a moment before continuing. "Does this upset you, this class? We're dealing with a very mysterious subject."

"A little bit, yes," John says. "It's upsetting to see how our lives inhibit us. It seems horrible that we're so conditioned to keep everything in. Now, all of a sudden, it's our job to let everything out."

"That, my friends, is why we're all here," Meisner says.

· · ·

"What play is this?" Meisner asks Joseph and Bette.

"*All Summer Long*," Joseph replies.

"What happens before this scene begins?"

"Our little brother has seen two dogs mating and Bette has told him the facts of life."

"Such as?" Meisner asks.

"What mating's all about," Joseph says. "And I've taken him under my wing, trying to educate him about life and the world—"

"You see how intellectual this talking is?" Meisner says, interrupting Joseph. "It's very *logical*. What if I said to you, 'That bitch of a sister of mine, who hates sex, saw two dogs mating and pointed out to my little innocent brother—innocent!—how dirty it was! I could kill her!' What's the difference?"

"You're talking about the difference between emotion and what you said was logical."

"So when you come in to talk to her, are you logical?"

"No, I'm emotional."

"In other words, you're in a rage, and that's your preparation. Can you see anything in what she told your brother that is morally sickening?" Meisner asks, and Joseph looks confused. "If somebody you love is an observer of a natural process which is a part of life, and is frightened to death because he's told it's filthy, immoral, dirty, it could have a very bad effect on him, couldn't it?"

"Yes."

"Well, that's what she did. She's neurotic, right? She hates sex. Why do you hate sex, Bette?" Meisner asks.

Bette, who is four months pregnant and very large, bites her lip but doesn't reply.

"She can't imagine hating sex," Meisner says, and the class laughs. "That's a character element. This is a character part for you in the sense that the attitude of this girl toward sex is alien to you."

"I'm trying to find a way to put it without intellectualizing it," Bette says.

"Well, why don't you emotionalize it? All you have to know is that two dirty dogs fucking in public disgusts you. It's disgust-

ing, and anybody who disagrees with you can go sit on a tack—
and that includes your dumb brother!"

"That's her point of view," Joseph says. "It's not mine."

"What's yours?"

"That she destroyed my younger brother by telling him that
sex is dirty."

"What did the kid do?"

"He ran away."

"Isn't that pathetic?"

John nods. Meisner turns to Bette.

"How do you feel about the fact that he ran away?"

"I think he must have had some filthy thoughts and must be
feeling guilty."

"To hell with him!"

"Yes! He deserves it. He should have run away!"

"Are you glad you did it?"

"Yes."

"Are you maliciously glad?"

"Yes."

"To prepare, just sit down and tell yourself all of the things
you hate most in the world." Meisner pauses. "Is this beginning
to make sense to you? Preparation is the worst problem in acting.
I *hate* it."

"So do I," Anna says.

"You hate it? Why?"

"The frustration I feel in trying to find something that will
self-stimulate me is fantastic. Then, when I finally do get something, I lose it unless it's very strong and very deeply rooted.
Unless it's strong enough to overcome the inhibition and shyness
and self-consciousness, it disappears."

"Well, play with it. Little by little you'll get it."

"Sandy," Joseph asks, "how do you know if you're in the right
ball park for your preparation if you don't watch it?"

"Let the director tell you, because if you watch yourself
you'll never get there." He pauses for a moment. "Self-stimulation. Ambition or sex. You know what sex is?" he asks
Bette.

"Filthy!" she exclaims. "Disgusting!"

"Right!" Meisner says, and the class laughs. "Ambition or sex. That's according to Dr. Freud, and I believe it. Let's assume that you're in a realistic play about economically very modest people. You're playing the part of a clerk in a store wrapping packages who gets a promotion to become the overseer of the entire wrapping department, and gets five dollars more a week as a raise. Now, to the actor playing that part, according to the play, that five bucks is ecstasy! And this actor knows that to get there all he has to do is to sing to himself the 'Ode to Joy' from Beethoven's Ninth Symphony. It's gigantic, and when he sings it, it lifts him off his feet! That's one of the choices he can make in order to induce in himself the transcendent happiness of the little shlemiel who got a five-dollar raise. The *worst* thing he could do is to try to imagine what he can do with the five dollars. That's ridiculous, because we all know only too well what you can do with five dollars now. So the less realistic, the more fantastic a way you can charm yourself, the more valid your happiness seems, and the more important the five dollars become. The guy with the five-dollar raise comes in and is jumping with joy, but it may actually have come from the fact that some girl has said, 'Okay, I'll go out with you tomorrow night.' "

He nods to Bette and Joseph and they return to their chairs. Because of her size, she lowers herself into the chair very slowly. "How long are you going to be able to stay in this class?" Meisner asks.

"Right through," Bette replies. "I'm not due until July, though I know it doesn't look that way." She laughs. "Did you hear what Ralph said to me?"

"No."

"Ralph, tell Sandy what you said."

Ralph smiles and then sings the theme used at the Miss America pageant: "Here she comes—North America!"

The class laughs.

February 23

"I think one of the problems that you all have with preparation," Meisner says, "is that you try to make it too big. It isn't enough to be in good spirits; you have to be hysterical with pleasure. That's too much. One of the things about emotion is that it has a way of coloring your behavior and that you can't hide it. You simply can't hide it."

He pauses for a moment before slowly standing to face the class. "What's my mood now as I am talking to you?" he asks.

"Serious," Bette says.

"Concerned," Joseph adds.

"One of those would do. I think you're making a problem out of stimulating in yourself too big an emotion. If you're in good spirits, that doesn't mean you're hysterical; if you're depressed, that doesn't mean you're funereal. You say that right now I'm thoughtful, concerned. But I'm also very depressed. Now, that comes from my day at home-sweet-home, from my personal life. It's possible to have a day at home-sweet-home when you want to kill yourself. That's what's affecting me now, and if my partner in a scene said to me, 'How do you feel today?' I'd say quietly, 'Lousy.' That's perfectly acceptable. I don't have to take a pistol out and shoot myself or writhe on the floor.

"There's another thing you have to realize about emotion. You can't hide it. You can mask it, but you can't hide it. All I'm trying to say is that's it's fairly easy to put yourself in a state of good spirits. That's not so difficult, you know? But if you feel you have to have ten thousand pounds' worth of good spirits, then you get in trouble."

Meisner returns to his desk and sits. "A couple of classes ago —you were all here—Joseph Morgan did an exercise with Rachael. There was no doubt that he was depressed. The way he lay his head against her shoulder—it was as if his heart had broken. You played a dirty trick on someone and it hurt your conscience, right, Joe?"

"Right."

"My point is that his acting was emotionally clear. But had this been a play and not an exercise, on some nights during its run it could be fuller, and on some nights it could be emptier. But if he attempted a herculean preparation to work himself up into the lowest depths of misery, the audience would all be as old as I am by the time he finally made his entrance. Do you understand?

"You cannot hide emotion, but you don't need three tons of it in order to color your behavior properly. It's just that you must not be empty. See, I maintain, and will continue to maintain, that Laurence Olivier is not a great actor. Did you see *The Entertainer*? In that play he needed to master the characteristics of a vaudevillian—the speech and manner, the sleaze of that office building at Broadway and Forty-seventh Street where all the vaudevillians hang out. He did it very well because he's a good actor and a thoughtful one, and if he decides to do this"—he sticks his thumb in his ear—"he gets a laugh! But when it came to the emotion of the part, there was nothing. There were two scenes in that play where he had to break down, and it was pathetic how empty his emotion was." He holds his hand to his face and skillfully indicates how Olivier indicated sobbing.

"In the nineteenth century, there was a great English drama critic, William Hazlitt. He said of the great English actor Edmund Kean, that watching his emotion subside after a big scene from Shakespeare was like watching the tide go out. You follow? Mrs. Siddons, another great actress, was so strong as Lady Macbeth that women in the audience were terrified and would run out of the theater. Nobody has ever fled because of an emotional moment from Olivier, and unless you have that, you're not a great actor."

Meisner pauses to adjust the microphone. "But the emotion of Kean and Mrs. Siddons did not, I think, come from preparation. Preparation is what you *start* with. Preparation is to acting what warming up the motor is to driving a car on a cold day. Could anything be simpler? Do you understand what I'm talking about?"

He scans the faces of the class. "Ray, you don't?"

"I think so," Ray says. "But on the one hand you explain how simple preparation is, and on the other you talk about great actors in a way that sounds like they have *tons* of emotion."

"But their emotion arises from the given circumstances of

the play, the situation they imagine themselves to be in."

"It's not necessarily something they bring on with them?"

"No. When Kean played Othello and found out his wife was unfaithful to him, it was his *talent* that made that scene look as if he'd had an epileptic fit. That's talent; you can't do anything about that. I say occasionally—not too often—that someone is a 'talented actor.' I see things. All I'm saying is: Don't be empty or you'll turn into Laurence Olivier."

The class laughs.

February 27

"Let's talk about this," Meisner says. "Ralph, you have an emotional block about this scene."

"I guess I do," Ralph says with a plaintive sigh. He sits on the edge of the bed. "I feel very self-conscious and I have real difficulty getting a hold on it. It's like mercury. I tried to practice preparation all week, and every time I tried to induce this emotion it just didn't work."

"Ralph, in this scene your girl is sleeping with Joe Schmidt. The mystery is why you don't blow up right away. I don't understand that."

"That's the thing. For some reason I can't get pissed off here. Sometimes I'm walking down the street and involuntarily think of some guy I hate, and I want to punch him in the head. Then I try consciously to do it here and it doesn't happen."

"You have to be more open to suggestion."

"You know what it is? You told me once that I always have to be the champ. I try to be good *all* the time. I was trying to give the best performance instead of concentrating on my partner and the emotional circumstances of the scene."

"What do your eighteen analysts say about your difficulty?" Meisner asks.

"There are twenty of them, every one of them is baffled," Ralph says. "Actually, you know what they say? They say, 'You're *afraid* to be angry, aren't you?' I used to have a violent temper when I was a little kid."

"Get it back," Meisner says and the class laughs. "Seriously, Ralph, I think you're right," he continues. "Your problem arises from trying too hard to be good. It's understandable, but there's a danger in trying too hard to be good. That's why the rookie ballplayer strikes out and the intern gets slapped with a malpractice suit."

March 1

"What are you doing, Ralph? This is no good, you know?" Meisner interrupts the exercise which Ralph and Rachael began only a few minutes ago.

"Well, last night I met the *Penthouse* magazine 'Pet of the Month' at a bar, and I had her laughing all night," Ralph says nervously. He holds a notebook and a pencil in his hands. "I told her I'd write her a funny poem about how to go from being a fold-out to real life—"

"The difficulty in that is that your imagination is without reality. That's one problem, which I'll discuss later. Another is that you're forcing all sorts of dialogue to happen so that you'll feel you're continuously active. You keep talking, keep relating to her not on the basis of what she's doing, but in order to perform. I don't know how to make this clearer to you."

"I understand. I felt that I was performing too. I was forcing it."

"Why do you do it?"

"I don't know. It comes down to the old thing, I guess: wanting to be the champ."

"Exhibitionism," Meisner says. "That's not necessarily bad. As an actor, you must have a certain amount of exhibitionism."

"Do you want me to say what that means to me? It means that I'm trying to show off."

"That's right. What's the best way to act well?"

"The best way to act well is to live truthfully, and don't create a phony situation."

"Why do I have to ask you when you already know this?"

"Because my natural tendency seems to come out."

"Your *unnatural* tendency."

"Okay, my unnatural tendency. I was thinking about the preparation, and I guess I planned it too much. I was wanting to be good, instead of just—"

"Ralph, did you ever hear that phrase 'Don't do something until something happens . . .' "

" '. . . to make you do it,' " Ralph says.

"Right. What's that mean?"

"It means that I shouldn't have done anything to fill the gaps."

"That's right," Meisner says. "Who do you want to be, Milton Berle?"

"No."

"Thank God!"

"Though I guess somewhere inside I do," Ralph says, and the class laughs.

"The funniest thing—not the funniest, I've heard funnier—but the thing about you—I was thinking about it—is that I said something to you one day in class, and ever since then you've gone off balance. What was it I said?"

"Something about the fact that I'm blocked. I remember I couldn't get angry in a scene, couldn't prepare for it. I think that ever since then I've taken it to mean that I couldn't prepare at all, and so I've been trying to prove that I could."

"I never said that."

"I know you never said that. It was my, you know . . ."

"I liked your entrance very much. You came in singing. But if Rachael hadn't been there it probably would have been better. Why do I say that?"

"Because I wouldn't have felt the imperative to push anything. I would have had to do what I had to do—namely, write that funny poem—and not try to prove in neon lights that I can work off the other person."

"What should I do with you? You answer everything intelligently. Do you mind being a little stupid next time and simply react to the simple things you get from your partner? You can't play Hamlet every day. Ever since I told you that, you've had a problem.

"Well—that's—" Ralph stammers.

"That's right. It's my fault."

"That's okay," Ralph says, and the class laughs.

"Every actor is an exhibitionist. If you're not an exhibitionist, you're no actor. But to be a good actor . . ." He pauses. "Ralph, you see what's happening here, don't you?"

"Yes, I do."

March 5

Ralph enters the room, where Rachael sits at a table writing a letter. François Truffaut's book *Hitchcock* is open beside her. Without acknowledging her presence, Ralph crosses to the bed, sits on the edge, opens a spiral notebook and begins to write. They continue to write for what seems a very long time.

"What is this," Meisner asks, interrupting the silence, "the New York Public Library? Don't you have a relationship?"

"We're cousins," Rachael says, looking up from her letter.

"That's no relationship."

"We share a house together."

"What brings you together so that you share a house?"

"We're like brother and sister. We grew up together and we share this house."

"Look," Meisner says. "In the first moment there's got to be at least one circumstance that brings you together. I don't care if it's that he told your parents that you're living with a Russian spy. That's the root of a relationship. At least it justifies with theatrical reality that when he walks in—"

"I react to him."

"Yes, you might even say, 'Hello, Shit Face.' But there was *nothing* here. Do you follow?"

"I follow," Ralph says mournfully.

"Or, if you used only what exists, you might pick up from his withdrawn silence that he's notoriously antisocial. You might even say, 'The cat got your tongue?' And what you don't know is that he hates cats, so his reply might be, 'If you mention cats to me once more, I'll knock your teeth out!' What does it mean to use what exists, Ralph?"

"To let what's happening affect you."

"At least to be aware of it, right? What happened when you came in?"

"Nothing. She just sat there with her back to me."

"That's not *nothing*. That's *something*. What's that mean?"

"No response is a response."

"There's no such thing as nothing."

"I didn't want to force something. I guess I didn't want to make the mistake I did last time," Ralph says.

"Forget your past!"

"I just felt like . . . It's frustrating, that's all."

"You're a little self-conscious, aren't you? You want to be right, don't you?"

"Yeah."

"Who doesn't? 'There's no such thing as nothing.' Rachael, what does that mean?"

"There is always something even if it's silence."

"Even though it's nothing."

"Yeah."

Meisner pauses while deciding how to continue. Finally he says, "Ralph, go out and come in again. Leave your notebook here on the table. You can come in and find it. Where are you coming from?"

"From work."

"That's meaningless."

"I had a very bad time at work—"

"Why did you have a bad time?"

"I was asked to take out the garbage, and I wasn't hired for that."

"How do you feel about that?"

"Pissed off. I want to quit. I want to write a letter of resignation."

"Does that mean angry?"

"It means angry."

"So you're coming home from work after having been humiliated. Let me see you do that. Take your coat with you and spend some time preparing."

Ralph leaves, closing the door. Meisner signals to Rachael to give him Ralph's notebook, which he hides in a drawer in his desk. Then he asks Rachael, "What are you doing?"

"I'm writing a letter to someone I want to seduce, and he knows a lot about Alfred Hitchcock."

"You want to be seduced?"

"I want to seduce someone."

"Alfred Hitchcock?"

"No, the person I want to seduce loves the work of Alfred Hitchcock, and I'm trying to compose a letter thanking him for lunch which contains all sorts of references to Hitchcock films."

"Okay," Meisner says. "Don't tell Ralph that I've got his notebook."

Ralph enters the room, closes the door quietly and stands still for a moment before taking off his coat. He is visibly upset and slams his coat onto the bed before crossing to the table, where he remembers leaving his notebook. Its absence is a genuine surprise to him, and the resulting exercise, though brief, has vitality.

"All right," Meisner says after a few minutes. "Now tell me, what did I do? Not what did *you* do, but what did *I* do?"

"You made something happen," Ralph says. "You made me want something. You created a need and made it impossible for me to—"

"I made it more alive," Meisner says. "Right? How did I do that?"

"You gave me something to do."

"I made you come from something that had happened, right?"

"Right. You made it more specific."

"And what happened because of that?"

"The scene came more alive. It got on the edge of something more important."

"It came to life. Were you working off each other?"

"Yes."

"Ralph, what I did to you—and this is no disgrace, quite the contrary—was to pull you back almost to the beginning. Why did I do that?"

"Because I got lost."

"So I gave you a compass."

"Right."

"And that's where you're going to stay until I feel that you're strong in yourself again. It won't last long—one or two weeks."

Ralph nods, and he and Rachael return to their seats.

Meisner pauses for a moment before turning to the class. "The principle is 'Don't do anything until something happens to make you do it.' In this exercise Ralph came in from having an altercation at work; he wouldn't empty the garbage. The boss was nasty, and he came in to write a letter of resignation. The first time he had no preparation. He came in, went right to the pad on the table, wrote his resignation, and it was as if we were in the public library. The second time he had his anger, which had to be prepared for, and it was good!"

Ralph grins shyly.

"Don't come in from nowhere," Meisner continues. "Come in from some situation which has a circumstance in it that gives you a foothold for a preparation. You follow? There was nothing wrong with Ralph as an actor at the beginning of this class last fall, before he started learning with a capital L. Then, for one reason or another, he got sick. What did I have to do? I had to give him an inoculation. What was the inoculation? *No acting, please.* Ralph, that was good. Very simple, but you were working off each other. What's wrong with that? It was good."

Ralph sighs with relief.

"Don't be an actor," Meisner says. "Be a human being who works off what exists under imaginary circumstances. Don't give a performance. Let the performance give you."

March 8

"Wait a minute. I assume that you know all the lines."

"I'm really shaky on my last speech before the end," Ralph says.

"I'm shaky on my life," Meisner says and the class laughs. "Look, have you got anything here that you can use as an independent activity?"

"Yes. I could write a letter."

"An *important* letter. Get your pen and paper. And you, Rachael, straighten up the room so that it's as neat as it possibly can be while you say the lines."

"Should we do the lines mechanically?" Rachael asks.

"No. As he concentrates on writing his important letter and you concentrate on fixing up the room, adjust to each other."

She nods and they begin. Ralph sits at the table and begins to write his letter and Rachael straightens the books piled onto the bookcase. The words of their lines are actively filtered through his concentrated struggle to write a difficult letter and her determined efforts to straighten up the cluttered room.

After a few minutes Meisner interrupts the scene. "Okay, I want to play with this. The color of that text, the way it came out of you, depended on what you were physically doing at the moment: organizing the books, making the bed, writing the letter. Now let's try something new. In this case the organic—a big word—color of the text will depend on what's going on inside of you emotionally. In this scene, Rachael, the father whom you love is about to commit suicide; he's ill, it's terminal, it's painful. And you, Ralph, are her rich, playboy brother from Southampton. Your sister has telephoned you, and you've just jumped into your Jaguar to rush over to East Hampton where she lives. To begin with, your dominant emotional color is your irrepressible good humor. Then it will change by itself, just as the color of the text changed depending on whether you were reshelving the books or making the bed or what you were writing in that letter. The color changed depending on what you were doing at that particular moment, right?"

They both nod in agreement.

"So Rachael, you'll start off with a preparation, an inner emotional state—no more fixing books. When you enter, it's as if you were coming from your father's sickbed, where the doctor has told you about his depression. Emotionally, the key is that you love your father. But the key to your inner life, Ralph, is that you're playing the female lead in the Southampton Country Club production of *The Merry Widow*. Why do I say that to you?"

"Because it's funny. It's a light and humorous thing to do."

"Do you remember what I said to you a week or so ago about the river and the canoe floating on it? Rachel, earlier, the river for you was getting the room organized. Ralph, the river for you was your writing the letter. Now we're advancing. The river is inner; for you, Rachael, it revolves around the fact that your father is dying. For you, Ralph, the river is that you're the star of *The Merry Widow*. Now, each river is going to have many kinds of currents as it moves along. Do you understand?"

"Yes," they both say.

"Fine. Don't try to do the whole thing. Do as much as you can do securely for next time," Meisner says, "on Monday."

March 12

Joseph and Anna quietly read their scene from *The Girl on the Via Flaminia* by Alfred Hayes.

Meisner interrupts. "Listen to me carefully. Anna, here's a girl who comes from a very respectable middle-class family. She's decent, sensitive and well educated—a superior girl. In the war she and her family were starving. Things were terrible in Italy during the war. So what does this eminently superior girl do? She deliberately goes with an American soldier because the Americans are rich and have everything. But it's interesting; she doesn't pick a bum, she picks someone who in his own way is as superior as she is. Then the police come, and this sensitive girl is arrested and tagged; she's registered as a common prostitute. For her this is total demolishment. When she comes into the room she's absolutely destroyed. That's the background for her emotion."

"Does the family know?" Anna asks.

"No. But the family downstairs knows because they tell the soldier. Now, Joseph, you find out before you come upstairs what's happened to her, and whether you like it or not, you're the cause."

"Of her being tagged a prostitute?"

"Right! So you feel all her humiliation and degradation too, because of what you did to her without meaning to. Do you follow?"

"Yeah."

"Anna, I can give you one thing. Next time get against a wall, break down and try to disappear into that wall like a cockroach! Take the emotional part of it very easy to begin with, because you have to read the script. Don't try to do the whole scene next time, just get it started emotionally. Do you understand, Joseph?"

"When I say, 'If there was anything I could have done, I would have done it,' isn't that where I find out?"

"No, they've already told you downstairs."

"So when I say my first line, 'Would you like some cognac?,' that's the beginning? I start the emotion there?"

"The emotion starts downstairs. 'Would you like some cognac?' is just a way of trying to cheer her up."

"So you want me to come in with a preparation and start the scene right there? 'Would you—' "

" 'Would you like some cognac?' I want you to start the scene emotionally there. Any questions? Don't learn the lines; let them happen. Improvise, do anything you want to bring to life the feeling of your degradation, Anna, and the feeling of your guilt, Joseph. You know what I said about the river and the words like the canoe that floats on it? Well, I want you *gradually* to start the river flowing."

March 15

Anna enters, closes the door, crosses to the bed against the wall and wraps herself in the dark green bedspread. After a few minutes she begins to sob. Joseph enters and the scene begins. His preparation is not deep and quickly subsides. He is grave, considerate, concerned, but not emotional. Anna is excellent; her emotion is full and deeply affecting. The only impediment is her insecurity with the lines.

"Let's talk about this," Meisner says. "That was a big advance over last time. Learn as many lines as you can, because when you have to start thinking about what the next line is, it breaks the flow of the emotion. Yet the problem here is not how to learn the lines; you know how to do that. The problem is emotional, and you've come a good way in finding that in yourself. Do you know that?"

"Yeah, I do," Anna says while wiping her eyes.

"Joseph, you can go further, especially at the beginning. It's almost as if you have to wait outside the door in order to get some kind of control over yourself so that she doesn't see how badly you feel. Do you understand?"

"Yeah."

"Look, if you get fifty percent of this scene, you're fifty percent ahead of yourself. You follow?"

"I do."

"So I'm patient, and *you* should be patient. The problem is emotional. It's to bring yourself emotionally to the text so that, as I said before, that river—I'm talking to you, Joseph—starts to flow with a reasonable degree of fullness. So if you get fifty percent of it, that's a big advance, isn't it?"

"Yeah," Joseph says. He seems discouraged.

"Joseph Morgan. I wonder," Meisner says, "I just wonder whether you go far enough away from the play into yourself for your preparation. Do you understand?"

"Yeah, I do make it personal," Joseph says. "But somehow it takes a while for me to connect . . . I don't know how to talk about it. Somehow the circumstances have to become real to me."

"Maybe you want to make it too personal?"

"I don't know about that. Usually at some point something kicks in and it becomes real to me. My preparation was very personal—it had to do with my family—but if it leaves me, it leaves me."

"Don't try to get it back," Meisner says.

"I don't. You know, I think it's a matter of time."

"I agree. Just because we talk about it on Thursday doesn't mean that you're going to come in all set on the following Monday. It moves slowly, you see? The difference between Anna today and Anna on Thursday was a very real advance, and it was having its effect on you. You follow?"

Joseph nods and Meisner pauses for a moment.

"Suppose that you saw—you can't even remember when or

where—one of those poor guys who sleep on the street. Say you saw him eat out of a garbage pail and it turned your stomach. That might be just fine for this scene. Now that's personal to me, but it springs from my imagination. The highly personal nature of preparation does not mean *literally* personal. When my father died, we, the family, were standing by the grave." Meisner stands up, puts the voice transmitter into the right pocket of his jacket and picks up his cane. He walks around the desk to face the class. "While they were lowering the coffin, I realized what I was doing with my foot. As the coffin was going down, the foot was going like this." His right shoe begins to shift on the ball of his foot as if he were methodically grinding out a cigarette or crushing a cockroach.

"Oh, my God," Anna says quietly.

"You see! Look at her reaction!" he says, pointing to Anna. "Look at yours!" he says to Bette. "You were shocked, and she was shocked in a different way. Yet at that gravesite, I felt nothing except *Don't ever come up again!* Now, what could be more personal than that? Yet now it doesn't do a thing for me, except perhaps to make me giggle a little bit. I tell you this to point out the fact that you'll never know how something will affect you emotionally. If I had any shame or self-respect, I wouldn't tell you that story. But I don't have."

As Meisner returns slowly to his desk, Anna raises her hand. "Sandy, when you say personal—and you just pointed out that something can be extremely personal and really not have any kind of deep emotional effect on you—is it also possible, as you said to Joseph, that something can be *too* personal? That when something is very personal you want to keep it private, and therefore it inhibits you even though it affects you very deeply?"

"Right! And only you can know the difference."

"When something is personal and affecting but you don't feel the need to keep it private?"

"Yes. I told one of my forty-two analysts this story about my father, and he was very impressed with its meaning."

"I'm sure," Anna says.

"The other forty-one didn't say anything. They never do, you know."

Scott Roberts enters Meisner's office.

"Yes, that's the book," Meisner says. "I gave it to the library thirty years ago."

Scott hands him the small red book, Sigmund Freud's *A General Introduction to Psychoanalysis*,* and Meisner flips through it for a few minutes. "This is the passage you asked me about," he says, finally, pointing to a page toward the end of the volume. "It's marvelous. I can't tell you how much this discussion of fantasy helped me clarify my thoughts about the dreadful problem of preparation."

He returns the book to Scott. "Please, read this aloud," he says. "I can't see well enough."

Scott clears his throat and begins to read Freud's pioneering text: "Before you leave today, I should like to direct your attention for a moment to a side of fantasy-life of very general interest. There is, in fact, a path from fantasy back again to reality, and that is—art. The artist has also an introverted disposition and has not far to go to become neurotic. He is one who is urged on by instinctual needs which are too clamorous; he longs to attain to honour, power, riches, fame, and the love of women; but he lacks the means of achieving these gratifications. So, like any other with an unsatisfied longing, he turns away from reality and transfers all his interest, and all his libido too, onto the creation of his wishes in the life of fantasy, from which the way might readily lead to neurosis. There must be many factors in combination to prevent this becoming the whole outcome of his development; it is well known how often artists in particular suffer from partial inhibition of their capacities through neurosis. Probably their

*Sigmund Freud, *A General Introduction to Psychoanalysis*; trans. Joan Riviere (New York: Pocket Books, 1953), 384–385.

constitution is endowed with a powerful capacity for sublimation and with a certain flexibility in the repressions determining the conflict. But the way back to reality is found by the artist thus: He is not the only one who has a life of fantasy; the intermediate world of fantasy is sanctioned by general human consent, and every hungry soul looks to it for comfort and consolation. But to those who are not artists the gratification that can be drawn from the springs of fantasy is very limited; their inexorable repressions prevent the enjoyment of all but the meager daydreams which can become conscious. A true artist has more at his disposal. First of all he understands how to elaborate his daydreams, so that they lose that personal note which grates upon strange ears and become enjoyable to others; he knows too how to modify them sufficiently so that their origin in prohibited sources is not easily detected. Further, he possesses the mysterious ability to mould his particular material until it expresses the ideas of his fantasy faithfully; and then he knows how to attach to this reflection of his fantasy-life so strong a stream of pleasure that, for a time at least, the repressions are bout-balanced and dispelled by it. When he can do all this, he opens out to others the way back to the comfort and consolation of their own conscious sources of pleasure, and so reaps their gratitude and admiration; then he has won—through his fantasy—what before he could only win in fantasy: honour, power, and the love of women."

Roberts closes the book and places it on Meisner's mahogany desk.

"Isn't that marvelous?" Meisner asks. " 'Then he has won—through his fantasy . . . honour, power, and the love of women.' I just love it."

9 The Magic *As If:* Particularization

MEISNER: I'm going to tell you all something.
The text is your greatest enemy.

April 26

The class begins with Bette and Beth performing the final scene from Lillian Hellman's *The Children's Hour.* At the end of the scene, Meisner begins his criticism.

"Acting in my terms, in all our terms except for the English —the Americans, the Russians, the Germans—is an emotional creation. It has an inner content. Unlike the English, who know intellectually what the character should be feeling and indicate this through the way they verbally handle the text, we work from living truthfully under imaginary circumstances. Beth, I'll take this very slowly. The play says that the man you love leaves you because he suspects that you're a lesbian, right?"

"Yes."

"Let's say that this doesn't mean anything to you as a person. You don't know the sensation of being a lesbian, or the experience of it. It's alien to you, but you have to play the part, right?

"To him a lesbian is an appalling pervert, but his accusation touches off nothing emotional in you. It's just words on paper, a cold text. How do you solve this problem? In this case, let's say that this is *as if* you were accused of something which is horrifying to you. Now, I don't know what's horrifying to you, but if you're honest with yourself, you'll find something in your experience or imagination. What could it be? It doesn't have to be sexual. Let me talk in a personal, yet imaginative way, about something that, had it happened to me, I would never tell anybody. Suppose that when the actress playing this part was five years old, a gang of four or five local ruffians dragged her into a deserted lot and ripped off her clothes. The horror, the disgrace of this experience is still so alive in her that whenever she recalls it she breaks down. So that might be a useful preparation for the opening of this scene, Beth, because what you're doing now is reading lines in a kind of sad way, but it has no life, no emotion."

"Yes," Beth says, "I felt that I couldn't get the top off, somehow."

"That's what you prepare for. I can't think of episodes or incidents for you which arouse in you terror, horror, shame—call it what you like. You have to do it by yourself. But if it's just words, it's not good enough. That's the point. This phrase, 'it's *as if*,' is called a 'particularization' in the pure terms used by Stanislavsky.

Here Beth is required to act a scene in which her boyfriend, the man she loves—it's real love, very rare—leaves her because he thinks she's a lesbian. If she reads the lines—and they're just lines—" Meisner says and then paraphrases the text: " 'He went away.' 'Is he coming back for dinner?' 'No.' 'You mean he's coming back late?' 'No, he's not coming.' 'Not coming at all?' 'No.' 'Well,' her partner says, 'I'll just light the burner under the goulash.'

"This is where the *as if* comes in. It's pure Stanislavsky. It's *as if* she were a five-year-old kid and something dreadful happened to her—something miserable, something degrading. Or it could be *as if* she were in a state of total shock, or *as if* she were suddenly paralyzed with fear or tension. In that particularization is the preparation."

"Sandy," Beth says, "I don't know what my problem is, but when I sit at home I can find memories or fantasies that arouse certain emotions in me. But here, sometimes they work and sometimes they don't. When I was trying to prepare out in the hall, I felt that I was trying to force something. It wouldn't come and I got nervous, and the more I tried to force it, the less it happened."

"It didn't mean anything to you."

"But when I was by myself it did."

"Then change the preparation. How many times have you heard a piece of music and after about ten repetitions you say to yourself, 'If I hear that once more, I'm going to break the record!' Change it! That will revitalize your preparation."

He pauses to adjust the microphone.

"But a particularization, an *as if,* is something else. It's your personal example chosen from your experience or your imagination which emotionally clarifies the cold material of the text."

"Would you say that again?" John asks.

"What did I say?" Meisner asks Lila.

"You said it's your own personal example which clarifies," Lila says. "I didn't hear the end of it."

Meisner says, "Look, I'm going to stay on this subject maybe for the whole class. It's about time I did. What have I said so far, Ray?"

"That when you come up against a text that's cold to you, which doesn't mean anything because the circumstances are alien to you, you use a particularization—another way to say that is '*as if*'—to describe for yourself a situation that would bring you *personally* to the emotional place you need to be in for the sake of the scene."

"Don't say 'describe.' Say 'evolve.' Bring to life in you. Let's take another example from this scene, and then we'll go on. Beth, you're not a lesbian, are you?"

"No," Beth says.

"But you have to say to Bette, 'He thinks we are.' What kind of particularization could you think of which would clarify the way in which you tell her that your ex-boyfriend thinks you're lovers?"

"I have two problems," Beth says. "One thing I think of is that I'm feeling sad because my boyfriend left me—"

"Forget the story!"

"I guess I'd think that if someone who really loved me left me because—"

"Forget love!"

"Well, if he thought I was involved with someone else sexually, and I wasn't, and he was falsely accusing me—"

"Forget sex! You've got a one-track mind!"

The class laughs.

"Sex or ambition," Beth says. "Didn't you say there's nothing else?"

"Suppose it was *as if* you told her that your boyfriend thinks you both take heroin. It's a deadly secret, isn't it? Or it's *as if* he suspects you both have prison records or jointly murdered an illegitimate child or were practicing witchcraft. You see, this is an area of acting which makes its demands entirely on your imagination. Suppose that Ralph and John were cast as players on the same football team, and suppose that in the play, Ralph, you're hurt on the field and are brought into the locker room and are lying there unconscious while your team is waiting for the ambulance to come. And suppose that I, as the director, said to you, John, 'Stand there and watch him *as if* he were your wife who is dying.' Now, God knows that has little to do with two football players, but we, the audience, will never know where you got your emotion, John, although we will be responsive to it. And if anybody says to you, 'Where did you get that moment? It's very touching,' your answer is, 'Buzz off!' "

"What the director said to John was just to clarify the situation," Ralph says. "It's not a particularization he has to keep forever, is it?"

"To clarify what part of the situation?" Meisner asks.

"To clarify his feeling about what he's watching."

"His emotion."

"But is there a difference between what he feels about my injury and his emotion?"

"The audience attaches the emotion to what he's doing. He's standing there watching you bleed to death, and we see that he's very moved. But we do not know where his emotion is coming from."

"So a particularization is similar to a preparation," Joseph says, "only it's for a specific moment."

"It has to be chosen," Meisner says.

"And it must be personal."

"Yes. And it's worked on in rehearsal."

"So it's what you do your homework on and bring into rehearsal," Joseph says.

"Is the particularization then a permanent part of the performance?" Rose Marie asks. "If I'm doing my two hundredth performance of *Death of a Salesman*—"

"Oh, by that time you may have had fifty different preparations, but the particularizations—the *as ifs* which have been worked out in rehearsal and are now those elements that give form to your role—remain constant."

Ray holds up his hand. "So when you choose a particularization, you choose what the moment is about emotionally. How do you make those choices? Is that the subject of a different class, or can we talk about it now?"

"They come from your instincts."

"Your instincts in relation to that particular scene?"

"Of course."

"As a result of how you either understand it or misunderstand it?" Ray asks.

"Of course! Let me ask you a question. Is there *ever* a time, no matter how many times Beth plays in *The Children's Hour,* when that character is not going to have to squirm with misery when she announces that her boyfriend is never coming back?"

After a pause, Ray says, "You put me in a spot because I want to say, 'No,' but at the same time I want to say that an equally valid reading would be if she were pissed off at the woman she lives with because of what has happened, and so anger comes out instead."

"Then it's a mischoice."

"Okay, that's what I'm asking. How do you make the *right* choice?"

"Your instinct!"

"Also," Rose Marie says, "there's a director."

"Yes," Meisner says, "there's a director. The director is going to let you know what he wants you to project emotionally. Look, Chopin wrote a piece called "The Revolutionary Étude." *Everybody* has played it. Can it ever be anything but"—and he mimes playing the triumphant piece on the top of his desk—" 'The Revolutionary Étude'? Do you understand?"

"I do," Ray says, "but I want to say that everybody who plays it will play it differently, and everyone who has to get to that emotion which the director wants gets there differently, personally."

"*Real* pianists who play it will play it differently, but they will all play the same notes."

"Are you saying," Beth asks, "that if they play the same notes, the color or emotional tone will be the same?"

"More or less," Meisner says. "Can you imagine a *cheerful* Hamlet?"

"No, I honestly can't. But perhaps this is only my problem. Sometimes during the preparation I start observing myself instead of simply doing it, and when I start judging it, I stop feeling it. Then, as in this scene, I freeze up."

"Look, this is the tenth time you've told me that you watch yourself. It's a particular problem which remains unresolved in your technique."

"I'm trying to figure out how not to do it."

"I'm trying to figure out how to tell you what to do," Meisner says. "Wait a minute. There's a certain element—would that it weren't there, but it is—in preparation which makes you aware of yourself. But the moment you play the scene and your attention focuses on something else, that self-consciousness diminishes. Do you understand?"

"Yes, I do. Thank you."

"Particularization," Meisner says, "is really very simple and not nearly as complicated as preparation—nor as subtle. Let's say I make up my mind that I hate to teach, see? That's all I have to say." He gets up and goes to the door of the room. "So I come into the class . . ." He hobbles into the room, glares at the students and says, "Oh, shut up!" The class laughs. Then he repeats the entrance, except that this time he waltzes in, delighted to see his students. "Is everybody here?" he asks, and they laugh again. "Now, I didn't have to work that out. I just know what 'I *hate* to teach'—'I *love* to teach' does to me emotionally. The only thing I cannot do is to do *nothing*—that is, *not* to interpret. It's really very simple if you are imaginative. It's instinctive."

Meisner returns to his desk. "Do you know the Ibsen play *Hedda Gabler*? She burns the manuscript at the end of the play. Do you remember that? Once I talked to Harold Clurman about that scene, and Harold said that when Hedda burns the manuscript, she's burning *him*! That's not just his book, it's her unfaithful lover! Now, the difference between burning a manuscript and burning a man is enormous. *That's* a particularization! That manuscript is him! Not his book, but *him*!"

Meisner sits at the desk, removes the transmitter from his pocket and places it on the desk top.

"Let me tell you something here. There are some roles, for any given actor, which cannot be particularized. If Helen Hayes tried to play Hedda Gabler, it would be ludicrous, right?"

The class agrees.

"The text would be spoken—even Judith Anderson learns her lines—but it would come out without the underlying emotion."

"She would make the correct choices," Anna says, "do the right things, but it would come out—"

"She'd play the obvious play."

"That's my worst fear," Bette says.

"*That's* your worst fear?" Meisner asks, and the class laughs.

"It's in the top ten, yeah," Bette says. "I'm constantly afraid of that because I—"

"I'll tell you something about that," Meisner says. "You are what you are. Your personality is what it is. There are some things that you cannot change and that you may as well accept in your-self. Each of us has a certain scope and certain limitations. That's our nature, our theatrical nature. We are limited by our theatrical nature, which can be very narrow or very broad. Duse could not play Shakespeare. She tried but she failed. You should read George Bernard Shaw's articles on Duse and Bernhardt to understand on the highest level the difference in theatrical personalities."

Meisner pauses for a moment before continuing. "You know, Maureen Stapleton is a wonderful actress, but if you ask her to play the mother in *The Glass Menagerie* she's not very good. There's something in her temperament which doesn't come together with that character. But give her the lead in *The Rose Tattoo* and nobody can touch her. There are some parts we don't have the temperament for even if we understand them, and there are some parts we are so right for that we don't even know that we understand them."

"So temperament means *emotional* understanding?" Joseph asks.

"What's wrong with that?" Meisner asks. "I wish you could see me play Macbeth. You see, you laugh. What's more, *I* laugh. What's the harm in being told that certain parts are not right for you? The Group Theatre had a custom. The directors would read the new play to the whole company before they cast it and we went into rehearsal. Well, after one or two plays, when they read the new play and it turned out that during the course of the action a sideboard was moved and something crept out that hadn't been seen for years, I'd say to myself, 'Good God, that's *my* part!' And you know, I was hardly ever wrong. The truth is, there are some roles we can play better than others."

Rose Marie raises her hand. "Do you think that if you're playing in *One Flew over the Cuckoo's Nest* it's necessary to go to an insane asylum to see how the people behave?"

"No."

"All you have to do is to go to Forty-second and Eighth, right?"

"If you want to go even that far," Meisner says. "You know, when I played the young son, Julie, in the Odets play *Paradise Lost*, I had to play a boy who was dying of sleeping sickness. Did I go to a hospital where they had sleeping-sickness patients? No.

But I did ask a doctor what the symptoms were, and he said, 'You get paralyzed.' So I paralyzed my left side—not my right side, because I had to use it. That's all. You pick out one or two things and don't try to duplicate realistically all the symptoms."

"I think it's important to get information," Rose Marie says. "Observation. Particularization."

"Right. It's like your talking about wearing the emerald dress to the White House. I don't have to make a field trip to the White House or study all the emeralds at Cartier's; all I have to think about is not having to serve cheeseburgers anymore. If I make it personal to me, the rest will follow."

Meisner nods in agreement.

"So what have I clarified in the way of particularizations, *as ifs?* Catch yourself in real life. You're constantly talking *as if.* 'When the secretary said the producer wanted to see me in his office, it was *as if* my heart stopped.' See? 'It was *as if* I felt myself breaking into a cold sweat!' You use them all the time. And it's the particularization that makes the acting have a point. You were all here at the beginning when Beth read Miss Hellman's lines very straight, with an overtone of sadness. It was no good. That's what made me bring up particularization. Her reading was straight, and consequently meaningless. But if she had prepared and also had chosen apt particularizations, it would not be meaningless. The way I greeted you when I felt I *loved* to teach was quite different from the way I greeted you when I hated the job." He pauses before adding, "So have I made any impression today?"

"I think we did a lot today," Bette says.

"That's a generalization," Meisner says.

"I'll have to qualify it—"

"A lot!" Meisner says, and the class laughs.

"Seriously," Meisner continues, "how does it feel to have an acting class and not act?"

"It feels fine," Anna says.

"You liked it?"

"It's nice once in a while," John says. "It really is."

"It's rather like Stella Adler," Rose Marie adds, and Meisner laughs.

"Yes, Stella does a lot of talking. I love Stella," Meisner says.

"I really do. She's my best friend. She is! I learned an enormous amount from her. Do you know that at the end of her classes she turns to the hordes of students before her and says, 'Do you love me?' "

He raises his arms above his head and the class laughs and voices cry out, "Yes, yes!"

"Swear it!" Meisner says.

"I swear! I swear!" voices shout, and the class applauds as Meisner looks ecstatic.

April 30

"I told a couple last week that they had to have more conviction about their material and suggested that an apt particularization, an *as if*, would deepen their playing. In the scene which we have just watched, the simple reality you had between you was very nice. It was definitely the behavior of two human beings. Shaw said, 'Self-betrayal, magnified to suit the optics of the theater, is the whole art of acting.' What does that mean?"

"It means to find in yourself and reveal what's true about the scene," Anna says, "and to let it rise to a level where it communicates in a real way."

"Suppose you said to me, 'I'm going to buy you a red tie from Countess Mara.' Acting is the art of self-revelation, so I have to understand how I feel about red, because my answer in the script is 'Not red!' " He turns to Bette. "Tell me you're going to buy me a red tie from Countess Mara."

"Sandy," Bette says, "I'm going to buy you a red tie from Countess Mara."

From looking delighted when hearing the first part of the line, Meisner grimaces on hearing the word "red." His line bursts forth: "Not red!"

"Blue?" Bette asks.

Meisner smiles with pleasure and the class laughs.

"Now, what did I just do?"

"You found a reaction in yourself, something that was big enough—"

"Spontaneous, right? Tell me you're going to invite me to dinner when you finish decorating your dining room, and that the main course is going to be artichokes."

"Sandy, when my dining room is finished, I'm going to invite you to dinner and the main course is going to be artichokes."

Again, from looking pleased, on hearing the word "artichokes" Meisner's face contorts with displeasure.

"You don't like artichokes?" Bette asks.

"That's quite clear, right?" Meisner asks, and again the class laughs. "That is material raised to the optics of the theater, you follow?"

"Yes."

"What do you follow?"

"It's not a little reaction. It's a reaction that's raised to a point where . . ."

". . . it needs to be. You have to know what you're saying *means to you.* That, in large measure, is how you work on a part. You follow?"

"So you should explore a part for the things to which you can react personally?" Beth asks.

"*After* you've achieved the basic reality. Let's talk about this. Ray, what do you think?"

"Well, what's curious to me is that you said that this exploration should wait until *after* you've achieved the basic reality of the scene. It's something I'd never thought of before and it seemed to make a lot of sense, because then you prevent yourself from making too much of something and falsifying it as a result. Am I understanding you correctly?"

"Or from falling into a cliché."

"So if you can get the basic reality at the conversational level, and then discover the deeper meanings that fuel it with the optics of theater, it's not built on a bed of clichés," Ray says.

"What does it mean, 'the optics of the theater'?"

"It means that when you put the real situation on the stage, you need to keep its reality so that it's believable both to you and to the audience, but you have to raise it to a level above real life. Otherwise it doesn't communicate."

"You're talking about emotion?" Meisner asks.

"Yeah, I guess. That's part of it, but I was also thinking in terms of energy."

"Energy will come with it. The trouble with English actors is their use of energy. It's got to be there, but they think of it as stage energy, with no emotional backbone, no support."

"So if you have the emotion first, the energy comes as a result of how deeply you feel the emotion, as opposed to going for an energy that has no base."

"Tell me again you're going to buy me a tie."

"Sandy," Bette says, "I'm going to buy you a red tie from Countess Mara."

This time Meisner's face puckers and he says in a prissy voice, "Uh . . . red!"

"See, this time I'm trying to do it all in my vocal intonation, whereas before when Bette said 'a red tie' it was *as if* she had said 'Hitler' to me." His expression is one of deep revulsion. "I'm overdoing this a little bit, but just a little. First the reality; that you have. Now the fullness with which you express yourself. To put this onstage it has to be the art of self-revelation raised to the optics—the eye, the level, call it what you like—of the theater. In this scene, for example, she asks you if you have sex with your husband, doesn't she? What's your answer?"

"That it's only animal," Anna says.

"You're so right," Meisner says with an expression of mild disgust. "You follow? That's basically an organic reading. What does that mean, an 'organic reading'?"

"No chemicals," Bette says, "no preservatives."

"No bullshit," Ray says.

"No bullshit," Meisner repeats. "That's the higher criticism." The class laughs. "So the problem is solved *if* you just make sure you know how you feel about what you're talking about. You know, I find this very difficult to make clear: how you express yourself with a *full* meaning. Next time I plan to do the *Spoon River Anthology* with you. Then you'll see something!"

"I think everybody's afraid of doing anything phony," Rose Marie says, "so the tendency is to underplay—"

"So I'm egging you on!"

10 "Making the Part Your Own"

MEISNER: The American actor is very lucky. Why? Because so little is asked of him.

May 3

"Is everybody here?" Meisner says as he quickly enters the classroom. Scott Roberts surveys the room and nods. "Good," Meisner says and sits behind his desk. "Let's start easily. Today we are going to begin to work with texts taken from Edgar Lee Masters' collection of poems called *The Spoon River Anthology*. For our acting purposes these are not poems, nor are they in any sense to be taken as monologues or solo performances. Instead, we should consider them as speeches in a play which are preceded by a cue that I'll describe in a minute. Ray, which one have you chosen?"

"I have about five which I haven't decided among."

"Decide."

"Immediately?"

"Immediately. The simplest one. The one that's most you."

"I'm not so sure what you mean by 'simple.' "

"One that's simple, personal, and that you have a genuine feeling for."

"Okay," Ray says. "I'll read 'Robert Southey Burke.' " He sits on a gray metal folding chair in the center of the acting area and begins to read in a clear, quiet voice:

"I spent my money trying to elect you Mayor,
A. D. Blood.
I lavished my admiration upon you,
You were to my mind the almost perfect man.
You devoured my personality,
And the idealism of my youth,
And the strength of a high-souled fealty.
And all my hopes for the world,
And all my beliefs in Truth,
Were smelted up in the blinding heat
Of my devotion to you,
And molded into your image.
And then when I found what you were:
That your soul was small
And your words were false
As your blue-white porcelain teeth,
And your cuffs of celluloid,
I hated the love I had for you,
I hated myself, I hated you
For my wasted soul, and wasted youth.
And I say to all, beware of ideals,
Beware of giving your love away
To any man alive."

"Okay," Meisner says. "Now, the cue for that speech in a play could be, 'Ray, why did you turn so suddenly against'—what's his name?"

"Blood. A. D. Blood," Ray says.

"—'A. D. Blood, when once you *adored* him? Such a question

could be asked of you; and that speech is your answer to the question."

"So I make up the question that's the cue?"

"Who's your partner?"

"Rose Marie."

"She could ask you the question. What's your answer?"

"This speech?" Ray asks.

"Yes. It's not a monologue. It *is* an answer to a question, right?"

"Yes."

"Well, just for the fun of it, Rose Marie, ask him why he turned so against A. D. Blood. Ray, you put the book down and answer her."

"Why did you turn so against A. D. Blood?" Rose Marie asks.

"Because I spent all my money trying to get him elected mayor," Ray says in an intense, even and quickly inflected voice. "I thought he was the greatest politician in the world and I worked real hard for him. Then I discovered what a fake he really was, and when I found it out I hated the fact that I had liked him so much. I hated myself for thinking he was a good person and for not knowing the truth."

"Okay," Meisner says. "That's the beginning of the idea. Ray, what are the last two lines of the speech?"

Ray picks up the book from the floor and finds the poem. " 'And I say to all, beware of ideals, / Beware of giving your love away / To any man alive.' "

"How do you feel about that?"

"It's harsh! I feel betrayed and angry."

"Could you prepare for that?"

"Yes."

"Okay. Listen, everybody. The emotional essence of each of these speeches usually comes in the last two lines. In this case it's *I hate fake idols!* Right?"

"Right," Ray says. "Now I know what you mean by a personal response to it."

"Good. Now I'll show you something, and let's see if it means anything to you. Let's imagine I have a short speech in a play, which I'll deliver in a moment. It's hard for me to laugh, but here goes." Instantly Meisner looks as if he is delighted by something wondrous and claps his hands in pleasure.

"My speech begins, 'I was in the worst taxi accident of my life! Two people were killed!' Then, after more laughter and more words, I get to the last line, which is, 'But I came out safe and so did my companion!' The emotional essence is in the last line, and once you have prepared that gaiety, *then* you start the speech, even though the first line of it is 'I was in the worst taxi accident of my life!' In these texts it's the last two lines which determine the emotional color of the whole piece. To continue with this example, suppose your partner says to you in the scene, 'You're always so happy. Why are you always laughing?' Your response is, 'I was in the worst taxi accident of my life!' And then, eventually, 'And I thank God I'm alive!' Do you follow the logic of what I'm talking about?"

Ray nods.

"Okay, rehearse with Rose Marie. She'll have one too. You get the preparation from the last two lines, and then invent—just for the exercise—a simple cue that motivates the speech. Let me repeat: this has to be treated like a speech in a play, with a cue and then an answer. It is not a solo."

"So when I say the words that appear on the page, I say them to Rose Marie?"

"Yes. You make clear to her why you're so bitterly angry. So what do you start with?" he asks Rose Marie.

"You start with a preparation based on the last two lines of the speech."

"And you take your time preparing," Meisner adds. "Then you improvise the speech, making a response in your own words which contains as least some of the elements of the speech. Then prepare and read the actual text. Improvise, then read it, then improvise—always with a preparation. Next class I won't ask you to do the actual speech. You won't do it until I sense that you have a secure emotional grasp of the material. You must make a reality of that speech—make it your own—by giving it a real preparation derived from the end of the speech and then relating its content in your own words to your partner. Any questions?"

"Yes," Rose Marie says. "In that speech about A. D. Blood, can

Ray do it for the purpose of the improvisation without ever mentioning A. D. Blood?"

"Of course!"

"He could just say something like, 'I hate it when people treat me unfairly'?"

"Right! The speech is not about A. D. Blood. The speech is about false idols, right?"

The class nods.

"All right, Ray, sit down," Meisner says. "Beth, have you got one?"

Beth comes forward. Her luxurious hair is tied back and she is wearing gray slacks. She sits and begins to read the poem "Ida Frickey":

"Nothing in life is alien to you:
I was a penniless girl from Summum
Who stepped from the morning train in Spoon River.
All the houses stood before me with closed doors
And drawn shades—I was barred out;
I had no place or part in any of them.
And I walked past the old McNeely mansion,
A castle of stone 'mid walks and gardens,
With workmen about the place on guard,
And the County and State upholding it
For its lordly owner, full of pride.
I was so hungry I had a vision:
I saw a giant pair of scissors
Dip from the sky, like the beam of a dredge,
And cut the house in two like a curtain.
But at the 'Commercial' I saw a man,
Who winked at me as I asked for work—
It was Wash McNeely's son.
He proved the link in the chain of title
To half my ownership of the mansion,
Through a breach of promise suit—the scissors.
So, you see, the house, from the day I was born,
Was only waiting for me."

"What's that speech about? Don't give a lecture. Tell us in your own words about a personal experience."

"It's about going into a place and feeling isolated and locked out, but having a vision that somehow you belong there and helping, through your own work, to open the doors, to make the place home—proving that it was home all the time."

"That's not what the speech is about," Meisner says. "Look, I'll do it for you." His face lights up in a delighted smile. "I got off a train in a strange town," he says. "I didn't know anybody, and nobody knew me. It was early in the morning and I walked and passed a great big mansion. I was so *hungry* that I had a vision of the house being cut in half by a giant pair of scissors! I went into the hotel and some guy there winked at me, so what do you think I did? I winked back! He bought me something to eat. We went to bed together, and eventually he promised to marry me. But when he didn't, I sued the pants off him! And I was awarded the mansion! Me! Which only goes to prove that *nothing* you wish for in this life is going to remain foreign to you! Isn't that wonderful?"

His enjoyment of the speech is infectious and the class laughs delightedly.

"That's what that speech means, you see?"

"Yes," Beth says.

"What's the emotional preparation for that speech, do you think?"

"To me it's that anything's possible. It's a dream, imagining it—"

"That's not an emotion; that's a sentence. Are you ticklish?"

"Not really."

He points to Bette, who is sitting in the front row of chairs. "Go tickle her," he commands. "Tickle her!"

Bette approaches Beth and, reaching around her from behind, begins to tickle her waist.

"Really!" Beth says. "I'm not ticklish!" She begins to laugh a large, genuine laugh and the whole class joins in.

"Now," Meisner says. "Tell her the story! Hurry up!"

"I got off the tra-han-ain," Beth exclaims, "and I saw this gorgeous mansion! And, oh, God, I was so hungry! I started walking to the inn to ask for work—" At this point, Bette joins in the laughter delightedly. "And I met this guy there and he happened to be the owner of the mansion!" The two women laugh with increased pleasure. "And he promised to marry me, and when he didn't," Beth continues, "I sued him for every cent he had! And do you know what?" Beth asks, and Bette shakes her head. "I won!" They laugh warmly together for a few seconds more.

"What does that prove?" Meisner asks.

"If I'm ticklish," Beth says happily, "anything's possible!"

"Are you beginning to get the idea?" Meisner asks the class.

"So," says John, "what we use from the last couple of lines, we use right from the first word? At first I thought we were to prepare for that but were to keep it only for the last couple of lines. But you want the whole thing done that way, right?"

"What was my example about the taxi accident?"

"It was right from the beginning."

Almost as if intoxicated, Bette and Beth burst into laughter again.

"Hold on to that until next Monday!" Meisner says, and the class laughs. "Dave? Did you choose one?"

"Yes."

"Let's hear it."

Dave reads "Dr. Siegfried Iseman" in a loud, clear voice:

"I said when they handed me my diploma,
I said to myself I will be good
And wise and brave and helpful to others;
I said I will carry the Christian creed
Into the practice of medicine!
Somehow the world and the other doctors
Know what's in your heart as soon as you make
This high-souled resolution.
And the way of it is they starve you out.
And no one comes to you but the poor.
And you find too late that being a doctor
Is just a way of making a living.
And when you are poor and have to carry

The Christian creed and wife and children
All on your back, it is too much!
That's why I made the Elixir of Youth,
Which landed me in jail at Peoria
Branded a swindler and a crook
By the upright Federal Judge!"

"What are the last two lines?" Meisner asks.

"Well, the last four lines are: 'That's why I made the Elixir of Youth, / Which landed me in jail at Peoria / Branded a swindler and a crook / By the upright Federal Judge!' "

"How do you feel about that?"

"Resentful."

"What's stronger than resentful?"

"Hate."

"All right. What else do you feel?"

"That it's a joke."

"What kind of a joke?"

"That there's no such thing as being 'upright.' "

"Wait a minute. What did you observe in Beth's exercise?"

"That her preparation—the laughing—got her involved in what she was doing."

"What was the meaning of my being funny when I said, 'I was in the *greatest* taxi accident *ever!*' What did you observe about that?"

"That you were saying one thing and were feeling another."

"True enough." Meisner pauses for a moment. "What are you going to do about the almost insane bitterness of this man? I say this man is almost insane in his impotence. The cue for this speech is very simple. 'Good God, Dave, how did you ever land in jail?' When you work with Sarah at home, take a couple of pencils and break them into a thousand pieces as a release for your venom, and when you have that, then, tell Sarah in your own words how you happened to land in jail. Do you follow?"

"Yes."

"Listen, people, I just gave him a character to play. He doesn't have to change his face; he doesn't have to shave off his moustache; he doesn't need an accent. He needs only one thing: *murder in his heart.* He's insane. Do you get that? Character comes from *how you do what you do.* It's not easy to give release to that kind of venom."

Meisner pauses for a moment. "You know, there's another way you could play this—in tears, crying, broken down by the tragedy of your life. So far, you've all picked such emotionally complicated ones. There are simple ones in this book. But if you understood Beth's hearty laughter—that's the essence of this exercise. Mary, your turn."

Mary Franc, a blond woman in her late forties, has been an auditor in the class from its beginning. With the expulsion of Vincent, she has joined the group of active students. "This is 'Hannah Armstrong,'" she says.

> "I wrote him a letter asking him for old times' sake
> To discharge my sick boy from the army;
> But maybe he couldn't read it.
> Then I went to town and had James Garber,
> Who wrote beautifully, write him a letter;
> But maybe that was lost in the mails.
> So I traveled all the way to Washington.
> I was more than an hour finding the White House.
> And when I found it they turned me away,
> Hiding their smiles. Then I thought:
> 'Oh, well, he ain't the same as when I boarded him
> And he and my husband worked together
> And all of us called him Abe, there in Menard.'
> As a last attempt I turned to a guard and said:
> 'Please say it's old Aunt Hannah Armstrong
> From Illinois, come to see him about her sick boy
> In the army.'
> Well, just in a moment they let me in!
> And when he saw me he broke into a laugh,
> And dropped his business as president,
> And wrote in his own hand Doug's discharge,
> Talking the while of the early days,
> And telling stories."

"Okay," Meisner says, "I'm going to give you an interpretation. From the speech we learn that Lincoln was a good man, right? A sweet man—helpful, human. What are the last two lines?"

"The last two lines are: 'Talking the while of the early days, And telling stories.' "

"So what do you feel about that?"

"I feel like she's—"

"You! You!"

"That I'm glad to find out that this great man remembers me."

"That's the story. He *remembers* you. That has emotional implications."

"It makes me feel proud and loving."

"All right, I'm going to show you something. I want you to imagine an experience that was so good and so sweet and so much a tribute to the goodness of human beings that you can't think about it without crying. Don't look for a real experience; I doubt whether you'll find it. Go to your imagination, and come up with a human kindness which is so rare that you can't think about it without crying. When you're fully prepared, tell that story to Ralph. Do you follow?"

Mary nods uncertainly.

"It's as if I said, 'You know, I can't think of my mother without wanting to break down. I'll tell you a story about the kind of person she was. . . .' That's what I'm doing, except now my text is: 'I was in terrible trouble and I remembered my old friend, Abraham Lincoln, so I went to visit him. They finally let me in. There he was, just as he used to be. It's heartbreaking now that he's dead.' I involve myself emotionally in something which I respond to, such as the sweetness and goodness of some people. It's as if the whole speech was held together by 'I'll tell you a story of what an *angel* he was.' And if you *let yourself alone emotionally*, something will happen. Now, if you can follow that, then you prepare and float on what you've got, and in your own words tell it to your partner. Right?"

"Right," Mary says.

"You pick such difficult ones!"

"They're all difficult," Mary says.

"They're not. You'll see. Joseph Morgan, what have you got?"
" 'Harry Wilmans.' "
"Read it."

"I was just turned twenty-one,
And Henry Phipps, the Sunday-school superintendent,
Made a speech in Bindle's Opera House.
'The honor of the flag must be upheld,' he said,
'Whether it be assailed by a barbarous tribe of Tagalogs
Or the greatest power in Europe.'
And we cheered and cheered the speech and the flag he waved
As he spoke.
And I went to the war in spite of my father,
And followed the flag till I saw it raised
By our camp in a rice field near Manila,
And all of us cheered and cheered it.
But there were flies and poisonous things;
And there was the deadly water,
And the cruel heat,
And the sickening, putrid food;
And the smell of the trench just back of the tents
Where the soldiers went to empty themselves;
And there were the whores who followed us, full of syphilis;
And beastly acts between ourselves or alone,
With bullying, hatred, degradation among us,
And days of loathing and nights of fear
To the hour of the charge through the steaming swamp,
Following the flag,
Till I fell with a scream, shot through the guts.
Now there's a flag over me in Spoon River!
A flag! A flag!"

"What do you feel about the last two lines?" Meisner asks.
"I feel that I could kill somebody for taking my life from me."
"Are you furious?"
"I went to war for them and they killed me."

"They made a gullible fool out of you, didn't they?"

"Yeah."

"How do you feel about that?"

"Like I want to kill somebody. Like I want to kill Henry Phipps. Like I could *scream.*" Joseph bangs his fist onto his leg.

"So do it next time in your own words—scream it! You made a fool of yourself, didn't you? A jackass! How would you feel if your were fifteen and you went to a Christmas party and said, 'But where's Santa Claus?' and everybody was rolling on the floor laughing at you. How would you feel?"

"I'd feel stupid."

"How would you feel if they gave you a stuffed Santa Claus for your *seventeenth* birthday?"

"I'd want to hit somebody!"

"*That's* the way you begin. Are you following the logic of this?" he asks the class and they nod. "How come you have a flag on your grave when nobody else does? Put the book away!"

"Because to me it's something they did as an empty symbol for having given my life to the country."

"What happened?"

"I was shot."

"What's the beginning of it—in your own words."

"Well, I went to hear a pompous ass stand up and make a speech about how we have to defend the country, and I was young and believed what he said. So I went off and joined the army—"

"I think there is more self-hatred than that. 'I *hate* what I did. I *hate* what they put me through. I *hate* what they did to me when I came back!' Does that mean anything to you?"

"Yeah."

"When it comes right down to it, it's Joseph Morgan's emotion. It's Joseph Morgan absolutely beside himself. When it comes down to it, it's always *you.* What did I just say to you?"

"That the emotion comes from me."

"Do you have a temper?"

"Yes, I do."

"Then, where does the control come from?"

"Probably it's from the way I was raised."

"I *hate* parents!" Meisner exclaims and the class laughs. "How would you like to be operated on without an anesthetic?"

"No, thank you."

"That's what this is, Joe. That's what this is."

May 7

"You people are judging material from your heads, not from your hearts. You judge from what you understand, and because all of you, unfortunately, have been to college there are no words in these texts that are difficult for you to understand."

"Would you rather I picked something else?" Sarah asks. She has just read a philosophical poem about an elderly milliner.

"Something simple," Meisner says. "Something that makes you laugh or cry or get angry. I'm talking about emotions! Have you got another?"

"Well, I'd rather put it off until Monday if that's all right with you."

"Sure. Listen, people, when I was twenty or thereabouts, my favorite composer was Chopin. Romantic, melodious, emotional. And my friend, Aaron Copland, used to die with laughter because he liked composers who were avant-garde, atonal and dissonant. *I* was smart. He wasn't. Who knows, that may have been smart for him, but what I liked was right for me. I wish I had a piano here so I could show you." He begins to play a lush, Chopinesque melody on the top of his desk. "Gorgeous! I say, pick from your heart! Don't pick from your head! Why not be simple? What's the crime in being simple?" He pauses for a moment. "You know, my biggest job in teaching you as actors is to bring you together with yourself. That's the root of creative acting." He turns to Ray. "What are you learning from the *Spoon River* exercises?"

Ray says, "The thing that's coming home to me is how you make this material your own. If we do it first in our own words and are fully prepared, then it's an easier jump to the actual words of the piece. And when we make the jump, the words of the text are like our own and we're less hampered by them. They come from *us.*"

"Did Chopin compose music in order to imitate Mozart?" Meisner asks.

"I say he didn't," Ray says.

"Well, who did he imitate?"

"I think he wrote to make music that pleased him. He was writing from his own instinct and spirit."

"His own what?"

"Instinct and spirit—his soul."

"Do you know the painter Cézanne? Did he paint to imitate Rembrandt? He didn't? Are you sure? Who did he imitate?"

"He didn't imitate anyone."

"What did he do?"

"He painted for himself."

"Where did he get his ideas?"

"From his instincts, his imagination."

"Who did Duse imitate? Well, you never saw her. What's the point I'm making?"

"That your work comes from within yourself," Beth says. "Even though the material already exists, the life you bring to it is your own. It's unique for each person who does it."

"You know," Meisner says, "learning to act takes time. It's made out of the human being who's doing the work. Each of you in your own way has certain human elements which are on the surface and are easy to play. Other elements are more difficult, but whatever you get from every exercise is part of your learning and improvement. You know, if you were a painter or a musician, you'd choose material because it already meant something to you, but in acting you have a much more difficult problem. More often than not you're given material which is *not* related to you, and you have to learn how to make it your own. You have to learn how to use yourselves as actors. There are very few character actors. There should be more, but actors today don't know how to make use of what doesn't come spontaneously to them. Television is a perfect example of your playing *that* deep," —he holds his thumb and index finger together before him— "according to the way you look."

"What instrument do you play?" Meisner asks Beth.

"I don't," Beth says.

"You just want to be a star?"

"I'm a writer."

"You're a writer?"

"Yes, I play the typewriter."

"Who do you imitate?"

"Nobody."

"What does it mean when you say an artist is original?"

"It means that he works from within himself," Joseph says.

"Are you learning that here?"

"Yes."

"What does it mean, to work from within yourself?"

"To express yourself impulsively, not to think about what it is that you're doing or watch yourself self-consciously."

"To express yourself impulsively. According to what standard?"

"Of being true to yourself."

"That's right," Meisner says. He pauses to adjust his microphone. "What does it mean that you can't be an actor and a gentleman?"

Joseph says, "You're allowed to do things onstage that you don't do in life. You're permitted to express yourself on stage and don't need to hold yourself back as you must in life."

"What does it mean, 'to hold yourself back?'"

"To censor yourself. Society sets the standard, but that has nothing to do with acting."

"That's true, but what do you mean?"

"Acting doesn't have anything to do with everyday life."

"It has to do with truth," Meisner says.

"It has to do with truth, yeah," Joseph says, "but it doesn't have anything to do with conventional life outside the theater."

"That's true. I've heard Maureen Stapleton at a party talk like a cultured woman. Who's she kidding? That's not what she lives by on the stage."

"Well, they're two different things."

"What do you mean?"

"Well, you bring your special self, your actor's self, to your work, and it's different from the way you are outside."

"You bring your *real* self, right?"

"Your truthful self," Joseph says.

"That's why you should never pick material in response to your ambition or your intellect. You should pick material that comes out of your gut. Unless you need a job," Meisner adds, and the class laughs.

May 10

"Which one?" Meisner asks Bette.

"I was going to ask you about it," she says. "A woman who married about eight times who ends up in Paris and gets poisoned."

"I don't think that one's right for you."

"Okay," Bette says. "The one I really liked was 'Elsa Wertman.'"

"Do it."

Bette sits down and begins to read:

"I was a peasant girl from Germany,
Blue-eyed, rosy, happy and strong.
And the first place I worked was at Thomas Greene's.
On a summer's day when she was away
He stole into the kitchen and took me
Right in his arms and kissed me on my throat,
I turning my head. Then neither of us
Seemed to know what happened.
And I cried for what would become of me.
And cried and cried as my secret began to show.
One day Mrs. Greene said she understood,
And would make no trouble for me,
And, being childless, would adopt it.
(He had given her a farm to be still.)
So she hid in the house and sent out rumors,
As if it were going to happen to her.
And all went well and the child was born—They were so kind to me.
Later I married Gus Wertman, and years passed.

But—at political rallies when sitters-by thought I was
crying
At the eloquence of Hamilton Greene—
That was not it.
No! I wanted to say:
'That's my son! That's my son!' "

"How do you feel about those last two lines?"
"They kill me."
"All right, prepare to be killed! Start crying! Start crying, and
when you have trouble controlling it, tell us the story."
Without a pause Bette says, "Okay. I came over from Ger-
many—"
"No! You're not prepared."
Bette takes a deep breath and covers her eyes with her hands.
After a moment or two she begins to shiver; a long, low sigh
escapes her lips and her large, brown eyes fill with tears.
"Now start," Meisner says.
"I came from Germany when I was very young," Bette says,
the tears streaming down her cheeks. "And the first job I had was
with Hamilton Greene. They were very nice people, but one day
she went out and he came into the kitchen and—"
"Cry!" Meisner exclaims encouragingly. "It's okay to cry. Let
out what you're feeling!"
"He came into the kitchen and he started to kiss me and I
pulled my head away and he kissed me on my neck." She is crying
softly. "I don't know what happened after that, but I got pregnant and I was so ashamed. Then she said she understood what
was happening—"
"Cry more!" Meisner says. "Don't be afraid to let yourself go!"
After a pause Bette begins to weep movingly. "She said she
would keep the baby, and so she told everybody that she was
pregnant and she stayed in the house for nine months. And I had
the baby and she took him!" Because of the weeping, her voice
has become very thin and high. "And now, when I go to political
rallies I start crying because"—she pauses in an effort to control
herself—"and everybody thinks I'm crying because he speaks so
well. But that's not it! It's because I want to say, 'That's my son.

That's my son!' " She covers her face with her hands and continues to sob.

"That's right," Meisner says. "Well, the defects are technical, purely technical. We can't understand you."

"Okay," Bette says and begins to laugh.

"*That's* what I'm talking about! Do it in your own words, and after you've done it, go through the script as written, then go back to the free improvisation—always prepared."

"Even when reading it?" Bette asks.

"Even when reading it *and* when telling it. Both."

"But I shouldn't look in the book to check some words?"

"No! They'll gradually come to you."

May 14

"In your own words, tell the class about yourself."

"I became very ill," Rachael says in a subdued voice, "which left me a shell of myself."

"What kind of surgery? Don't guess, it's quite obvious."

"Cancer."

"You left the hospital a shell of yourself, which is the way cancer leaves you. Tell them the story as it occurs to you."

"I had cancer and I had surgery for it, which left me just a part of myself. On my wedding anniversary, when I felt that I was somewhat myself again, my husband and I went for a walk in the woods. We talked about everything but what we were really feeling, and we tried to act as if everything was as it always had been. But it wasn't the same. And it depressed me more when he"—she begins to cry softly—"when he left me alone for a few minutes, and I saw myself in the mirror and realized that I was really half-dead! And that I might as well be completely dead!" She is crying fully, the tears streaming from her eyes. "So I killed myself, and I wondered if he ever understood why."

"That's nice," Meisner says after a few moments, when Rachael's emotion begins to subside. "What you ended with is what you should prepare for and then begin with. The preparation has something very concrete; it has to do with a once young, hopeful person who knows that her life is really over and how she feels about it. It's as though your partner says to you, 'Why did a young and lovely girl like you shoot yourself?' Your answer is this speech. That's turning poetry into a living, acting part of a role, not a poem. Do you remember John Gielgud? He did a program of poems, all from Shakespeare. He has a beautiful voice. He started off in C major; then he went to D minor, and he did each speech in a different key. There is no key here; there is only you. And don't finish until the emotion subsides."

"When I practice it, do you want me to do it in my own words?"

"You may want to try different emotional approaches in the preparation, but what you did just now was essentially what it's all about."

Rachael looks pleased and the class laughs.

May 17

"Which one is it?"

"Another suicide," Rose Marie says. " 'Julia Miller.' She takes morphine. She's thirty years old and married to an aging man."

"Read it."

"We quarreled that morning,
For he was sixty-five, and I was thirty,
And I was nervous and heavy with the child
Whose birth I dreaded.
I thought over the last letter written me
By that estranged young soul
Whose betrayal of me I had concealed
By marrying the old man.
Then I took morphine and sat down to read.
Across the blackness that came over my eyes
I see the flickering light of these words even now:
'And Jesus said unto him, Verily
I say unto thee, To-day thou shalt
Be with me in paradise.' "

"That's a difficult one. Why is it difficult?"

"The text is based on the hope that there will be something better for me and my baby in heaven."

"Do you hope or do you know?"

"I know. God will be there."

"How do you feel about it?"

"I feel relieved. I'm scared, but I'm also relieved."

"Relieved?"

"I feel almost happy. They can't touch me anymore."

"That's difficult," Meisner says. "Anything that has to do with religious pleasure is very difficult to act. I'll tell you a story as an example of what it might mean. In Florence, Italy, there's an old monastery, and in it you go up a flight of steps and at the top there's a landing, and on the far wall there's a mural. What I saw there was the angel telling the Virgin Mary about the future birth of Christ. But it was so human, so inspired! Mary's face! I still see it very clearly. She's still—"

"Are you saying you saw a painting or you saw a vision?" Rose Marie asks.

"I saw a painting by Fra Angelico called *The Annunciation*. My suggestion is that you treat this speech as if it were a prayer in which you, having taken morphine, know you're going to die and that you're going to heaven. There life is going to be full of wonderful peace and quiet for you. That's quite a problem. Do you want to do it?"

"Yep."

"The preparation has to do with what?"

"Absolute, blinding joy, tears of joy that I'm finally getting the one thing I want."

"And what would that be?"

"Pure happiness."

"Okay. Don't talk about it any more. In this speech that's comparable to the angel's announcement to Mother Mary that she's going to give birth to Christ. It's a prayer of joy!"

"Then the morphine is a blessing?"

"Yes, that's a good way to look at it. I hate to talk about it because it's so delicate, but in the hush, in the quiet of a rare moment of joy, you open your heart. Does that touch anything in you?"

"Yes."

"Are you going to do it now?"

"I'll try it," Rose Marie says, and after a moment she continues. "He can't touch me anymore. He can't get near me. I don't even know why I married him. Yeah, I know why I married him." She is crying quietly. "He . . . saved me from what I couldn't take. The young man didn't want me anymore, so—" Her emotion renders the rest of the phrase unintelligible. "I'm nervous, but I'm not really . . ." Because of the crying, her speech is unclear. "Because I know that this time, right now, I'm coming home! I see the black before my eyes, but I'm not afraid of that either. Because I remember reading—I can't even see the page—I remember reading that very soon I'll be home, and my baby will be with me. And nobody can . . . nobody can ever hurt me again!"

"That's the idea. I was thinking that it's as if it were a prayer to the one saint you believe in. Are you a good Catholic?"

"I'm lapsed, but there was a time when I prayed to the saints."

"Work on that."

May 21

"I was sick, but more than that I was mad at the police and at the crooked game of life—"

"What's that mean?"

"That they cheated and lied, that they're hypocrites, and I'm going to expose them," Rachael says. "They're covering up."

"For whom?"

"For the rich guy I shot and killed."

"What was he doing in your room?"

"I was a prostitute."

"Go on."

"So I wrote to the chief of police in Peoria, 'I'm here in my girlhood home of Spoon River gradually wasting away. But come and take me. I killed the son of the merchant prince in Madam Lew's. The newspapers that said he killed himself in his home while cleaning a hunting gun lied like the devil to hush up the scandal for the bribe of advertising."

"For what?"

"The newspapers were bribed. His father owns the town."

"Go on."

"I shot him at Madam Lew's because he knocked me down when I said that in spite of all the money he had, I was going to see my lover that night. I insulted him, so he knocked me down and I shot him."

"And who was your lover?"

The question has not occurred to Rachel, and she is at a loss for words.

"It doesn't say in the text. You've got to make it up out of your imagination," Meisner says. "Look here. The questions I'm asking you are not technical questions as such; they're *imaginative* questions. This is part of a process called 'making the part your own.' Suppose that you had told this rich man's son, 'I'm not going to sleep with you tonight. I'm going to sleep with Tony, who drives your father's coal truck. *He's* my real lover, not you!' And when you taunted him with this, he got so furious that he dropped the gun. You picked it up and shot him. But the police and newspapers are so corrupt that they'd never report such a scandal. Do you remember what they did when Rockefeller died?"

"I was thinking about that the whole time," Bette says.

"The hypocrisy, the deceit, the corruption of the newspapers sickened you, right? Finally, since you're dying anyhow, you say, 'Here's the *truth,* you bastards!' This strikes me as someone taking revenge with such relish—"

"Very pleased with herself," Rachael says.

"Very! 'Everybody knows you're a crook and nobody wants to tell you but me. Now go do something about it!' You see? This is 'making the part your own.' The process of filling a cold text with your life is what this process is in a nutshell."

"Sandy," Bette says. "I loved what you just did with Rachael. Those are the questions that I have to learn how to ask."

"That's the way you work on a part. Work on these speeches has everything to do with interpretation. My provocative remark is that by doing the *Spoon Rivers* you all should have learned something very substantial and clarified about how you approach a character. Suppose an actor who was about to play Othello said to the director, 'Explain this jealousy thing to me.' What does that imply?"

"I'd think that he should never play the part," Bette says.

"No doubt about that. How does one know that *Othello* is about great love and great jealousy?"

"You read the text and it hits you," Beth says. "It hits something in you."

"It hits you. I like that phrase. It hits you. There are some people in this class who are very concerned with the problem of character. But what is character? How do you answer that question?"

"Why are you looking at me?" John asks.

"Your questions have concerned me because to me they mean that you have an inorganic preoccupation with character. What does that mean? 'Inorganic preoccupation with character'?"

"It's mental," Bette says.

"Where do you get it from?"

"Your brain. From outside."

"Where should you get it from?"

"Your guts."

"What you do and how you feel about the script which makes you do what you do determines the character. I would think that the *Spoon River* pieces have contributed hugely to your knowledge of how you find the character in you. Let's talk about character. Let's see what this means to you. I once asked you out of the sheer devilment that's a part of me, 'How many of you are not learning anything?' Do you remember? Do you remember Vincent, who said he wasn't?"

"I'll never forget it," Bette says.

"And what did I do? I threw him out. So you saw two sides of my character. My mischievousness and my conceit. Character, you can say, is determined by what you do."

"And *how* you do it, right?" Rose Marie asks.

"That depends on you and your imagination. The emotion comes with how you're doing what you're doing. If you go from moment to moment, and each moment has a meaning for you, the emotion keeps flowing. I would sum it up by saying that the interpretation is best found in what really moves you. Not complicated, not necessarily original. *You.* It's you. And I think that much has been learned from this work on the *Spoon Rivers,* don't you?"

May 24

"What's the matter?" Meisner asks Ray.

"I felt on the spot, so I was a little uncomfortable, though I forgot about you."

"Oh, to hell with me. Listen, you played the villain in *The Octoroon.* Do you know what that is?"

"I don't know what *The Octoroon* is. I assumed when I did the poem that it was some pageant that happened around Halloween."

"No, it's a famous play with a wonderful villain. Make them laugh by the way you do that line."

" 'I played the coronet and I painted pictures and I modeled clay—' " Ray's voice has risen an octave and then plunges into a full bass register for the end of the line: " 'And I played the villain in *The Octoroon.*' "

"Twirl your moustache," Meisner says.

Ray twirls an enormous imaginary moustache and the class laughs.

"What does your family think of you?"

"They think I'm a genius."

"Act out that you're a genius," Meisner says, and he points to his brain with the index finger of each of his hands. The class laughs again.

"Oh," Ray says timidly, "that kind of thing." Without any gesture he continues, "They thought I was a genius."

"No," Meisner says. "I mean—" and he makes a broad, slightly wacky gesture of pointing to his cranium with both index fingers.

Ray repeats the gesture and says, " 'My parents thought I was going to be as great as Edison, or greater.' " He laughs nervously and says, "I don't know what to do. I'm stuck."

"That's okay. Jump to the end of the speech. Now you've thought it through. What was the truth about yourself?"

" 'The truth was this—' "

"Jump up!" Meisner exclaims, and Ray does so before completing the line: " 'I didn't have the brains.' " The class laughs.

"You see, what I'm telling you is to find, like *The Octoroon*, elements you can act out almost in pantomime which tell us what that's all about. For example, 'I studied and I studied and I studied!' " And with each repetition Meisner bangs his fist on his head.

"I see," Ray says. " *'Thinking, thinking, thinking!'* " he says, attempting to duplicate the gesture Meisner has given him.

"Yes," Meisner says, "but with a sense of the ridiculous. 'I was thinking!' " His index finger grinds like a drill bit into his brain. "Do you follow?"

"I do," Ray says, "but I would have been afraid to do that before seeing you. You know what I mean?"

"I *guess* I know what you mean. You think you'd be indicating."

"Exactly."

"I would tell you if you were. This particular *Spoon River* lends itself to dramatizing all the nonsense. 'Do you know what the truth of the matter is?' " Meisner asks, pointing to his head and crossing his eyes. The class laughs. "You were afraid to do that."

"Yep, I was. What's interesting is that it's the kind of acting I used to do most easily," Ray says, laughing, "before this class. Not with the emotion behind it, but that sort of broad cliché. I would hit those clichés real hard."

"Well, there's nothing wrong with a cliché if it belongs. What's that mean?"

"It means that if the style lends itself, and the emotion is real behind what you're doing, a cliché can enhance the piece instead of make it worse."

"Right," Meisner says. "Say 'a can of peas' to me."

" 'A can of peas,' " Ray says.

Meisner reacts broadly, yet believably, as if in saying the *p* in "peas" Ray has spit in his eye. "Why can't you do that?"

"Oh, I can. Honest, I can," Ray says.

Meisner pulls the right side of his suit jacket open, peers into the inside pocket and whispers, "Did you hear what he said?" The class laughs and Bette applauds. *"Farce comedy!* Please don't make all these pieces momentous. Did you ever hear Beethoven's *Für Elise?* I can't sing. It goes ta, ra, ta, ra, ta, ta, ra, ta, ra, ta. It's a simple, kind of naïve piece of music, but it's by *Beethoven,* so it better be *deep!* Wrong! Don't try to work *too* significantly."

Ray nods.

"Ask me how old my mother was when she died."

"How old was your mother when she died?" Ray asks.

"She was eighty-five!" Meisner exclaims in such a way that the meaning is, Isn't it wonderful she lived to such a ripe old age! "Ask me again."

"How old was your mother when she died?"

Meisner seems about to burst into tears, and can hardly answer the question. "She was," he says, "eighty . . . five." The class laughs. "Now, *that's* a cliché: mother—dying—you've *got* to cry. Do you know," Meisner asks with great solemnity, "I happened to hear that there are teachers of acting who can't teach unless they feel deeply. Ask me what I had for breakfast this morning."

"Sandy, what did you have for breakfast this morning?"

The class begins to titter because Meisner seems so full of emotion that he can hardly speak. Finally he forces himself to say, "Corn . . . flakes." The class laughs. "You follow? It's got to be *deep,* or otherwise how can I be a good teacher? But I'm here to say, 'Be yourself! Accept whatever comes out spontaneously!' If you're treating it too casually or too deeply, I'll be the first to tell you!"

"Sandy," Scott Roberts says, "in the early 1940s—after the Group Theatre folded—you directed three plays on Broadway. Were you dissatisfied with being an actor and did you think, 'Maybe I'll direct as well as teach?' "

"I think I went any way the wind blew me," Meisner says.

He takes a sip of his drink. They are sitting in the living room of Meisner's apartment. The play Scott has directed for the Circle Repertory Company is about to open, and he has come by to take Meisner to a preview.

"I wasn't a very good director," Meisner says. "The reason is that I don't handle adults very well. I don't have confidence. Something in my psyche makes me restricted and inhibited by adults, and so I was timid about my authority. This is in contrast to the Playhouse, where I did really good productions and worked with freedom. As I thought about it later, I realized that I had retained what I did as a child, when I directed pageants with my cousins. I could deal with young people, but I couldn't deal authoritatively with established adults. I have always thought this was one of the reasons that I didn't become a good director, because otherwise I have all the elements for it. With the students at the Playhouse I was in the same relationship as I was with my kid cousins when I was thirteen."

"In the class," Scott says, "is that the problem with Lila?"

"Yes, but I treat her like a young child," Meisner says.

"Yes, you do."

"See? I don't treat her like somebody with a reputation. I know what her problems are as an actor, and I go after them. But all those people have a certain relationship to me, which is that of teacher/student. Within that, where I am and have to be the authority, I function. I don't know what it would be like now. Now I don't care one way or another."

"About being a director?" Scott asks.

"Yeah. Or acting, for that matter. It's the theater that interests me, not acting. I don't like actors very much, though I do like to act. It's enjoyable—sometimes. But I don't like what it brings to the surface in my personality: the self-centeredness, the childish vanity, the infantilism. That's what an actor has to have."

Scott looks at his watch.

"You're right," Meisner says and stands up stiffly. "Let's go take a look at your play."

11 Some Thoughts on Actors and on Acting*

STUDENT: Sandy, you wanted one of us to ask
you about punctuation in acting.
MEISNER: Punctuation is emotional, not grammatical.
If you say, "To be [*pause*] or not to be [*pause*]
that [*! pause*] is the question," there are three commas,
three *emotional* commas, and an exclamation
point in those lines, but they're not on the paper.

"A girl is seduced when she is eight, so everybody thinks she is
a whore and has nothing to do with her. Then a newcomer
arrives in town; he marries her and then finds out about her past
and abandons her. After that she just dies from not wanting to
live anymore. That's sad, don't you agree?

"Now there are many ways of expressing your sadness. You
don't have to cry. But you cannot be almost empty emotionally,

*The observations presented in this chapter were made during the thirteen
months the class was in session. They are grouped by topic and not, as in
the rest of this book, by date.

because your history is too strong. Christ on the cross must have been in unimaginable agony, but He didn't cry. He held back. But in order to hold back, you have to have something to *hold*."

"Fanny Brice, an incredible comic, told me that whenever she went on the stage she was like this—" Meisner's hands tremble violently. "And this was at the end of her career when her name was like that—" He holds his hands one above the other, about two feet apart. "And the title was like this—" His hands are six inches apart. "So you're going to be nervous! *Be* nervous! Did you ever hear that line—every actor knows it—'I thought I'd die until I got my first laugh!' You follow? The first laugh means 'We love you.'"

"That was very good."

"I lost the words."

"That's nothing. Let me tell you something, all of you. Sarah, you were really acting. The moments were coming spontaneously, and they had a meaning for you. God knows they've tried, but psychoanalysts really don't know where talent comes from. But one of the possibilities is that what gives talent life, what makes it occur, comes in part out of people's lack of confidence, out of their feeling that they're not loved. Now, what made me think of that? Well, any of the negative experiences that life has to offer have impacts of varying degrees. One of them is the feeling you're going to be told that you're wrong, that you're bad and unlovable when you're this high—" Meisner's hand indicates the height of a small child. "But this feeling that you're being mistreated, that you're no good, which is a holdover from way back when you were almost an infant, can be a potent force in your acting. But the confidence that permits you to say 'I *am* somebody' takes a long time to become secure in you. The problem arises when that feeling of worthlessness is juxtaposed with something that is part and parcel of this business—namely, that you can't learn to act unless you're criticized. If you tie that criticism to your childhood insecurities, you have a terrible time. Instead, you must take criticism objectively, pertaining only to the work being done. Imagine if you said to a plumber, 'I don't think you plunged that toilet well,' and he burst into tears! It's only in the creative arts that self-confidence is such a problem. Now, if Sarah did that speech many times, and if each time people said, 'You were lovely,'—her self-confidence would bloom! A good notice is like a kiss on your cheek."

"There's one thing that's clearly absent from this reading, Bette. You had it at the beginning and then you gave it up. What was it, do you know?"

"Contact?"

"A point of view. Look, I'll show you something. Beth, tell me something about the life of your character."

"My life?" Beth, Bette's partner, says quietly. "It doesn't seem too bright. My life seems kind of hopeless."

"Uh-huh!" Meisner says with a kind of ravenous enjoyment.

"It looks bleak," Beth continues.

"Ah," Meisner says with malicious pleasure.

"You think that's funny?" Beth asks in annoyance.

"No," Meisner says, smiling gleefully.

"You act like you seem to enjoy it!"

"I don't mean to," Meisner says in a conciliatory voice and then continues. "You see, Bette, there was a consistent point of view in my reaction to Beth. It's like this." He pauses. " 'My grandmother died a week ago.' 'Oh,' " he says, smiling in delight, " 'you've got to be kidding!' 'Yeah, she was cremated.' 'Ahooh!' " Meisner says with exaggerated false sympathy, and the class laughs. "It doesn't have to be logical. 'My grandmother was cremated two weeks ago.' " He claps his hands together in exuberant joy and says, " 'What a pity!' "

Again the class laughs.

"Do you understand, Bette? It's the opposite of what it should be. It's *opposite*. You follow?"

"Sort of. I think so," she says hesitantly.

"Ray, do you understand what I said to her?"

Ray nods but doesn't speak.

"Look, tell me something. Tell me something tragic."

"My sister has leukemia," Ray says.

"That's fatal!" Meisner says, positively savoring the tragedy. The class laughs.

"*That's* the way you should do this part. What I did with Ray is what I think you should do."

"Okay."

"What's your response when I tell you that my sister has leukemia? What do you do?"

"I laugh," Bette says.

"Let me hear that."

With a contented smile Bette chuckles quietly and says through lightly clenched teeth, "That's fatal," and the class laughs again. "Okay, I've got it," she continues. "Oh, God, I've got it!"

"The first thing you have to do when you read a text is to find yourself—*really* find yourself. First you find yourself, then you find a way of doing the part which strikes you as being in character. Then, based on that reality, you have the nucleus of the role. Otherwise every shmuck from Erasmus Hall High School is an actor because everyone there knows how to read. Let's say the script has the line 'Oh, I forgot.' Along comes the star of the Erasmus Hall High School Dramatic Club, and what you get is, 'Oh, I forgot.' It is a straightforward but uninteresting reading of the words. But then you get the dope who never went to school, and he says, 'Oh!' " Meisner's fists go to his temples in a moment of painful recollection. A long pause follows during which he realizes that it's too late now and he must make the best of it. Finally, almost with a shrug of his shoulders, he says casually, " 'I forgot.' Which one is the actor?"

"The dope," Bette says.

"Anybody can *read*. But acting is *living* under imaginary circumstances. A script—I may have said this before—a script is like a libretto. You know what a libretto is, don't you?"

"It's the text to which the composer adds music in an opera," Ray says.

"Right. The composer reads on the paper, 'How cold your hand is!' and the musician in him translates that into a glorious melody. An actor is like a composer. What you read in the book is only the merest indication of what you have to do when you really act the part."

"What a profession! I've been teaching acting for forty-seven years. I started when I was seven, and now I'm fifty-four." The class laughs. "What's so funny?"

"When did you start teaching?" Joseph asks. "In 1935?"

"Yeah, about then."

"You were still working with the Group Theatre, right?"

"Until 1940, the year it ended."

"Where did you start teaching—here, the Neighborhood Playhouse?"

"Professionally, here. I did my apprenticeship at various places."

"How did you start teaching here?"

"Through my friend Clifford Odets."

"Really?"

"He had a girlfriend who was a student here, and they were looking for somebody to come in and direct their final play. She had suggested him, but *Awake and Sing!* had just opened and he was famous—the cover-of-*Time* kind of famous. So he said to me —he was my best friend—'You go.'"

"Was Martha Graham teaching here then?"

"Yes. She taught the movement classes for years."

"Do you still play the piano?"

"I quit. On Bequia I play the church organ."

"This is very indiscreet of me, so promise that you'll only tell it to thirty people. A woman by the name of Mrs. Cartier—they have a little jewelry shop on Fifth Avenue—is after me—this is true—to meet with a group of her friends. They want to know more about acting, so that when they pay forty dollars a ticket for a show, they'll know why they're being cheated. This kept me up almost the whole night. They want a course."

"Are you serious?" Joseph asks.

"There's a play in there somewhere," Bette says.

"Such an old-fashioned play. She called last night."

"Maybe they'll learn something," Joseph says.

"Who gives a shit?"

"They probably don't know what good acting is," Joseph says.

"Most people don't. Can you imagine Mrs. Cartier and Mrs. Guggenheim doing the word repetition?"

" 'I love your tiara.' 'You love my tiara?' " Ralph says and the class laughs.

"Once in California, I gave a speech at a big theater downtown, and I talked about the things that I have always believed in. But at the end somebody said, 'What can we do? This is Hollywood.' And I answered, 'I have never let myself forget what the theater can be, and I'll stick to my guns.' What else can I do? I was in the Group Theatre. That was something. I couldn't speak to Mrs. Cartier the way I talk to you. She's a nice woman. She's got a thirty-seven-carat diamond ring, but she's a nice woman. Believe me, I've got nothing against that diamond."

"Sandy," Ray says, "are there ever any circumstances in a play when you can legitimately decide that your character is trying to hide his real feelings?"

"You wouldn't hide them. You wouldn't try. You'd have them, but you wouldn't let them out. You follow?"

"No. Don't Chekhov's people always hide what they're feeling? I mean, they feel it, but they try to hide it."

"Ah, Chekhov! That's a big question. *The Three Sisters** opens with Masha, the middle sister, bored to death. Her speech beginning, 'Father died a year ago today,' is full of melancholy, but she is not sitting *shivah*. She talks about the past with a certain mood.

---

*The events described in the following are out of sequence; however, their emotional importance is accurately conveyed.

Then Masha's husband, a teacher who's a big bore, comes in. He comes to get her but she hates him and sends him away, saying she'll come home in a minute. Then Vershinin comes in and fascinates the whole family with his personality. After a long time, Masha—who hasn't said a word, not *one* word—suddenly announces, 'I think I'll stay to lunch!' Now, why does she do that?"

"You tell me."

"She's fallen madly in love with Vershinin. But she doesn't say a word to him and he hardly knows she's in the room."

"So does the actress playing Masha try to hide from the others the fact that she's falling in love with him?"

"His being there changes her. He says something which inspires her, or she thinks he's sexy. Who knows? The point is, it's typical Chekhov, and the emotion is entirely internal. She doesn't *do* anything, does she?"

"Not until she says, 'I think I'll stay to lunch.' "

"Until then. But she started out the act by complaining, 'I've got to go home. God help me!' That radical change in her is entirely internal. In the first line of *The Seagull*, another teacher, Medvedenko, says to another Masha, 'Why do you always wear black?' And she says, 'I'm in mourning for my life.' Can you imagine how many choices the actress has to motivate that line? Maybe she decides that Masha is in love with her father, maybe she has *never* been in love. The actress has to choose *something*, and then hide it behind a smile as if it were a joke."

"So there *are* certain cases where you feel something inside and yet hide it."

"No, you've got to give some indication that you think of it as a joke in order to *mask* the truth, which is that you wear black because you are literally in mourning for your life. Do you understand the difference? Chekhov writes from such a deep source! At the end of *The Cherry Orchard*, Madame Ranyevskaia says to the man who's chopping down the cherry trees, 'So long!' It's rather cheery, but it happens to be the end of an era! Chekhov is terrible!"

"Why?" Ray asks.

"Because he's so inscrutable."

"What writers aren't terrible?"

"Chekhov," Meisner says. "But look how difficult he is. A line says, 'Ivan, bring me a pound of tomatoes from the market,' and the stage direction reads, 'She bursts into tears.'" The class laughs. "Yes, he's wonderful, but there's no question but that he's very difficult!"

"I have one more question, but it has nothing to do with class," John says. "I want to know about when you were in the Group Theatre and Stella Adler came back from Paris and said, 'Listen, what's going on here with Lee Strasberg isn't what Stanislavsky really meant at all,'" John says. "Did you and the other actors suspect that your work process wasn't right even before Stella talked to Stanislavsky?"

"It wasn't prevalent. They may have had suspicions, but that's all. Among other things, she brought back 'given circumstances' —how you get to the essence of 'given circumstances.' You know, Stella and Strasberg were enemies even before we started the Group. She said, 'He's a fake' before we ever began."

"Then how do you explain the quality of acting of some of his students?" Ray asks. "You say you can show somebody the best way to bring out the best acting that he or she can do. But underneath it all is *talent*, and you don't know what that is. You know that it has something to do with imagination, but you don't know what—nobody does. So it seems to me that if what Strasberg did was, in effect, to introvert actors who were already introverted, to make them have private experiences on stage that aren't expressed, then the people that came out of his classes and his technique and acted beautifully must have done so in *spite* of the training."

"That's right. Like who?"

"Pacino."

"Al Pacino has been that way for twenty-five years!"

"I think so too—as an actor, as a talent and as an individual. But isn't that always true?" Ray asks.

"What do you mean?"

"What I mean is that if you can't act, you can't act, right?"

"Right."

"But if you can act very well, if you're one of those people who let beautiful acting come out of them because that's the way they're made, then you can do it under any circumstances."

"Yes, and you know what? Strasberg would see that talent and invite someone to join the Studio, all those famous, talented people, and then say later, 'He was my student!'"

"Did he do that with Duvall?" Joseph asks.

"Duvall studied with me."

"I know he studied with you first, but he also went to the Studio afterwards."

"To work on himself, not to learn to act! It's quite different."

"What do you mean, 'to work on himself'?"

"It was a place where there were other actors. That was the merit of the Actors Studio."

"To get back to what I asked," John says, "when Stella came back from Paris, did the two of you have a series of meetings—just the two of you—where she said, 'Sandy, this is *really* what it's about'?"

"Clurman. Harold Clurman was there too."

"And the three of you started working out this system we're learning now?"

"More or less, yes, though Stella doesn't teach the way I do."

"Not at all!" Rose Marie says.

"Did you develop the repetition exercise then?" Ralph asks.

"No, much later. I invented it with people in my classes."

"How did you know that was the way to go?" Joseph asks.

"Instinct."

"You knew that if the partners repeated lines back and forth, the very repetition would give rise to something new—that it would change organically?"

"Yes, I more or less knew that. I found out by working here at school and in my private classes that it produced the kind of life that had nothing to do with introverting you. Also the problem of preparation; I took great exception to Strasberg on preparation."

"You developed the repetition after the Group Theatre," John says.

"Yes, but it wasn't until the late 1950s or early 1960s that it took the form it has now."

"Was there anything similar that you used to do in the Group?"

"No."

"It was more in line with the method that Strasberg taught?" Rose Marie asks.

"More or less, yes."

Ralph holds up his hand. "Did Harold Clurman have any technique or theories about acting?"

"He had a general, sensitive knowledge of acting."

"Was he primarily a director?"

"Yes, a historian, too. His books are very good."

"Yes, they are," Rose Marie says. "Clurman was a director, but you were an actor, and you understood what it meant to lead that life. And from what I hear, you were a very good actor. Apparently Strasberg wasn't very successful as an actor. Is that true?"

"He was a terrible actor."

"So maybe that says something."

"He was a librarian; that's what he was. I don't want to go into it, but in the back of the Neighborhood Playhouse brochure which we send to prospective students there's a list of the graduates. If you want to amuse yourself in a sickening kind of way, go through that list and see how many people he invited to the Studio and then said, 'He was my student.' It's amazing."

"How many of the men in this class have wanted to be teachers?"

Ray holds up his hand.

"You have?"

"When I went to college I thought I'd be a teacher."

"An acting teacher?"

"I've thought of being an acting teacher, but—"

"Just before you all came in, I saw a Playhouse class.* It really slayed me how awful it was. Terrible."

"The students themselves were bad," Joseph asks, "or the work was bad?"

"The work was very bad."

"So how many new teachers are you looking for?" Bette asks.

"Two or three, but where are they?"

"And you're only hiring men?" Rose Marie says.

"Not necessarily."

"But aren't all the Playhouse teachers, those who teach the younger students under your direction, former students of yours?" Joseph asks.

"They were all trained by me."

"I'm not so sure it's the teachers' fault anymore," Rose Marie says. "I think it has to do with the students today. I think that when a lot of young people read that Robert Duvall and Diane Keaton studied here and that you were their teacher, they decide they want to be like them, but they don't understand the work that goes into it."

"They worked like dogs, those people."

"I believe it. I don't believe they were just natural talents. I think they worked very, very hard."

"With natural talent."

"With natural talent," Rose Marie agrees.

"How do you teach somebody," John asks, "to be a good acting teacher? It seems to require—"

"You don't!"

---

*The Neighborhood Playhouse School of the Theatre, 340 East 54th Street, New York, offers a two-year training program for the theater to a maximum of 110 students, most of them in their early twenties. It has a faculty of fourteen, of whom four teach acting under Sanford Meisner's supervision. Other courses include speech and vocal production, singing, stage movement, dance, fencing, makeup and a course in acting period plays. In addition to his work with these students, Sanford Meisner has traditionally taught a class, like the one described in this book, for older professionals.

"That's what I mean," John says. "I agree, because it seems to be the most sensitive kind of teaching there could ever be."

"I think," Ray says, "that half the people teaching don't know what good acting is. What drives me forward in the class is my belief that you know what you're looking at, and that it means a great deal to me if you say I'm going in the right or the wrong direction. That's where the drive comes from; I believe you know what you're talking about. I believe it because of two things: your reputation, and the way you discuss what you see in class. You *know* what you're talking about."

"I'll tell you something," says Meisner, "and I'm really speaking objectively—there are practically no acting teachers who *see.*"

"There are many supposed techniques around, but nobody with a really clear vision of what to do," Ralph says. "At least that's my experience. I'm a person who needs some kind of clarity in being taught—you know, step-by-step. I've worked with a lot of people who teach scenes, who know what to do in any number of given scenes, but who have no clarity, no technique, no way to help the student go step-by-step. They're confusing!"

"There are no teachers of acting technique around. They're fakers! I say this impersonally. I've seen their work. I don't know how we got on this subject, but I once saw a picture of a well-known French painter who was painting with his back to the photographer. On each hand he had tied brushes because he was so old and paralyzed with God knows what. But he couldn't stop painting. I'm the same way. I can't stop teaching. Good or bad, I can't stop. I'm old enough to stop. I can't see, I can't talk, I can hardly walk."

"Why did you begin teaching?" Anna asks.

"Why does any artist begin doing what he's made for? Even he doesn't know. He's just following a need within himself."

"And the Playhouse?" Ray asks. "What should happen to it?"

"After I leave?"

"Yes."

"Objectively? Impersonally? I hope they close it down. It will have done its work."

. . .

"Sandy," says Scott Roberts, "I should change your battery."

"Well, change it."

Scott sits beside the gray desk, removes a new nine-volt battery from its package and opens the case of a small transmitter resting on the desk top, which sends Meisner's voice to the amplifier and the loudspeaker across the room.

"I wish I could kill myself."

"Really?" Anna asks. "Are you serious?"

"I don't have the nerve; that's why I can say it."

"Why do you wish you had the nerve?"

"When he fixes this so I'm sure you can hear my answer, I'll tell you."

Scott snaps the new battery into the transmitter, closes it and returns to his seat beneath the controls of the amplifier across the room.

"Because life stinks."

"You're right," Anna says, "it does."

"I've had enough of it."

"That's a given, though," Ray says. "What does that have to do with anything? You can't help that."

"It's a full moon, Sandy," Beth says. "You'll feel better next week."

"A full moon always affects you emotionally," Bette says.

"Next week you'll want to live and dance," Beth says.

"In a play that I did—Scott saw it, a Sam Behrman play—what was the name of it?"

"*The Cold Wind and the Warm*," Scott says.

"*The Cold Wind and the Warm*. I played the part of a fat, rich, insensitive businessman—a horrible character. In one scene I say to a young girl—Suzanne Pleshette—'Will you marry me?' Well, she almost falls off her chair in amusement. To a *sensitive* person her amusement would mean, 'Are you kidding? *Me* marry *you?*' But to a big lump like the character I was playing it meant—" He smiles in delight and clasps his hands before him as if savoring a victory. The class laughs. "I took the meaning of her laugh from my character, which means that I know something about the nature of an insensitive lunkhead. It's all in the instinct."

"But in the moment, too, right?" Ray asks.

"It comes *out* of the moment. Character reveals itself by *how* you do *what* you do. I say, 'Will you marry me?' and she laughs derisively. I'm insensitive. I think she's accepting me."

"There are many people who would play that as if they realized what she meant," Rose Marie says, "but you played it as if you didn't even see it."

"No, I *saw* it, but I misinterpreted it because I was insensitive."

"It was a character choice," Rose Marie says.

"But you made that choice instinctively, not intellectually," Ray says.

"When I was working on the part I could *decide* how to do it."

"So," Ray says, "your character's insensitive, and when the girl laughs, you decide that that she's accepting you, because you missed her meaning. But isn't there a danger that if you make too many of those choices by going through the script and picking them out of here"—he points to his head—"the performance is bound to be artificial?"

"Yes."

"So even though there's a balance between making those kinds of choices emotionally and making them as a result of reading the script with your head, even the ones you decide on intellectually are not something that you said to yourself, 'Oh, *this* would be interesting to do.' If so, in the long run it would be better for some other actor to do the part."

"Say that again."

"You didn't make a choice based on ideas that would have worked better if somebody else had the part," Ray says.

"Right."

"That is what I want to learn," Bette says. "I want to find out where my limitations are—which parts I should be going for or avoiding. I have a *feeling* for all of it, so how do I know if I can't do it?"

"Do you have a feeling for *Peter Pan?*"

"Yeah."

"Well, you're not right for it."

"Okay," Bette says, "that's one down. That's what I want to know."

"Life, life, life, life."

"In time I'll find out?"

"The last play the Group Theatre put into rehearsal was *The Three Sisters* by Chekhov. Luckily, we never performed it. They gave me the part of Baron Toozenbach. I said, 'I won't play it. A minor German nobleman in prerevolutionary Russia?' It didn't mean a thing to me—not a thing. Do you understand?"

"I used to think," Rose Marie says, "that if I didn't like a part and refused to do it, it was because I wasn't any good as an actress. If I were *really* good, I'd be Meryl Streep, who can do anything."

"No, she can't."

"You're right," Rose Marie says.

"I always get cast as the bright, happy-go-lucky girl next door," Bette says. "I never get the roles I'd really love to do."

"Like what?"

"The killer parts."

"That's our theater."

"Now, *that's* encouraging," Bette says, turning to the class. "He didn't say I couldn't do those parts, but that *they* didn't think I could do them, or that *they* didn't want to see me do them. They don't want people to act. They want people to be what they *appear* to be. If you look a certain way, that's what they want or don't want. They don't think of anything else."

"All casting is like that. We had a student here—a black boy, very talented. He graduated, read for a part and got it. They said, 'Come back tomorrow to sign your contract.' He went back—this is God's honest truth—and the lady who was producing it said, 'Oh, by the way, how old are you?' He said, 'Twenty-three.' And she said, 'The character is twenty-one.'"

"Ah!" gasps the entire class.

"That's happened to me," Bette says.

"It's part of the business."

"Hollywood is terrible," Anna says.

"It's just as bad here," Meisner says.

"There they want sixteen-year-olds for everything."

"Or seventy-five-year-olds."

"Yeah, they're getting into that," Anna says.

"Have you noticed that on television all the heroines are blond and all the heroes have curly black hair?"

"A blond man isn't taken seriously," Rose Marie says.

"Tell that to Robert Redford," Ray says.

"She's right," Meisner says, "not for another three years."

The class laughs.

"Blond women do okay, though," Bette says.

"For three years," Meisner says. "Then they're going to switch."

"In three years," Bette says, stroking her braided black hair, "my ship will come in."

"Once I took my courage in both hands and told a little parable about the two barrels to a famous psychoanalyst, and instead of dropping on the floor with amusement, he said he saw some truth in it. The story goes like this:

"All of us have two barrels inside us. The first barrel is the one that contains all of the juices which are exuded by our troubles. That's the neurotic barrel. But right next to it stands the second barrel, and by a process of seepage like osmosis, some of the troubles in the first barrel get into the second, and by a miracle that nobody fully understands, those juices have been transformed into the ability to paint, to compose, to write, to play music and the ability to act. So essentially our talent is made up out of our transformed troubles."

Meisner pauses for a moment.

"I'd always thought that two of the luckiest, happiest people I could imagine were Shakespeare and Beethoven, but the doctor to whom I told this parable said, 'No, no. Shakespeare had plenty of trouble—that is, neurosis—and so did Beethoven,' and he pointed out some of their more obvious troubles. This proved to me that the osmosis between the barrels doesn't work completely. There is always some juice in the trouble barrel, no matter how full the talent barrel is. The trouble cannot transpose itself into talent without leaving some residue behind, even in the most talented of human beings."

"The moment in the play in which Duse performed in London in 1895, when she sees her lover of thirty years ago, the man who is the father of her child, and tries to be quite pleasant, but then suddenly finds herself blushing, is pure genius. You can't fake a blush; you can't run into the dressing room for a pot of rouge. It also cannot be prepared for. It cannot be premeditated. George Bernard Shaw, in the famous review he wrote about her performance, said he was curious, in a professional way, whether it happened all the time. I think that it happened when it happened. That's all. That blush can't be prepared for, that's my point; what's more, if the script says, in so many words, 'She begins to blush,' *cross it out.*"

"Why?" Ray asks.

"You cross things like that out because they are anti-intuitive. Those little words in parentheses underneath the character's name in the script, like 'softly,' 'angrily,' 'entreatingly,' or 'with effort,' are aids for *readers* of plays, not for *actors* of them. Cross them out immediately."

"Tell us why you cross them out," Ray says.

"Because they dictate a kind of life which can only be there spontaneously."

"That's good to remember," Bette says.

"Did you ever read any of the late plays by Eugene O'Neill? They have so many stage directions that, if you're cast in one, the first thing you have to do is buy a pencil and cross them all out, because nobody, not even the playwright, can determine how a life is going to live itself out sensitively, instinctively, on the stage. But I add this caveat: the life of the actor *must not* annihilate the deeper implications of the play which the playwright has written."

Ray Stanton enters Meisner's office and says, "Scott told me you wanted to see me."

"Yes. Come in and sit down. Perhaps you've heard that Scott has successfully directed a play downtown."

"Yes," Ray says, "at Circle Rep. It got great reviews."

"So great," Meisner says, "that he has decided not to assist me for much longer. He thought you might like to have the job. Yes?"

"Good God," Ray says, "I'm stunned, but I would. Thank you."

"Scott reminded me that you once said in class that you aspired to become a teacher. Is that true?"

"Yes."

"Good. We'll see. Give Scott a call. He'll tell you when he's leaving and what the job is all about."

September 27

Spring Awakening by
Frank Wedekind*
act 3, scene 5

A bedroom. Doctor, Wendla and Mrs. Bergmann.

*Tom Osborn, trans. (London: Calder and Boyars, 1969). First published in
Zurich in 1891.

194

Exeunt Doctor with Mrs. Bergmann

WENDLA: The leaves are turning yellow on the plane trees.
Sometimes I feel so happy—full of joy and sunlight.
There's a warm glow round my heart. I want to
walk in the sun in the evening, through the fields
and under the trees, and sit on the river bank and
dream ... And then my pain comes back and I think
I'm going to die tomorrow. I go hot and cold and it's
all dark in front of my eyes, and a monster comes
floating into the room ... Whenever I wake I see
mother crying. That hurts, Mother, why do you cry?

MRS. B: *(Returning)* He thinks the sickness will soon pass and
then it's perfectly all right for you to get up. I think
it would be better for you to get up soon too.

WENDLA: What else did he say out there, Mamma?

MRS. B: He said nothing—he told me about the young Bar-
oness who also used to faint. That is a common
symptom of anaemia.

WENDLA: Did he say I had anaemia?

MRS. B: He wants you to drink milk and eat plenty of meat
and green vegetables as soon as your appetite returns.

WENDLA: Oh Mamma, I don't believe I've got anaemia.

MRS. B: You have got anaemia, Wendla. You must rest now.
You have got anaemia.

WENDLA: No Mamma—I know that's not true. I can feel it's
not true. I haven't got anaemia. I think I've got
dropsy.

MRS. B: You've got anaemia—that's what he told me, that
you've got anaemia. Try to rest now, Wendla, it'll
get better.

WENDLA: It won't get better. I've got dropsy. I think I'm going
to die, Mamma. I'm going to die.

MRS B: You won't die, my daughter—you won't die ... Oh
merciful God ... You won't die.

WENDLA: But you're crying, Mamma, then why are you crying?

MRS B: You won't die—Oh Wendla. It's not dropsy. You've
          got a baby ... You've got a baby ... How could you ...

WENDLA: How could I what?

MRS B: Don't go on denying it—I know. I just couldn't say
          it before. Wendla, my Wendla ...

WENDLA: But it's not possible, Mamma. I'm not married ...

MRS B: Oh God, give me strength. That's just it, you're not
          married. That's the terrible thing. Oh Wendla, how
          could you do it?

WENDLA: But what did I do? We lay together in the hay ...
          I've never loved anyone but you, Mamma, only
          you ...

MRS B: My dearest girl ...

WENDLA: Oh Mamma, why didn't you tell me it all ...

MRS B: It won't help now, it won't help now, weeping and
          reproaches. How could I tell you—a fourteen-year-
          old girl ... My mother told me no more than I did
          you—it would be like the sun not rising one day
          ... We must put our trust in God now, Wendla, in
          His mercy. Nothing has happened yet. If we can be
          courageous now, God will stay with us. Be brave,
          Wendla, be brave ... What's the matter?

WENDLA: Someone knocked at the door.

MRS B: I didn't hear anything.

WENDLA: Oh yes, I heard it very clearly. Who's there?

MRS B: No one. Mrs. Schmidt from Garden Street. Come
          up, Mrs. Schmidt. I was expecting you.

"If one is foolhardy enough to put a fragile canoe into a tempestuous river, what dictates the movement of the canoe?"

"The current of the river," Sarah says.

"The river. You know all this. The river is equivalent to the
emotions, right? Now, you have to know something about this
play. It was written as a passionate rebellion against the ignorance of children. Fourteen—she's a child, Sarah, you follow? To
be pregnant at fourteen is the equivalent of your mother finding
out that you're going to jail for life for heroin or murder. It's a
scene about fatality. Do you understand?"

"Yes," Sarah says.

"Now, the problem of the scene is in the preparation, the tempestuousness of the river, and in your understanding of the fact that this is a play which is a violent protest against keeping young people ignorant. It's *as if* you and your mother have just found out that your young husband of two days was killed in an accident. It's a scene of bereavement against the misfortune of life."

"You mean this terrible thing has happened to me and there's nothing I can do about it?"

"There's nothing you can do if the judge says, 'You're in for life!' Nothing you can do. The play takes place *as if* this room were your prison cell! Do I make myself clear?"

"Yes," Sarah says, "very clear."

"If I were you, I'd do an exercise which will release for you the emotional content of the scene. What I said before about a canoe in a typhoon is an example which explains the rhythm and the content of this scene. Any questions?"

"Are you talking about the emotional life of both these people?" Lila asks.

"You're both in the same canoe."

"Okay, they're both in this typhoon together. But is it important that the mother feels more responsibility and guilt for the daughter's ignorance?"

"You don't have to worry about that because it is revealed during the course of the play. You just have to get the canoe into that river."

"Get the canoe into the water?" Sarah asks.

"That's the preparation. You know, it's such a short scene that you might—"

"We'll do it on Monday," Lila says.

"Learn the lines. You'll *start* it on Monday, right?"

"Right," Lila says. "I mean, we can do it without the book on Monday."

"If you're in the canoe!"

October 4

"Stay where you are. Put your book away. Lila, sit down. Sarah, take that bedcover off you. Lila, you've just found out—I'm talking about imagination—that your daughter is going to prison. Anything! I don't care! See? I don't care what you think of. Cry! And don't stop crying until I tell you to. That's right. Begin to cry! Now, Sarah, you're an actress. If a doctor told you that you had lung cancer, would it upset you?" Sarah nods and Lila begins to cry. "That's right. Sarah, if somebody told you that your mother was about to die, would it upset you?"

"Yes."

"Okay, so start to cry."

After a pause Lila says, "The doctor said that you're—"

"No text! No text! Only emotion! If you want to use words, you can them based on what I said about cancer or prison." They both are crying quietly. There is a pause. "If you remember any of the lines—if you can say them to each other—you can have a conversation. *If* you remember. If you don't, that's okay too."

The crying increases. Lila is weeping openly; the tears stream from her large blue eyes, and the mascara on her lashes begins to run. The women begin the scene and the text floats on the surface of Lila's deeply felt emotion. Sarah, however, seems quiet but unmoved.

"Cry, Sarah!"

"Ah!" she shouts and hits the bed with her fists in frustration. In a moment she begins to sob. It is heartbreaking. "I don't have anaemia! I know it!" she cries.

After a moment, when her grief permits, Lila says in little panting breaths, "You have . . . anaemia . . . and it . . . will get better. . . ."

Sarah shouts, as if in great pain, "It won't get better! It won't get better!" Then, calming herself, she says, "Oh, Mother, I've got to die."

"You don't have to die," Lila sobs. "You don't have to die. Merciful heavens! You don't have to die!"

"Then," Sarah says accusingly, "why do you cry so much?"

In a tiny voice strangled with tears, Lila says, "You don't have to die. . . . You only have dropsy. You have . . . you have a baby! What have you done to me?"

"I haven't done anything to you!"

"Oh, you lied to me. I know everything. I just couldn't say anything before now. Oh, Wendla!" She is overcome by more tears.

Sarah is stunned and says in a whisper, "It's not possible. I'm not married."

"God, that's just it. You're not married. Oh, what have you done?"

"Mother, I've never loved anyone except you. You, Mother!"

The reading sounds forced and Meisner interrupts her. "That's out of the book!" Lila continues to sob. "I feel good about this because *that's* the scene—the scene without those screwy words. The scene is about two people going through a terrible experience, and I don't know any floozy—I'm not talking about either of you—who can't learn those lines if she's asked to. But I told you last time—this isn't criticism—about the canoe! *That's* the canoe. It comes first, and when you are full and you can remember an occasional line, throw it out! It can't hurt!" The class laughs. *"This is the scene.* No book. No text. I don't have to say any more. Can you grasp that?"

"I think so," Lila says wiping her eyes on a silk handkerchief. "I thought of a very strong preparation for—"

"Where was it?"

"Well, I didn't feel that she had reached the point—"

"It says so in the book."

"I mean at the beginning. I was working my way into it."

"There are too many line actors in this world! That's for stock! In New Hampshire! In the summer! We're talking about acting! What's the character? A woman terrified of scandal because of what her daughter has done to herself. A daughter who will be broken by the scandal of what she's done! Do you follow?"

"Yes."

"Did you understand what I meant when I said, '*This* is the scene'?"

"The preparation has to be *that* full?" Sarah asks.

"Yes! When you rehearse, you should prepare, play it freely

with no book, then quit. Talk about the President, have a cup of tea, then rehearse again."

"I'm still confused," Lila says. "I mean, I understand what you're talking about, and you obviously want it from the very beginning. I was prepared to move emotionally. I was trying to hide from her at the onset of the scene—"

"You weren't hiding. You can't kid me when it comes to emotion."

"Well, that's what I was attempting to do."

"Don't talk about it. I told you that *this* is the scene. In time, tack on the text. Talk to each other. What's so mysterious about that? You don't understand?"

"Do you want us to continue with it?" asks Lila.

"Damn right. That's what it's all about."

"I thought I was moving in that direction—"

"You don't *move* in that direction. You're right *there.*"

"But what do you do," Lila asks, "when that emotional preparation is for something that is not at the very beginning of the scene?"

"There's no such thing. A preparation is only for the *beginning* of the scene, and each moment feeds it and changes it. You're not going to get it from the text!"

"Then I misunderstood," Lila says. "This has been a very painful rehearsal time for us."

"I say it should be very simple. Prepare for the hysteria, gradually learn the lines, then put the two together. If you prepare and then work moment by moment off her and with her, you'll always be riding on a very stormy river. Do you understand what I'm talking about? What do you know before you begin?"

"I know that my daughter is pregnant."

"That's all you need. That means your daughter's dead! Cry! What could be simpler? Who is Mrs. Schmidt, the lady from Garden Street?"

"I assumed, for the sake of the scene," Lila says, "that she's an old friend—"

"No! She's the abortionist!"

"Oh, my God," Lila says.

"Cry, both of you, *then* talk. That's my method of acting: cry, then talk. Don't talk and *then* expect to cry, because you won't! When you began you didn't have anything. This time you had it! Next time I bet you will too!"

October 11

Lila and Sarah repeat, for the last time, their scene from Wedekind's *Spring Awakening*. It is full of tears and emotionally moving, but the amount of their emotion and inexperience in handling it makes it difficult for the audience to understand every word.

"Okay, blow your noses. Emotionally—" The two women are still crying, so Meisner stops. "Lila, laugh! Sing 'The Star-Spangled Banner'!"

" 'Oh, say can you see?' " Lila sings in a blowzy, teary voice and then begins to giggle.

"That's right! Sarah, tickle yourself!"

Sarah begins to laugh and the class joins in.

"Emotionally, that is the scene. Do you see the difference between last time and this time?"

"Yes," Lila says.

"You do? My chief concern is for you—for anybody—to act out the life of the scene as intended by the playwright. Technically it was faulty in its lack of clarity, but I don't care about that. The problem is to be understandable without losing the emotional life of the scene, which you now have. Getting used to having the emotion will help greatly; the clarity will come by itself. The canoe won't capsize. You follow?"

"I think so," Sarah says. "What you're saying is that the more we rehearse it—"

"The clearer you will be without losing the life of the scene. *If* you do it like this."

"Are you saying that the emotion shouldn't be at this peak for the whole scene?" Lila asks.

"Right, not all the time."

"But you wanted for us to go for it—"

"You *start* from there."

"Right."

"This *is* the scene as written by the playwright. I'm pointing out that emotionally it was where it should be, but that technically it was weak. But this happens all the time."

"Do you mean in plays or in life?" Lila asks.

"In plays, not in life. You're not forced to live life, you know."

October 18

| A Palm Tree in a Rose Garden* by
| Meade Roberts
| from act 3, scene 1

. . .Charlie and Barbara enter L. ~~Both are tight, Barbara the more so, and she immediately heads for one of the beach chairs and flops into it.~~

BARBARA: (~~Sighing with relief.~~) Oh. (~~She kicks another chair lightly with her foot.~~) Sit down.

CHARLIE: I can't stay long. I've an early appointment with Victor.

BARBARA: Victor, Victor, Victor! Where were we tonight?

CHARLIE: (~~Sits.~~) At Victor's.

BARBARA: I know we were at Victor's. Where's Victor's?

CHARLIE: On North Rodeo Drive.

BARBARA: Silly name, North Rodeo. And La Cienega's a silly name, too. And Las Palmas!

CHARLIE: All right, Barbara!

BARBARA: How could anybody in his right mind name a street Las Palmas? I'll never live on Las Palmas. Never, never!

CHARLIE: So don't live on Las Palmas!

BARBARA: You don't much care where I live, do you?

CHARLIE: No, I don't!

*Meade Roberts, *A Palm Tree in a Rose Garden* (New York: Dramatists Play Service, 1958), 51–56.

BARBARA: You'd much rather forget where I live. Like you almost forgot this afternoon! If I had any pride, I wouldn't have gone with you tonight! I shouldn't have anyway. It wasn't much fun!

CHARLIE: Well, you were the one who wanted to sulk! Nobody else was sulking. Everybody was having a fine time! Everybody was joking and singing songs! Everybody was having a fine time!

BARBARA: Were you?

CHARLIE: Sure I was.

BARBARA: You weren't joking and singing songs. You were with Victor in a corner—talking! Gab, gab, gab, all night long. Everybody felt sorry for me!

CHARLIE: Nobody felt sorry for you! (*Half rising.*) I got to go home.

BARBARA: Sit down!—There's something I have to ask you! Did you talk to Victor tonight?

CHARLIE: (*His voice rising.*) You know I talked to Victor tonight! What's the matter with you? You crazy?

BARBARA: —I mean, did you talk to Victor about me?

CHARLIE: (*Hedging.*) Sure, sure, I talked to him about you. (*Rises and crosses away a bit.*)

BARBARA: And?

CHARLIE: (*After a pause.*) He's not making the picture.

BARBARA: Not making—! What in hell do you mean?

CHARLIE: What in hell do you think I mean? He's not making the picture.

BARBARA: (*Building.*) So I don't have a part in the picture! I'm out? So I'm in the doghouse again!

CHARLIE: Listen, will you—

BARBARA: (*Near shouting now.*) I'm in the doghouse again!

CHARLIE: Shut up!

BARBARA: You're a liar! A goddamned liar! He is making the picture! You never mentioned me to him!

CHARLIE: (*Angrily.*) Call him, if you don't believe me!

BARBARA: (*Rises.*) I don't have to call him! I'll go see him! *Right now!* Who is he anyway?

CHARLIE: Listen! (~~But Barbara is sobbing now, and Charlie loses his anger and takes her in his arms.~~)

BARBARA: (~~Crumpling.~~) Charlie—Charlie—Charlie—

CHARLIE: Now, it's not that important—

BARBARA: (~~Sobbing.~~) But it is, it is—

CHARLIE: (~~Quietly.~~) Why don't you just go inside and lie down?

BARBARA: (~~A little girl again.~~) Will you go inside with me?

CHARLIE: It's late—

BARBARA: (~~Shouting again.~~) All right, don't go inside with me! I don't want you to anyway! You're not that good. I just thought you wanted to! (~~. . . . Barbara starts toward the house, then stops and faces him, a queer expression on her face.~~) Charlie?

CHARLIE: What?

BARBARA: (~~Slowly—quietly.~~) Charlie—if the deal is dead—why are you seeing Victor in the morning?—You're hiding something. What is it?

CHARLIE: I'm not hiding anything.

BARBARA: (~~As matter-of-factly as possible.~~) Yes, you are. I can tell. What are you hiding?

CHARLIE: I—

BARBARA: Come on. (~~Laughing in spite of herself.~~) Mama wants to know! (~~There is a long, long moment during which Charlie averts her glance.~~) Come on.

CHARLIE: I'm—leaving, Barbara.

BARBARA: Leaving? What do you mean, leaving?

CHARLIE: I'm going to Rome with Victor.

BARBARA: Rome?

CHARLIE: Victor's doing a picture there.

BARBARA: When did all this come about?

CHARLIE: Tonight.

BARBARA: You mean it was all thought up and decided tonight?

CHARLIE: More or less.

BARBARA: I see. (~~Exploding suddenly.~~) How can you lie in my face like that? How can you stand there expecting me to believe you?

CHARLIE: Barbara!

BARBARA: And don't tell me to quiet down! 'Cause I won't! Let

204

everybody hear! I want them to hear! —How stupid
do you think I am?

CHARLIE: I refuse to discuss this with you if you're going to
be hysterical!

BARBARA: I'll be as hysterical as I want! I don't get ditched that
easy, my friend.

CHARLIE: (*Flaring up.*) What do you expect me to do? Turn
down the job? —Are things so hot for me now that
I can turn it down? What do you expect me to do?

BARBARA: (*Petulantly.*) Take me to Rome, that's what I expect
you to do! Take me to Rome with you!

CHARLIE: I can't do that.

BARBARA: —Yes, you can—

CHARLIE: —I can't—

BARBARA: You have to! You brought me back!—

CHARLIE: —I can't discuss this until you're calm!—

BARBARA: I'm not going to be calm. What's going to happen to
me? Where'll I go? You expect me to go back to
Cleveland?—

CHARLIE: (*A way out.*) You have your family—

BARBARA: The hell with my family! They don't care whether I'm alive or dead! —Why should I go back to
them?—

CHARLIE: —Then don't go back!

BARBARA: What am I going to do?

CHARLIE: (*After a pause—quietly.*) It's time you figured that out
for yourself. —Good night. (*He exits to the street.*)

BARBARA: (*With terrifying frenzy.*) It's not going to be that easy,
you hear! (*. . . Shouting after Charlie.*)—It's not going
to be that easy! You'll be sorry, Charlie! I'll make
you sorry! You'll see I'll make you sorry! (*Sobbing
convulsively, Barbara rushes about wildly and violently
needing something to destroy picks up a small stone and
flings it. . . .*)

"Emotionally, this scene is a Hollywood scene. That means that
everybody in it is a liar. Wendy, why did you go to the party?"

"I think that I went there to get a job, an acting job," Wendy says.

"Ralph took you there to introduce you to a director who was going to give you a part. Did he talk to the director?"

"Yes. He talked to Victor."

"Did you get the part?"

"No."

"Why aren't you getting it?"

"He talked to the director only about himself."

"Of course. That's Hollywood. First he tells you that they're not going to make the picture; then he admits that they are, and that he's going to Rome and act in it, right?"

"Yes."

"What does that make him?"

"A liar."

"What does that make you?"

"A nothing," Wendy says.

"So you're a nothing? How did you do at the party?"

"Not very well."

"Why not?"

"Because he was talking to the director all the time and wasn't talking to me, and I was sulking and everybody was feeling sorry for me."

"*Who* was feeling sorry for you?"

"*I* was. I was feeling sorry for me."

"What were the other people doing?"

"They were laughing."

"Having a good time?"

"Yes," Wendy says.

"One of the big stars said, 'Here, girlie, get me a drink.' How did you feel about that?"

"I wanted to die."

" 'I want to *die* because of what happened' is the preparation for this scene. You follow?"

"Yes."

"But if you're in a condition where *you honestly want to die*, it doesn't last for only a minute, it goes on and on. Do you understand?"

"Yes."

"Charlie never introduced you; he never even mentioned you. 'I want to die' is a good emotional springboard for this exercise." Meisner turns to Ralph. "Did you get work?"

"Yeah."

"Did she get work?"

"No."

"How do you feel about that?"

"I don't want to hear it."

"Why not?"

"Because it's a downer. It's just negative. I've got better things to do."

"To hell with her! Let her go back to Topeka, right?"

"Yeah, it's not my responsibility."

"Sure! So it's a scene about a girl who, rightly or wrongly, is desolate about the death of someone or the loss of something that's precious to you, Wendy, and that you, Ralph, don't give a damn about. Did you understand that? What did you write down?"

"I wrote down," says Ralph, who has been making notes on the pages of a small notebook, " 'She is desolate and I don't care.' "

"Instead of 'I don't care,' write down, 'indifferent—i-n-d-i-f-e-double-r-e-n-t.' Then prepare and work with the script. We'll see what you do."

October 25

"Wait a minute. Wait a minute. Do you know the lines more or less?"

"Some I do, some I don't," Wendy says.

"All right. Throw yourself on that bed. Throw yourself!"

Wendy walks to the foot of the bed and sits.

"That's throwing?" Meisner asks and the class laughs. "Now —and this is the worst direction of all time—get hysterical! I don't hear anything. More!" Wendy begins to sob out loud. "More. Hit the bed! Kill the bed!" She lets out a loud cry of pain. "That's good! Now say your lines!"

"Sit down," Wendy says to Ralph.

"Never mind him. Just stay hysterical."

"I can't stay long," Ralph says. "I have an appointment with Victor in the morning."

"Victor! Victor! Victor! Where were we tonight?"

"At Victor's."

"I know we were at Victor's. Where's Victor's?"

"On North Rodeo Drive."

"I know North Rodeo—that's a silly name! And La Cienega's a silly name and so is Las Palmas! I'll never," Wendy says with manic intensity, "live on Las Palmas! Never! Never!"

"So don't live on Las Palmas," Ralph says with such blatant indifference to her suffering that the class laughs in surprise.

"You don't much care where I live, do you?" Wendy says coldly.

"No, I don't care where you live."

"Don't look at him," Meisner says, "just stay hysterical!"

"You don't care where I live, do you?" Wendy says in a louder voice.

"Wendy, lie down!" Meisner says.

She lies back on the bed and begins to sob. "You don't . . . care . . . where I live . . . do you?"

"No, I don't care where you live," Ralph repeats calmly.

"Hit the bed!" Meisner says.

"This evening! It wasn't much fun!"

"You're the one who wanted to sulk. Everyone else was having a fine time. Everyone was joking and singing."

"Were you?"

"Sure I was."

"Yeah, you were having a fine time! You were over in the corner talking with Victor all night long! Gab, gab, gab! Everybody felt sorry for me," Wendy wails.

"Nobody felt sorry for you, Barbara. I'm leaving!" Ralph says. His turn toward the door prompts an unclear emotional outburst from Wendy. "Did you talk to Victor tonight?" she finally asks.

"Of course I talked with Victor tonight."

"I didn't see you talk to Victor about me!"

Meisner interrupts. "Don't look at him once!"

"Didn't you talk to Victor about me?"

"Sure. Sure."

"And?"

"He's not making the picture!"

"Ah! Why in hell isn't he making that picture?"

"What in hell do you think I mean?" Ralph says. "He's not making the picture."

"Ah! Ah! Ah!" Wendy exclaims, and with each cry she bangs her head against the wall. She is hysterical with frustration and anger, and her emotion is at once real and funny. "And I'm in the doghouse again!" she says, and the class laughs. "You're a liar. He *is* making the picture!"

"If you don't believe me, why don't you just call him up?"

"I'll call him! Who the hell is he, anyway?" She is sobbing loudly. "Oh, Charlie, Charlie, Charlie!"

"It's not that important," Ralph says firmly.

"Oh, it is!" she cries, and then, clenching both fists, she emits a cry of impotent rage—"Ahhh!"—and the class laughs.

"Why don't you lie down?" Ralph says.

"Will you lie down with me?"

"No, it's late. I got to go."

"Okay, go!" she says, suddenly directing her anger at Ralph. "You're not that good, anyway. I just thought you wanted to. Charlie?"

"What?"

"If he's not making the picture, then why are you seeing him tomorrow morning? You're hiding something from me! I know you're hiding something from me!" She suddenly bangs the back of her head against the wall once again. "You're hiding something from me. I know you're hiding something! Mama wants to know. Why?"

"I'm leaving, Barbara. I'm going to Rome with Victor in the morning."

"Ah!" she says, as if he has stabbed her. "Rome? When did all this come about?"

"Tonight."

"Was this all decided tonight?"

"More or less."

"I see," she says calmly, and then suddenly loses control again. "You stand there and lie to me like that! How stupid do you think I am? Don't tell me to keep quiet because I'm not keeping quiet! I'll be hysterical if I want to be! Ahhgh! Ahhgh! Ahhgh!"

"I'm not going to talk to you unless you calm down."

"I'm not going to calm down! I don't want to be calm! Take me with you! Take me to Rome!" This sudden shift is funny, and the class laughs. "You have to, you have to, you have to! What happened to me? What in hell happened to me? Where am I going to go? What am I going to do? I'll die if I have to go back to Cleveland!"

"Well, don't go there," Ralph says, then turns on his heel and walks out the door.

"I'll make you sorry. I'll make you sorry, Charlie!" Wendy says, and the class laughs.

"I liked that very much," Meisner says. "That's a picture of a Hollywood actress who didn't get the job. It happens about three thousand times a day in Beverly Hills," he adds. "*That's* the scene! A girl from Cleveland comes to Hollywood and she's been there for five years and hasn't even gotten into a manager's office. Her friend promises her he's going to get her a part, but he doesn't even mention her! You know, she makes fun of all the streets in Beverly Hills, right? That's like being so angry at New York that you go"—Meisner shakes his first—" 'Fifth Avenue, Fourth Avenue, Third Avenue, Lexington—I hate them all!' It's not a geography lesson." The class laughs. "Listen, Ralph, in this scene you find yourself in the presence of somebody who is beside herself over something you consider unimportant. It's *as if* you're saying, 'I'm going to the movies with another girl tomorrow night,' and she throws one of her temper tantrums. Well, you're still going."

Ralph nods.

"Ray, what did you think of it?" Meisner asks.

"It was wonderful."

"Tell them."

"Tell them? It was hysterical."

"Why?"

"There were two completely different things happening," Ray

says, "yet they were working off each other. She was terribly frustrated and he was blasé, and that's what real comedy is. For the third reading it was great."

"We've spent a lot of time—I don't know how much—on the problem of using yourself truthfully. Now we're beginning to edge up on the problem of playing the part. The emphasis has been primarily on 'This is what I'm doing and I'm doing it truthfully.' Now the question coming up is 'How do I do it?' Do you all understand? Is this shift clear?"

"So we're bearing on the problem of not only being truthful, but of playing the role," Ralph says.

"Of playing the part, yes. Wendy, did I force you to play the part of that dizzy Hollywood actress?"

"Yes."

"We're not only bringing truth to it. We're also doing something specifically dictated by the character and the circumstances," Ralph says.

"So what was the point of today's class?" Meisner asks Bette.

"We're supposed to look at the character instead of . . ."

"Instead of *merely* the truth," Meisner says, turning to the class. How many of you want to do this kind of work?"

Every student shoots up a hand.

November 1

Golden Boy* by
Clifford Odets
act 1, scene 4

A few nights later.

Joe *and* Lorna *sit on a bench in the park. It is night. There is carrousel music in the distance. Cars ride by in front of the boy and girl in the late*

*Clifford Odets, *Six Plays of Clifford Odets* (New York: The Modern Library, 1939), 262–267.

spring night. Out of sight a traffic light changes from red to green and back again throughout the scene and casts its colors on the faces of the boy and girl.

LORNA: Success and fame! Or just a lousy living. You're lucky you won't have to worry about those things. . . .

JOE: Won't I?

LORNA: Unless Tom Moody's a liar.

JOE: You like him, don't you?

LORNA: (*After a pause*) I like him.

JOE: I like how you dress. The girls look nice in the summertime. Did you ever stand at the Fifth Avenue Library and watch those girls go by?

LORNA: No, I never did. (*Switching the subject.*) That's the carousel, that music. Did you ever ride on one of those?

JOE: That's for kids.

LORNA: Weren't you ever a kid, for God's sake?

JOE: Not a happy kid.

LORNA: Why?

JOE: Well, I always felt different. Even my name was special—Bonaparte—and my eyes . . .

LORNA: I wouldn't have taken that too serious. . . . (*There is a silent pause. Joe looks straight ahead.*)

JOE: Gee, all those cars . . .

LORNA: Lots of horses trot around here. The rich know how to live. You'll be rich. . . .

JOE: My brother Frank is an organizer for the C.I.O.

LORNA: What's that?

JOE: If you worked in a factory you'd know. Did you ever work?

LORNA: (*with a smile*) No, when I came out of the cocoon I was a butterfly, and butterflies don't work.

JOE: All those cars . . . whizz, whizz. (*Now turning less casual.*) Where's Mr. Moody tonight?

LORNA: He goes to see his kid on Tuesday nights. It's a sick kid, a girl. His wife leaves it at her mother's house.

JOE: That leaves you free, don't it?

LORNA: What are you hinting at?

JOE: I'm thinking about you and Mr. Moody.

LORNA: Why think about it? I don't. Why should you?

JOE: If you belonged to me I wouldn't think about it.

LORNA: Haven't you got a girl?

JOE: No.

LORNA: Why not?

JOE: (*evasively*) Oh . . .

LORNA: Tokio says you're going far in the fighting game.

JOE: Music means more to me. May I tell you something?

LORNA: Of course.

JOE: If you laugh, I'll never speak to you again.

LORNA: I'm not the laughing type.

JOE: With music I'm never alone when I'm alone—Playing music . . . that's like saying, "I'm a man. I belong here. How do you do, World—good evening!" When I play music nothing is closed to me. I'm not afraid of people and what they say. There's no war in music. It's not like the streets. Does this sound funny?

LORNA: No.

JOE: But when you leave your room . . . down in the street . . . it's war! Music can't help me there. Understand?

LORNA: Yes.

JOE: People have hurt my feelings for years. I never forget. You can't get even with people by playing the fiddle. If music shot bullets I'd like it better—artists and people like that are freaks today. The world moves fast and they sit around like forgotten dopes.

LORNA: You're loaded with fireworks. Why don't you fight?

JOE: You have to be what you are—!

LORNA: Fight! see what happens—

JOE: Or end up in the bughouse!

LORNA: God's teeth! Who says you have to be one thing?

JOE: My nature isn't fighting!

LORNA: Don't Tokio know what he's talking about? Don't Tom? Joe, listen: be a fighter! Show the world! If you made your fame and fortune—and you can—you'd be anything you want. Do it! Bang your way to the light-

	weight crown. Get a bank account. Hire a great doctor with a beard—get your eyes fixed—
JOE:	What's the matter with my eyes?
LORNA:	Excuse me, I stand corrected. (*After a pause.*) You get mad all the time.
JOE:	That's from thinking about myself.
LORNA:	How old are you, Joe?
JOE:	Twenty-one and a half, and the months are going fast.
LORNA:	You're very smart for twenty-one and a half "and the months are going fast."
JOE:	Why not? I read every page of the *Encyclopaedia Britannica*. My father's friend, Mr. Carp, has it. A shrimp with glasses had to do something.
LORNA:	I'd like to meet your father. Your mother dead?
JOE:	Yes.
LORNA:	So is mine.
JOE:	Where do you come from? The city is full of girls who look as if they never had parents.
LORNA:	I'm a girl from over the river. My father is still alive —shucking oysters and bumming drinks somewhere in the wilds of Jersey. I'll tell you a secret: I don't like you.
JOE:	(*surprised*) Why?
LORNA:	You're too sufficient by yourself . . . too inside yourself.
JOE:	You like it or you don't.
LORNA:	You're on an island—
JOE:	Robinson Crusoe . . .
LORNA:	That's right—"me, myself, and I." Why not come out and see the world?
JOE:	Does it seem that way?
LORNA:	Can't you see yourself?
JOE:	No. . . .
LORNA:	Take a bird's-eye view; you don't know what's right or wrong. You don't know what to pick, but you won't admit it.
JOE:	Do you?
LORNA:	Leave me out. This is the anatomy of Joe Bonaparte.

JOE: You're dancing on my nose, huh?

LORNA: Shall I stop?

JOE: No.

LORNA: You're a miserable creature. You want your arm in *gek* up to the elbow. You'll take fame so people won't laugh or scorn your face. You'd give your soul for those things. But every time you turn your back your little soul kicks you in the teeth. It don't give in so easy.

JOE: And what does your soul do in its perfumed vanity case?

LORNA: Forget about me.

JOE: Don't you want—?

LORNA: (~~suddenly quite nasty~~) I told you to forget it!

JOE: (~~quietly~~) Moody sent you after me—a decoy! You made a mistake, Lorna, for two reasons. I make up my own mind to fight. Point two, he doesn't know you don't love him—

LORNA: You're a fresh kid.

JOE: In fact he doesn't know anything about you at all.

LORNA: (~~challengingly~~) But you do?

JOE: This is the anatomy of Lorna Moon: She's a lost baby. She doesn't know what's right or wrong. She's a miserable creature who never knew what to pick. But she'd never admit it. And I'll tell you why you picked Moody!

LORNA: You don't know anything.

JOE: Go home, Lorna. If you stay, I'll know something about you. . . .

LORNA: You don't know anything.

JOE: Now's your chance—go home!

LORNA: Tom loves me.

JOE: (~~after a long silence, looking ahead~~) I'm going to buy a car.

LORNA: They make wonderful cars today. Even the lizzies—

JOE: Gary Cooper's got the kind I want. I saw it in the paper, but it costs too much—fourteen thousand. If I found one second-hand—

LORNA: And if you had the cash—

JOE: I'll get it—

LORNA: Sure, if you'd go in and really fight!

JOE: (*in a sudden burst*) Tell your Mr. Moody I'll dazzle the eyes out of his head!

LORNA: You mean it?

JOE: (*looking out ahead*) Those cars are poison in my blood. When you sit in a car and speed you're looking down at the world. Speed, speed, everything is speed—nobody gets me!

LORNA: You mean in the ring?

JOE: In or out, nobody gets me! Gee, I like to stroke that gas!

LORNA: You sound like Jack the Ripper.

JOE: (*standing up suddenly*) I'll walk you back to your house —your hotel, I mean. (*Lorna stands. Joe continues.*) Do you have the same room?

LORNA: (*with sneaking admiration*) You're a fresh kid!

JOE: When you're lying in his arms tonight, tell him, for me, that the next World's Champ is feeding in his stable.

LORNA: Did you really read those *Britannica* books?

JOE: From A to Z.

LORNA: And you're only twenty-one?

JOE: And a half.

LORNA: Something's wrong somewhere.

JOE: I know . . . (*they slowly walk out as*)

Fadeout

"A certain kind of person could have many sides to his character or he could be simple. Now, we know from the play, Rachael, that you've been sent here to try to persuade him to fight."

"That's right."

"What do you know about him?"

"I know that he has two very definite sides to him. On the one hand, he wants to fight. On the other, he's sensitive, a musician, and he has to make a decision now that will affect the rest of his life."

"Why are you here?"

"I'm here because Tom Moody wanted me to convince him to fight."

"How do you feel about that?"

"I feel that I owe it to Tom. He's been good to me, and I'm doing it for him."

"So you're doing it to pay somebody back, would you say?"

"Yes."

"How do you feel about Joe?"

"I feel that he's very vulnerable, but I know he has a wonderful opportunity. He has a choice, and I really don't have a lot of sympathy with that. I sympathize more with Tom because he really doesn't have a choice. He's a loser."

"Does Joe make you nervous?"

"Yes."

"Why?"

"Because I feel drawn to him, and I don't want to be."

"What else do you feel about him?"

"Well, he's very different from the people that I'm used to."

"In what way?"

"I think it's mostly his sensitivity. A young man who's sensitive and intelligent. He's not the usual type hanging around boxing rings."

"Is that his dominant characteristic?"

"No, the most dominant is his anger. He wants to get back at the world because he hates it that people have made him feel different."

"Why do you want to get back at the world?" Meisner asks Ray.

"Because I'm different. Because people have made fun of me. Because I can't get ahead. Because I don't know which direction to go in." Ray pauses for a moment and then adds, "Because I've got a funny name and my eyes are weird."

"If you go into a butcher shop and ask for a couple of pounds of lamb chops and the butcher seems to hear you but waits on two other people before you, how do you feel?"

"I want to reach over the counter and grab him by the tie and tell him not to ignore me!"

"Why do you have that curious reaction?"

"Because people do it to me all the time. They behave as if I'm not there."

"The nature of neuroses is very peculiar. Why would your neuroses make you a good fighter?"

"Because it's power. It fuels my anger and it's what makes it possible for me to fight." Again Ray pauses for a moment. "Because everybody I fight is the rest of the world."

"What's the name of the heavyweight who just quit?"

"Muhammad Ali?"

"Yeah. Do you think that his neuroses were part of what made him a champion?"

"Yes."

"So Joe Bonaparte is like an unrecognized Muhammad Ali. Do you follow?"

"Yes."

"Rachael, how would you like to argue with Muhammad Ali that white people are superior to colored people?"

"I don't think I'd like to."

"Suppose you had to?"

"It would make me very nervous."

"To say the least."

"Yeah."

"So we're really talking about two neurotics, each in his own way, right?"

Ray and Rachael nod.

"All right," Meisner says, "prepare and let's hear a reading."

They leave the room to prepare and when the reading is over, Meisner says, "I want to talk about this. You've got something bordering on the character."

"Are you talking about me?" Ray asks.

"Yeah. Rachael, why does she say, 'I don't like you'?"

"She can't control him. He's locked inside himself and she can't get to him."

"I'll help you," Meisner says. "He's just told you about himself, hasn't he?"

"Yes."

"Ray, what did you say?"

"I told her that people always make fun of me and that I don't forget it. That I wish music could shoot bullets so that I could get back at those people. That music makes me feel like a man. I can say, 'Here I am and it's okay to be that.' But at the same time I feel that people who play music just sit around like forgotten dopes while the world passes them by."

"Where does she say, 'I don't like you'?"

"It's a little later on."

"It's after he asks her about herself," Rachael says.

"That's right. How does she feel about herself?"

"She doesn't feel good at all about herself."

"Her past is very sad, but she tells him about it, and then she says, 'I don't like you.' Why does she say that?"

"To change the subject?"

"No, he doesn't listen to a word you say. He's entirely wrapped up in himself."

"I see," Rachael says.

"How come I didn't know that?" Ray says.

"Because I'm smarter than you!" Meisner says, and the class laughs. "Ray, why does he like cars?"

"Because they make him feel that he's on top of the world. When he goes fast in a car the sensation matches the energy that's pent-up inside him and he feels more at peace. I'm making this up," Ray adds.

"Of course," Meisner says. "Where else are you going to get it? Cars are powerful." After a pause Meisner continues. "Don't you see how all of this, Rachael, has a tantalizing effect on you? He's pathetic, and yet there's something tragic about him, something dangerous."

"Yes."

"The cue is when you say, 'You know, I don't like you.' You get it, Ray, don't you?"

"Yeah. He's ready to punch you in the mouth one minute and then to apologize sweetly the next."

"Do you realize how much sadism there is in him when he says, 'If only violins had bullets'?"

"I had a sense of that, but maybe I didn't realize how much there is."

"Rachael, a person like that can make you nervous."

"Yes."

"Your walk with him from Moody's office to the park was nerve-racking, you follow? You're not using your powder puff because you want to make sure your powder is smooth. Why do you use it?"

"Sweat?" Rachael asks.

"Sweat! Have you got a clearer idea?"

"Yes," Ray says. "It's much clearer."

"Well, work on that."

November 8

"That was much better, but Rachael, it's not passionate enough. Lorna's feelings have been very hurt and I think that makes you angry."

"You mean it has to be more sad?"

"No, more vigorous! Why does she say, 'Tom loves me'? Why doesn't she say, 'I love Tom'?"

"Because she doesn't love Tom."

"Why does she live with him?"

"She owes him. He's been good to her and he loves her."

"It's because he loves her?"

"Yes."

"No, it's because she was tired of being treated like a whore!"

"I see."

"When you begin, how do you know Joe's not going to take a poke at you?"

"I don't know."

"Doesn't that make you nervous?"

"Sure, but I didn't really want to show him that I was nervous because I also have to convince him—"

"That's literary! You be what you are! If you were a salesman about to enter a fancy office and will come out with a big order and a big commission if you're lucky, would you be nervous?"

"Yes."

"But you'd try to stay composed?"

"Right. You mean in that situation?"

"In *this* situation!"

"I should try to stay composed? I don't understand."

"You're going to get a tremendous order. That makes you very nervous. *Try* to control it!"

"Okay."

"Ray, what does driving a car fast mean? Just power? You're going eighty miles an hour. Is it just power?"

"No, it's freedom, too. Also it's *calm*. The last time you asked me this question I said that it was as if he himself was going eighty miles an hour, so when he gets in the car and it goes eighty miles an hour it's almost peaceful. He *needs* to do it."

"It's sexual."

"You have a better vocabulary than I do," Ray says, and the class laughs. "No, I understand what you mean."

"What do you think of the street?"

"That it's war. That it's a place where I have to fight."

"How do you feel about that?"

"I hate it. I'm willing to fight back, but it makes me mad."

"You hate it."

"But I'm not going to get beat up by it. I'll strike back."

"It makes you feel like nobody. That's a terrible feeling to have."

"A different feeling, then. Feeling like nobody is different than feeling mad, isn't it? If it makes me feel like nobody, wouldn't it make the whole scene more introspective? That's what feeling like nobody means to me. But the street makes me mad, so it's the opposite of introspection."

" 'If a violin could only speak bullets!' That's a burning aspiration! It's too bad you're not Jewish!"

"Why? Do you have to be Jewish to play the scene?"

"You need that kind of intensity."

"He's Italian!" Ray says.

"The same thing."

"I'll get it."

"You had good moments this time. So did she, except she's not driving enough. Do you intimidate her?"

"You mean in reality? In the rehearsal process? No, I don't think I do. But it would help the scene, wouldn't it?"

Meisner nods.

| The Seagull by
| Anton Chekhov*
| from act 3

(Sorin and Medviedenko go out.)

ARKADINA: Oh, how he frightened me.

TREPLYOV: It isn't good for him to live in the country. He gets too depressed. If you suddenly felt generous, Mother, and lent him a thousand or even two he could spend a whole year in town.

ARKADINA: I don't have any money. I'm an actress, not a banker. *(Pause.)*

TREPLYOV: Will you change my bandage for me, Mother? You do it so well.

ARKADINA: *(Taking a bottle of iodine and a box of bandages from the chest.)* The doctor's late today.

TREPLYOV: Yes, he promised to be here at ten and it's twelve now.

ARKADINA: Sit down. *(She takes off his bandage.)* You look as if you're wearing a turban. Yesterday somebody asked them in the kitchen what nationality you were. The wound is almost healed. Just a little scar left. *(She kisses his head.)* You won't do anything silly again while I'm away, will you?

TREPLYOV: No, Mother. It was a moment of despair; I didn't have any control over myself. It won't happen again. *(He kisses her hands.)* You have such golden hands, Mama. I remember a long time ago when you were still playing in the state theaters—I was very young then—there was a fight in our courtyard and one of the other tenants, a washerwoman, was almost beaten to death. Do you remember? She was unconscious when they picked her up and you

*Jean-Claude Van Italie, trans. (New York, Hagerstown, San Francisco, London: Perennnial Library, Harper & Row, 1977), 50–53.

nursed her, you took medicine to her, and you washed her children in a tub. Don't you remember?

ARKADINA: No. *(She puts on a fresh bandage.)*

TREPLYOV: There were two young ballerinas living in that same house. You used to have them over for coffee.

ARKADINA: I remember that.

TREPLYOV: They were terribly pious, weren't they? (~~Pause.~~) These past few days, Mama, I've loved you as innocently and completely as when I was a child. Only why do you let yourself fall under the influence of that man?

ARKADINA: Konstantin, you don't understand him, he has a very noble character.

TREPLYOV: When he was told I was going to challenge him to a duel his noble character didn't stop him from being a coward. He's leaving. An ignominious retreat.

ARKADINA: Nonsense! It was I who asked him to leave.

TREPLYOV: What a noble character! You and I are almost quarreling over him in here and he's probably somewhere in the drawing room or the garden laughing at us—expanding Nina's mind, trying to convince her that he's a genius.

ARKADINA: You seem to enjoy saying disagreeable things to me. I've told you I respect him, and I'll thank you not to speak badly of him in my presence again.

TREPLYOV: But I don't respect him. You want me to think he's a genius, too. Well, I'm sorry, but I can't lie about it: his books make me sick.

ARKADINA: That's just envy. People with no talent are always putting down real genius. It must be very comforting to you.

TREPLYOV: (~~Ironically.~~) Real genius! (~~Angrily.~~) I've got more genius than any of you if it comes down to that. (~~Tears off his bandage.~~) You and he and your boring old ideas, you've taken over the arts, and you won't recognize or tolerate anything except your own conventional trivia. You want to sit and suppress everything else. Well, I don't accept your high artistic opinions of yourselves. I don't accept his and I don't accept yours!

ARKADINA: You're decadent, that's what you are!

TREPLYOV: Well, then go on back to your precious theater and act in your trashy third-rate plays!

ARKADINA: I have never acted in trashy third-rate plays. Why don't you leave me alone? You couldn't even write a cheap vaudeville sketch. Little middle-class inhabitant of Kiev! Sponger!

TREPLYOV: Miser!

ARKADINA: Beggar! (~~He sits down and cries softly.~~) Little nobody! (~~She walks up and down excitedly.~~) Don't cry! Please don't cry, Kostya. (~~She cries herself.~~) Darling, do stop! (~~She kisses him on his forehead, his cheeks, his head.~~) My darling, forgive me! Forgive your wicked mother. I'm such a miserable person, please forgive me.

TREPLYOV: (~~Embracing her.~~) If you only knew. I've lost everything. She doesn't love me now and I can't write. I have no hope.

ARKADINA: Don't feel like that, my darling. It'll all work out. He's leaving today. She'll love you again. (~~She wipes away his tears.~~) There, that's enough. We've made up now.

TREPLYOV: (~~Kissing her hands.~~) Yes, Mama.

ARKADINA: (~~Tenderly.~~) Make up with him, too. You don't really want a duel. It's too silly.

TREPLYOV: All right, Mother, only please don't make me see him again. That would be too much. I couldn't stand it. (*Trigorin comes in.*) Here he is. I'm going. (*He quickly puts the bandages and iodine back into the medicine chest.*) The doctor will bandage me later. . . .

"Mary, what do you think of your son? Have you thought about it?"

"Yes. I feel guilty about him, but I also feel threatened by him. He's a terrible nuisance and an embarrassment."

"Why?"

"He's critical of me and of my work. He dislikes my friends and is rude to them. I also don't like having a big, oafish son around all the time. He gets in the way of my life."

"So you just tolerate him."

"I keep him off on the farm, stuck out in the country."

"Why?"

"Well, in the first place I can't part with money. I just can't. It's like a physical incapacity. And it would take money to do anything with him. He'd have to have more education, better clothes. And his being as old as he is makes me feel my age and makes other people aware of it. I feel it might interfere with my career. I think she's desperate to keep her life as it is, and she doesn't want to have somebody around that she has to do something about. But also she can't stand anybody who is with her not to love her."

"All the things you say are true. John, what about you and your mother and the girl you love and the writer who is flirting both with the girl and your mother? They're all mixed up. Chekhov is a *terrible* playwright!" The class laughs. "What do *you* want?"

"I want her to care about me. I feel that she doesn't really pay much attention to me—"

"To say the least! What you want is love from your mother, the kind of love you get from a mother. How did you get that bandage around your head?"

"I tried to shoot myself."

"You must have been pretty unhappy. Why do you ask her to fix the bandage on your head?"

"So that I'll get some sympathy from her."

"But it doesn't come out that way."

"Right."

"She tells you the truth, probably for the first time, and you tell her how you feel about her. Bring in the scene for next time. Read it very easily. By 'easily' I mean don't try to make a performance out of it. Know why you say everything you say. Mary, how do you feel about his asking you to fix his bandage?"

"Well, I hadn't thought about that, but I don't think she minds."

"I think she does."

"You think she minds? Why? Because she resents his trying to kill himself and making such a fuss and getting all this attention and she has to do the dirty work?" Meisner nods. "I see."

"She's like a nurse who has to take care of a patient she has no sympathy for. That's why the last part of the scene comes out of her so easily. It's the way she thinks of him anyway."

"I see," Mary says.

"John, why don't you wait for the doctor?"

"Because I want my mother to do it as a gesture of caring and love."

"Next time take an easy reading of this text. Ask yourself all the questions that you need to ask. Why do I do this? Why do I say this? Try to understand the scene. Chekhov's terrible. He's really terrible."

"He crams too much humanity into his plays," Ray says.

"Why didn't you like Baron Toozenbach?" Scott Roberts asks.

"I couldn't understand him. I understand *this* scene. This is one of his easier ones. Provided you know that ninety circumstances go into each moment."

November 19

"You know, if you took a sensitive, tremulous young man—you can practically see the nerves quivering in his face—who believes that to be considered talented means to be loved, and his mother says, 'You're talentless,' then in essence his mother is saying that she doesn't love him. It's tough to take, isn't it? Basically, to be talented is to be loved. If I had the ability, the power, the influence to say to you, 'John, stay in your father's business because . . .' I'd like to see the scene when you're home by yourself remembering. That's how strong it is, except you experience it right here. Understand?"

"Yes."

"If you're trying to be an artist and she says to you, 'You have no talent,' what do you do?"

"I think I'd kill myself," John says.

"Yes. And Mary, you see you've gone a little too far. The other person is wounded. What do you say?"

" 'I'm sorry, I didn't mean that.' But I have a lot of trouble with that line. It leaves almost nothing for her to do in this scene. She really is affected by him, isn't she? Or is it all just superficial?"

"He's a *pest!* From the very beginning. She's the nurse, and when the patient says, 'Can I have a drink of water,' she gives it to him, but under her breath, she's saying 'Why doesn't he get out of here!' You follow?"

"I follow, but it's just . . . Why is she so bad?" Mary blurts out, and then laughs nervously. "She's selfish and she's—"

"She's a mother!"

"Yes."

"She's an actress!"

"Yes."

"She has a lover!"

"Yes."

"Who's playing around with her son's girl!"

"Yes."

"She's got a son who's older than the girl!"

"Yes."

"It's enough to drive her crazy!"

"Yes."

"You understand?"

"Yes."

"The rest of it is submerged, but it comes to the surface pretty quickly."

"I see. Yes."

"Now break him down!" Meisner says.

"Okay. In a way, it's all *his* fault. If he was man enough to keep his girl, we wouldn't all be in this mess."

"If he was man enough to at least move to another city!" Meisner says, and the class laughs.

Mary says, "I thought about that, Sandy, and my feeling is that it's not that she hates him; it's that all she can manage is—You don't buy that? I think there's a kind of gallantry in that she does what she can with her own life."

"But he exists!"

"And that's the insult?"

"Look what she calls him!"

"Yes."

"It's very destructive, isn't it?"

"Yes."

"Why does she say it? Does she mean it?"

"Yes, I think she does."

"Well, *mean* it!"

"Okay."

"Destroy him! This scene isn't about a bandage! The scene is about a mother's love—or lack of it! You could wait for a bandage, but you can't wait one second more for your mother's love. You follow, John?"

"Yeah."

"She gives you two *slaps* to the face, and that's all you feel! This has nothing to do with a bandage; it has to do with survival!"

"Yes," Mary says.

"Prepare much more—*much more.* Focus on the jealousy, Mary, and the desolation. I could go on, but go on yourself. You follow?"

"Yes, I do. Do you want us to throw away the book, or should we read it again?"

"It will come by itself."

"Okay."

November 8

> **Summer and Smoke by**
> **Tennessee Williams***
> **part 1, scene 6**

*Tennessee Williams's *Tennessee Williams: Four Plays* (New York and Scarborough, Ontario: New American Library, 1976), 72–83 and 112–120.

A delicately suggested arbor, enclosing a table and two chairs. Over the table is suspended a torn paper lantern. . . . John's voice is audible before he and Alma enter.

JOHN: *(from the darkness)* I don't understand why we can't go in the casino.

ALMA: You do understand. You're just pretending not to.

JOHN: Give me one reason.

ALMA: *(coming into the arbor)* I am a minister's daughter.

JOHN: .That's no reason. *(He follows her in. He wears a white linen suit, carrying the coat over his arm.)*

ALMA: You're a doctor. That's a better reason. You can't any more afford to be seen in such places than I can—less!

JOHN: *(bellowing)* Dusty!

DUSTY: *(from the darkness)* Coming!

JOHN: What are you fishing in that pocketbook for?

ALMA: Nothing.

JOHN: What have you got there?

ALMA: Let go!

JOHN: Those sleeping tablets I gave you?

ALMA: Yes.

JOHN: What for?

ALMA: I need one.

JOHN: *Now?*

ALMA: Yes.

JOHN: Why?

ALMA: Why? Because I nearly died of heart failure in your automobile. What possessed you to drive like that? A demon?

(Dusty enters.)

JOHN: A bottle of vino rosso.

DUSTY: Sure. *(He withdraws.)*

JOHN: Hey! Tell Shorty I want to hear the "Yellow Dog Blues."

ALMA: Please give me back my tablets.

JOHN: You want to turn into a dope-fiend taking this stuff? I said take one when you need one.

ALMA: I need one now.

JOHN: Sit down and stop swallowing air. (~~Dusty returns with a tall wine bottle and two thin-stemmed glasses.~~) ~~When does the cockfight start?~~

~~DUSTY.~~   ~~'Bout ten o'clock, Dr. Johnny.~~

~~ALMA.~~   ~~When does *what* start?~~

JOHN: They have a cockfight here every Saturday night. Ever seen one?

ALMA: Perhaps in some earlier incarnation of mine.

JOHN: When you wore a brass ring in your nose?

ALMA: Then maybe I went to exhibitions like that.

JOHN: You're going to see one tonight.

ALMA: Oh, no, I'm not.

JOHN: That's what we came here for.

ALMA: I didn't think such exhibitions were legal.

JOHN: This is Moon Lake Casino where anything goes.

ALMA: And you're a frequent patron?

JOHN: I'd say constant.

ALMA: Then I'm afraid you must be serious about giving up your medical career.

JOHN: You bet I am! A doctor's life is walled in by sickness and misery and death.

ALMA: May I be so presumptuous as to inquire what you'll do when you quit?

JOHN: You may be so presumptuous as to inquire.

ALMA: But you won't tell me?

JOHN: I haven't made up my mind, but I've been thinking of South America lately.

ALMA: (~~sadly~~) Oh . . .

JOHN: I've heard that cantinas are lots more fun than saloons, and señoritas are caviar among females.

ALMA: Dorothy Sykes' brother went to South America and was never heard of again. It takes a strong character to survive in the tropics. Otherwise it's a quagmire.

JOHN: You think my character's weak?

ALMA: I think you're confused, just awfully, awfully

confused, as confused as I am—but in a different way. . . .

JOHN: (*stretching out his legs*) Hee-haw, ho-hum.

ALMA: You used to say that as a child—to signify your disgust!

JOHN: (*grinning*) Did I?

ALMA: (*sharply*) Don't sit like that!

JOHN: Why not?

ALMA: You look so indolent and worthless.

JOHN: Maybe I am.

ALMA: If you must go somewhere, why don't you choose a place with a bracing climate?

JOHN: Parts of South America are as cool as a cucumber.

ALMA: I never knew that.

JOHN: Well, now you do.

ALMA: Those Latins all dream in the sun—and indulge their senses.

JOHN: Well, it's yet to be proven that anyone on this earth is crowned with so much glory as the one that uses his senses to get all he can in the way of . . . satisfaction.

ALMA: Self-satisfaction?

JOHN: What other kind is there?

ALMA: I will answer that question by asking you one. Have you ever seen or looked at a picture of a Gothic cathedral?

JOHN: Gothic cathedrals? What about them?

ALMA: How everything reaches up, how everything seems to be straining for something out of the reach of stone— or human—fingers? . . . The immense stained windows, the great arched doors that are five or six times the height of the tallest man—the vaulted ceiling and all the delicate spires—all reaching up to something beyond attainment! To me—well, that is the secret, the principle back of existence—the everlasting struggle and aspiration for more than our human limits have placed in our reach . . . Who was it that said that —oh, so beautiful thing!—"All of us are in the gutter, but some of us are looking at the stars!"

JOHN:	Mr. Oscar Wilde.
ALMA:	(~~somewhat taken aback~~) Well, regardless of who said it, it's still true. Some of us are looking at the stars! (~~She looks up raptly and places her hand over his.~~)
JOHN:	It's no fun holding hands with gloves on, Miss Alma.
ALMA:	That's easily remedied. I'll just take the gloves off. *(Music is heard.)*
JOHN:	Christ! (~~He rises abruptly and lights a cigarette.~~) Rosa Gonzales is dancing in the casino.
ALMA:	You *are* unhappy. You hate me for depriving you of the company inside. Well, you'll escape by and by. You'll drive me home and come back out by yourself. . . . I've only gone out with three young men at all seriously, and with each one there was a desert between us.
JOHN:	What do you mean by a desert?
ALMA:	Oh—wide, wide stretches of uninhabitable ground.
JOHN:	Maybe you made it that way by being stand-offish.
ALMA:	Oh, I . . . tried to entertain them the first few times. I would play and sing for them in the Rectory parlor.
JOHN:	With your father in the next room and the door half open?
ALMA:	I don't think that was the trouble.
JOHN:	What was the trouble?
ALMA:	I . . . I didn't have my heart in it. (~~She laughs uncertainly.~~) A silence would fall between us. You know, a silence?
JOHN:	Yes, I know a silence.
ALMA:	I'd try to talk and he'd try to talk and neither would make a go of it.
JOHN:	The silence would fall?
ALMA:	Yes, the enormous silence.
JOHN:	Then you'd go back to the piano?
ALMA:	I'd twist my ring. Sometimes I twisted it so hard that the band cut my finger! He'd glance at his watch and we'd both know that the useless undertaking had come to a close . . .
JOHN:	You'd call it quits?

ALMA: Quits is what we'd call it . . . One or two times I was rather sorry about it.

JOHN: But you didn't have your heart in it?

ALMA: None of them really engaged my serious feelings.

JOHN: You do have serious feelings—of that kind?

ALMA: Doesn't everyone—sometimes?

JOHN: Some women are cold. Some women are what is called frigid.

ALMA: Do I give that impression?

JOHN: Under the surface you have a lot of excitement, a great deal more than any other woman I have met. So much that you have to carry these sleeping pills with you. The question is why? *(He leans over and lifts her veil.)*

ALMA: What are you doing that for?

JOHN: So I won't get your veil in my mouth when I kiss you.

ALMA: *(faintly)* Do you want to do that?

JOHN: *(gently)* Miss Alma. *(He takes her arms and draws her to her feet.)* Oh, Miss Alma, Miss Alma! *(He kisses her.)*

ALMA: Not "Miss" any more. Just Alma.

JOHN: *(grinning gently)* "Miss" suits you better, Miss Alma. *(He kisses her again. She hesitantly touches his shoulders, but not quite to push him away. John speaks softly to her.)* Is it so hard to forget you're a preacher's daughter?

ALMA: There is no reason for me to forget that I am a minister's daughter. A minister's daughter's no different from any other young lady who tries to remember that she *is* a lady.

JOHN: This lady stuff, is that so important?

ALMA: Not to the sort of girls that you may be used to bringing to Moon Lake Casino. But suppose that some day . . . *(She crosses out of the arbor and faces away from him.)* . . . suppose that some day you—married . . . the woman that you selected to be your wife, and not only your wife but . . . the mother of your children! *(She catches her breath at the thought.)* Wouldn't you want that woman to be a lady? Wouldn't you want her to be somebody that you, as her husband, and they as her precious children—could look up to with very deep respect? (~~There is a pause.~~)

JOHN: There's other things between a man and a woman besides respect. Did you know that, Miss Alma?

ALMA: Yes. . . .

JOHN: There's such a thing as intimate relations.

ALMA: Thank you for telling me that. So plainly.

JOHN: It may strike you as unpleasant. But it does have a good deal to do with . . . connubial felicity, as you'd call it. There are some women that just give in to a man as a sort of obligation imposed on them by the . . . cruelty of nature! (~~He finishes his glass and pours another.~~) And there you are.

ALMA: There *I* am?

JOHN: I'm speaking generally.

ALMA: Oh.

(~~Hoarse shouts go up from the casino.~~)

~~JOHN.~~   ~~The cockfight has started!~~

ALMA: Since you have spoken so plainly, I'll speak plainly, too. There are some women who turn a possibly beautiful thing into something no better than the coupling of beasts! But love is what you bring to it.

JOHN: You're right about that.

ALMA: Some people bring just their bodies. But there are some people, there are some women, John . . . who can bring their hearts to it, also . . . who can bring their souls to it!

JOHN: (~~derisively~~) Souls again, huh? Those Gothic cathedrals you dream of!

(~~There is another hoarse prolonged shout from the Casino.~~)

Your name is Alma, and Alma is Spanish for soul. Some time I'd like to show you a chart of the human anatomy that I have in the office. It shows what our insides are like, and maybe you can show me where the beautiful soul is located on the chart. (~~He drains the wine bottle.~~) Let's go watch the cockfight.

ALMA: No! (~~There is a pause.~~)

JOHN: I know something else we could do. There are rooms above the casino. . . .

ALMA: (~~her back stiffening~~) I'd heard that you made suggestions like that to girls that you go out with, but I refused to believe such stories were true. What made you think I might be amenable to such a suggestion?

JOHN: I counted your pulse in the office the night you ran out because you weren't able to sleep.

ALMA: The night I was ill and went to your father for help.

JOHN: It was me you went to.

ALMA: It was your father, and you wouldn't call your father.

JOHN: Fingers frozen stiff when I—

ALMA: Oh! I want to go home. But I won't go with you. I will go in a taxi! (~~She wheels about hysterically.~~) Boy! Boy! Call a taxi!

JOHN: I'll call one for you, Miss Alma . . . Taxi! *(He goes out of the arbor.)*

ALMA: (~~wildly~~) *You're not a gentleman!*

JOHN: (~~from the darkness~~) Taxi!

ALMA: *You're not a gentleman!*
(~~As he disappears she makes a sound in her throat like a hurt animal. The light fades out of the arbor and comes up more distinctly on the stone angel of the fountain.~~)

"In a way, I liked this reading quite well. I think that you both had a feel for the characters. Joseph, the hedonism that you had in contrast to Anna's desperation about being in this situation was good. The things that were missing are relatively minor. For example, it was a little too glib, Joseph. What you do, you do partially to arouse her, to tempt her and to enjoy her shockability —which she responds to. Anna, you don't give enough time in the very beginning, when you almost have to come out of a faint. But essentially the spirit here was correct."

Joseph gives Anna a quick smile.

"Now I have taught you—or I have brought out of both of you, if you prefer—a degree of reality which is commendable. Every moment must have a reason for being there. You don't say to her, 'You know, they've got rooms upstairs,' without knowing damn well what it means, and the effect it will have on her. You know the effect, but you want to witness it. In a way, John is quite a sadist. You need to give her time to recuperate from the shock of your driving. Usually people make this trip from town in twenty-five minutes, and you made it in ten! But that's secondary. You got the devil-may-care quality of this man, and that's what's important. All in all, the general picture is essentially correct: it's a scene between a carefree guy and a neurotic woman. But the details are still not sharp enough, and you have to ask yourself what they mean to you. Do you understand?"

"Yes," Joseph says.

"Anna, this girl wants so many of the things that are associated with life, but she is constantly in conflict between her real wishes and her upbringing. I think that she's perpetually—I hate to use this word—*nostalgic* about being happy. Do you understand?"

"No," Anna says.

"If she looks through the window of her living room and sees a girl and a fellow walking down the road holding hands, it creates a great poignancy in her. You follow? She's deprived of life. She's afraid of life, but the deprivation hurts her just the same. That he brings her here to the casino, that he suggests that they go upstairs—everything he does is against her education. The point is she *wants to*, but she's *afraid*. It's tragic."

Anna nods and Meisner turns to Joseph again.

"That was all right. The liveliness of it, the ready acceptance of the facts of life—girls, cockfights and so on. It was much more relaxed emotionally, Joseph. You know, you're a different kind of actor now than you were six months ago."

"Am I? I don't know."

"You're freer."

Joseph laughs. "I hope so. I mean, that's what I'm working for."

"Emotionally freer, yet you still don't know why you say what you say at each moment. You should have both."

"Yes, I know. There were some moments I was able to work on. In others the realization isn't there yet."

"So do it again."

November 15

Joseph places two metal chairs together to form a bench on the right side of the acting area; then he and Anna, closing the door behind them, leave to prepare for the scene.

"The amplifier's not on, is it?" Meisner asks.

"No," several voices reply.

"But you can hear me anyway?"

"Yes."

"Cancer is a great thing."

"Did you say, 'Cancer is a great thing'?" Ray asks. "Why is that?"

"I can talk and I have no larynx," Meisner says, and the class laughs uneasily. "You don't see the humor in it?"

"I see the humor," Ray says, "but I missed the word 'black.' "

In a few moments the door opens, Joseph and Anna enter, and the scene begins. "I don't see why we can't go into the casino," Joseph says with a genial chuckle as if to say it would be fun, but that it's not important. "You do understand . . . you're just pretending not to," Anna says in a low, tense, breathy voice as if it were difficult for her to inhale this air. Her shoulders are wrapped in a white cotton shawl held tightly around her body more for protection than for warmth. She clutches a black leather handbag in her right hand.

"Give me one reason," Joseph says affably. "I'm a minister's daughter," Anna says softly, almost as if she were ashamed of the fact. "That's no reason," he says. "You're a *doctor*," Anna says proudly, "that's an even better reason. You can afford to be seen in such places even less than I can!" She gulps a large breath, crosses to the bench, sits, opens the handbag and reaches into it.

Their ensuing clash over the pills is surprisingly violent—her desperation is as strong as his concern—and his reading of the line "You want to turn into a dope-fiend taking this stuff?" sug-

gests that he really cares for her. The tremulous, breathy preparation Anna entered with justifies perfectly his line "Sit down
and stop swallowing air."

The shift in the conversation to the subject of the cockfight
now becomes John's way of covering up his concern for Alma.
Again his tone becomes light, slightly mocking, suggesting a
carefree quality. This mood continues into the discussion of his
proposed flight to South America. For Alma the questions she
asks suggest both her hunger for the least bit of information
about him and her irrational fear of anything foreign.

John's line defending the sensual life—he whispers the final
word, "satisfaction," seductively—prompts Alma to defend herself with the lyric speech about Gothic cathedrals. At the end, the
placing of her gloved hand on his seems accidental until, chal-
lenged, she says in a low voice with a false air of casualness,
"That's easily remedied. I'll just take the gloves off," and her need
for physical contact with him is painfully evident.

John's rejection of Alma prompts the discussion about the
desert, the "wide, wide stretches of uninhabitable ground,"
which she feels separate her from others. Perhaps it's his guilt,
perhaps his returning concern, but the questions John asks are
posed delicately, with care, as a psychiatrist might treat an especially troubled patient, until, with moving tenderness, he kisses
her. With tears in her eyes she hesitates, and these two touching
and very human characters play out the rest of the scene, moment
by moment, to its unsettling conclusion.

"Is that the end?" Meisner says after Alma's second "You're
not a gentleman!"

Anna nods and Joseph, who has left the room, returns.

"Sit down. That was good. I was thinking. There's a scene at
the end of the play where she is desperate with loneliness and
unhappiness, and is finally determined to go to him and propose
that they live together. Do you know the scene?"

"Is it in my office?" Joseph asks.

"Yes. Then finally you have to tell her the truth. She comes in because she can't stand it anymore, and she finds out that you're married. So in her pain, after she leaves—it's very moving—she goes
out and picks up a guy on the street, a traveling salesman. It's sad,

Joseph. You can do nothing for her, even though you like her."
"Yeah."
"*It might have been.* It might have been. There's something heartbreaking in that. And she makes one last desperate effort to see that tragedy doesn't happen to her. Read it. If you don't like it, do something else. If you like it, do it. Okay?"
"Okay," Joseph says.
"He's not cruel, as you'll see. He's a healthy man, and she," Meisner says, looking at Anna, who is radiant from the pleasure of having acted well, "is a pathetic old maid."
Anna laughs easily.
"Typecasting," Meisner says, and the class laughs. "You want to try it?"
"Yeah," Joseph says.
"Sure," Anna says, taking a deep breath and then letting it out slowly.

November 19

| Summer and Smoke
| part 2, scene 11

. . . *In* John*'s office* . . . John *is seated at a white enameled table examining a slide through a microscope.*

(*A bell tolls the hour of five as* Alma *comes hesitantly in. . . .*)

ALMA: No greetings? No greetings at all?
JOHN: Hello, Miss Alma.
ALMA: (~~speaking with animation to control her panic~~) How white it is here, such glacial brilliance! (~~She covers her eyes, laughing.~~)
JOHN: New equipment.
ALMA: Everything new but the chart.

JOHN: The human anatomy's always the same old thing.

ALMA: And such a tiresome one! I've been plagued with sore throats.

JOHN: Everyone has lately. These Southern homes are all improperly heated. Open grates aren't enough.

ALMA: They burn the front of you while your back is freezing!

JOHN: Then you go into another room and get chilled off.

ALMA: Yes, yes, chilled to the bone.

JOHN: But it never gets quite cold enough to convince the damn fools that a furnace is necessary, so they go on building without them.

(~~There is the sound of wind.~~)

ALMA: Such a strange afternoon.

JOHN: Is it? I haven't been out.

ALMA: The Gulf wind is blowing big, white—what do they call them? cumulus?—clouds over! Ha-ha! It seemed determined to take the plume off my hat, like that fox terrier we had once named Jacob, snatched the plume off a hat and dashed around and around the back yard with it like a trophy!

JOHN: I remember Jacob. What happened to him?

ALMA: Oh, Jacob. Jacob was such a mischievous thief. We had to send him out to some friends in the country. Yes, he ended his days as . . . a country squire! The tales of his exploits . . .

JOHN: Sit down, Miss Alma.

ALMA: If I'm not disturbing you . . . ?

JOHN: No—I called the Rectory when I heard you were sick. Your father told me you wouldn't see a doctor.

ALMA: I needed a rest, that was all . . . You were out of town, mostly. . . .

JOHN: I was mostly in Lyon, finishing up Dad's work in the fever clinic.

ALMA: Covering yourself with sudden glory!

JOHN: Redeeming myself with good works.

ALMA: It's rather late to tell you how happy I am, and also how proud. I almost feel as your father might have felt—if . . . And—are you—happy now, John?

JOHN: (uncomfortably, not looking at her) I've settled with life on fairly acceptable terms. Isn't that all a reasonable person can ask for?

ALMA: He can ask for much more than that. He can ask for the coming true of his most improbable dreams.

JOHN: It's best not to ask for too much.

ALMA: I disagree with you. I say, ask for all, but be prepared to get nothing! (She springs up and crosses to the window. She continues.) No, I haven't been well. I've thought many times of something you told me last summer, that I have a *doppelganger.* I looked that up and I found that it means another person inside me, another self, and I don't know whether to thank you or not for making me conscious of it! . . . I haven't been well. . . . For a while I thought I was dying, that that was the change that was coming.

JOHN: When did you have that feeling?

ALMA: August. September. But now the Gulf wind has blown that feeling away like a cloud of smoke, and I know now I'm not dying, that it isn't going to turn out to be that simple. . . .

JOHN: Have you been anxious about your heart again? (He retreats to a professional manner and takes out a silver watch, putting his fingers on her wrist.)

ALMA: And now the stethoscope? (He removes the stethoscope from the table and starts to loosen her jacket. She looks down at his bent head. Slowly, involuntarily, her gloved hands lift and descend on the crown of his head. He gets up awkwardly. She suddenly leans toward him and presses her mouth to his.)
Why don't you say something? Has the cat got your tongue?

JOHN: Miss Alma, what can I say?

ALMA: You've gone back to calling me "Miss Alma" again.

JOHN: We've never really got past that point with each other.

ALMA: Oh, yes, we did. We were so close that we almost breathed together!

JOHN: (*with embarrassment*). I didn't know that.

ALMA: No? Well, I did, I knew it. (*Her hand touches his face tenderly.*) You shave more carefully now? You don't have those little razor cuts on your chin that you dusted with gardenia talcum . . .

JOHN: I shave more carefully now.

ALMA: So that explains it! (*Her fingers remain on his face, moving gently up and down it like a blind person reading Braille. He is intensely embarrassed and gently removes her hands from him.*) Is it . . . impossible now?

JOHN: I don't think I know what you mean.

ALMA: You know what I mean, all right! So be honest with me. One time I said "no" to something. You may remember the time, and all that demented howling from the cockfight? But now I have changed my mind, or the girl who said "no," she doesn't exist any more, she died last summer—suffocated in smoke from something on fire inside her. No, she doesn't live now, but she left me her ring . . . You see? This one you admired, the topaz ring set in pearls. . . . And she said to me when she slipped this right on my finger—"Remember I died empty-handed, and so make sure that your hands have *something in them!*" (*She drops her gloves. She clasps his head again in her hands.*) I said, "But what about pride?" . . . She said, "Forget about pride, whenever it stands between you and what you must have!" (*He takes hold of her wrists.*) And then I said, "But what if he doesn't want me?" I don't know what she said then. I'm not sure whether she said anything or not—her lips stopped moving— yes, I think she stopped breathing! (*He gently removes her craving hands from his face.*) No? (*He shakes his head in dumb suffering.*) Then the answer is "no"!

JOHN: (*forcing himself to speak*). I have a respect for the truth, and I have a respect for you—so I'd better speak honestly if you want me to speak. (*Alma nods slightly.*) You've won the argument that we had between us.

242

ALMA: What . . . argument?
JOHN: The one about the chart.
ALMA: Oh—the chart!

(She turns from him and wanders across to the chart. She gazes up at it with closed eyes, and her hands clasped in front of her.)

JOHN: It shows that we're not a package of rose leaves, that every interior inch of us is taken up with something ugly and functional and no room seems to be left for anything else in there.
ALMA: No. . . .
JOHN: But I've come around to your way of thinking, that something else is in there, an immaterial something—as thin as smoke—which all of those ugly machines combine to produce and that's their whole reason for being. It can't be seen so it can't be shown on the chart. But it's there, just the same, and knowing it's there—why, then the whole thing—this—this unfathomable experience of ours—takes on a new value, like some . . . some wildly romantic work in a laboratory! Don't you see?

(The wind comes up very loud, almost like a choir of voices. Both of them turn slightly, Alma raising a hand to her plumed head as if she were outdoors.)

ALMA: Yes, I see! Now that you no longer want it to be otherwise, you're willing to believe that a spiritual bond can exist between us two!
JOHN: Can't you believe that I am sincere about it?
ALMA: Maybe you are. But I don't want to be talked to like some incurably sick patient you have to comfort. (A harsh and strong note comes into her voice.) Oh, I suppose I am sick, one of those weak and divided people who slip like shadows among you solid strong ones. But sometimes, out of necessity, we shadowy people take

on a strength of our own. I have that now. You needn't
try to deceive me.

JOHN: I wasn't.

ALMA: You needn't try to comfort me. I haven't come here on
any but equal terms. You said, let's talk truthfully. Well,
let's do! Unsparingly, truthfully, even shamelessly,
then! It's no longer a secret that I love you. It never was.
I loved you as long ago as the time I asked you to read the
stone angel's name with your fingers. Yes, I remember
the long afternoons of our childhood, when I had to stay
indoors to practice my music—and I heard your play-
mates calling you, "Johnny, Johnny!" How it went
through me, just to hear your name called! And how I—
rushed to the window to watch you jump the porch
railing! I stood at a distance, halfway down the block,
only to keep in sight of your torn red sweater, racing
about the vacant lot you played in. Yes, it had begun that
early, this affliction of love, and has never let go of me
since, but kept on growing. I've lived next door to you
all the days of my life, a weak and divided person who
stood. in adoring awe of your singleness, of your
strength. And that is my story! Now I wish *you* would
tell *me*—why didn't it happen between us? Why did I
fail? Why did you come almost close enough—and no
closer?

JOHN: Whenever we've gotten together, the three or four
times that we have . . .

ALMA: As few as that?

JOHN: It's only been three or four times that we've . . . come
face to face. And each of those times—we seemed to be
trying to find something in each other without knowing what it was that we wanted to find. It wasn't a body
hunger, although . . . I acted as if I thought it might be
the night I wasn't a gentleman—at the casino—it
wasn't the physical you that I really wanted!

ALMA: I know, you've already—

JOHN: You didn't have that to give me.

ALMA: Not at that time.

JOHN: You had something else to give.

ALMA: What did I have?

(~~John strikes a match. Unconsciously he holds his curved palm over the flame of the match to warm it. It is a long kitchen match and it makes a good flame. They both stare at it with a sorrowful understanding that is still perplexed. It is about to burn his fingers. She leans forward and blows it out; then she puts on her gloves.~~)

JOHN: You couldn't name it and I couldn't recognize it. I thought it was just a Puritanical ice that glittered like flame. But now I believe it *was* flame, mistaken for ice. I still don't understand it, but I know it was there, just as I know that your eyes and your voice are the two most beautiful things I've ever known—and also the warmest, although they don't seem to be set in your body at all. . . .

ALMA: You talk as if my body had ceased to exist for you, John, in spite of the fact that you've just counted my pulse. Yes, that's it! You tried to avoid it, but you've told me plainly. The tables have turned, yes, the tables have turned with a vengeance! You've come around to my old way of thinking and I to yours, like two people exchanging a call on each other at the same time, and each one finding the other one gone out, the door locked against him and no one to answer the bell! (~~She laughs.~~) I came here to tell you that being a gentleman doesn't seem so important to me any more, but you're telling me I've got to remain a lady. (~~She laughs rather violently.~~) The tables have turned with a vengeance! . . . The air here smells of ether—It's making me dizzy . . .

JOHN: I'll open a window.

ALMA: Please.

JOHN: There, now.

ALMA: Thank you, that's better. Do you remember those little

> white tablets you gave me? I've used them all up and
> I'd like to have some more.

JOHN: I'll write the prescription for you. *(He bends to write.)*

Joseph and Anna read. She is deeply prepared, weeping openly
at the beginning and throughout the scene. It is a moving performance. Joseph is stiff and uncommitted emotionally to the
material; yet it is obvious that his performance has great poten-
tial.

"What's this scene about, Joseph?"

"I'm in my office and she comes in to tell me that she's changed
her mind about being a lady, that she really wants to go to bed
with me, and I'm telling her that the human soul does exist and
that there's more to life than our physical desires."

"How do you feel about her?"

"I feel sorry for her."

"Is it a painful scene?"

"Not really, from the point of view of John. It hasn't reached
that point yet. I mean, it's hard—but I haven't really broken its
back yet."

"Knowing how you feel about her and that you are going to
marry someone else, emotionally aren't you really on her level?"

"Not really, no. There's a tremendous remorse and sadness on
John's part, but as far as what she's bringing to the work—the
crying and so forth—that's not the meaning of it for me."

"That's not the meaning of it for you?"

"No, but it's very touching. What almost was but never was.
What almost happened but never was."

"When are you going to cope with that?"

"When am I? I don't know," Joseph says and then pauses. "I
have to be honest with you. I have a hard time working off her
behavior when she's crying like that."

"Wait a minute," Meisner says. "This is a classroom."

"I understand that."

"And anything can happen in it which might not happen if
you were really onstage."

"You mean I should treat it more as if it's an exercise."

"That's right."

"I understand that, but if I were really to work off *her* behavior, *mine* would be different. It would be opposed to what I believe the scene is about. There's a lot of pain in what I have to admit to her—that I'm engaged—and if she comes in crying, my initial impulse is to put my arms around her."

"But if you hold back and just have it without actually *doing* anything about it, wouldn't it be helpful to you as an actor?"

"It would do something to me, yes."

"That's what I'm looking for."

"Okay."

"She's doing what I told her to, right?"

"I don't remember. Okay."

"She's doing what I told her to. I say you should allow the sensitive human being you are to respond to that."

"Okay."

"To throw out an example, if your best friend were in a terrible accident and you had to console his mother, who is destroyed, you'd be destroyed too, but something in you would say, 'I must try to be strong!' Don't you see?"

"Sure."

"From the point of view of treating this as an exercise, she's like the destroyed mother, and you, emotionally, are not far from where she is, but *you can't let it out!* Does that mean something to you?"

"Yes."

"It's as if you know why she's coming over to see you, and it annihilates you, but you have to contain yourself. Do you agree?"

"Sure."

"I don't want you to play this scene as it *theoretically* should be played. This is a device which will stimulate you emotionally. You know why she's coming over, and it does almost to you what it does to her, but whereas she lets it out, you try to contain it. The point is not to *play* the scene. The point is to use it as an exercise for a purpose. You understand?"

"I do."

"We are actors. We have more than one color in our personalities. You can laugh, cry, be sarcastic, be desperate—whatever. This is a classroom. Maybe you can't play the scene the way she did, but it has a value to her as an actor. You're permitting yourself to be a little too self-watchful. That's not the proper benefit to get from a class. You understand?"

"Yes."

"The difference between last class's reading and today's is enormous. What difference does it make if it's not quite right for the scene? A prizefighter with a rubber ball keeps squeezing it all the time, but he doesn't fight that way! It's to strengthen his muscles. Have I made myself clear?"

"Yes," Anna says.

"You can say to a pianist, 'That was all off when it came to interpreting the piece, but you had good octaves.' Well, gradually it all comes together. Am I making myself clear?"

"Yes," Joseph says.

"Okay. Feel free—without the book—to let it come out almost improvisationally. Do anything that will achieve your emotional freedom."

November 29

Joseph and Anna sit at the gray table. She is in the upstage position; he sits to the side giving prominence to her. The reading is quiet, yet full of exquisite emotion. There is a sense of concentration, of controlled direction to the scene. The acting is compelling. The observers forget the hardness of the metal folding chairs and the lateness of the hour. Anna is more subdued now than last week; the emotion is more controlled, bursting forth only toward the end of the scene. Joseph is quieter, more sober and reflective, feeling more deeply.

"It's coming along well," Meisner says.

"Next time should we try to incorporate some of the things that are suggested, like his taking my pulse?" Anna asks.

Meisner nods. "The guilty doctor. Start learning it now."

"Okay," Joseph says.

"Would you believe that a playwright who wrote such a lovely, lyric play as this would wind up the way he did? Well, that's *life!* But the delicacy of this is something I'm going to talk about, and . . . Well, we'll see."

December 6

Joseph sits at the gray table writing in a notebook. After a few minutes Anna enters. "No greetings?" she says. "No greetings at all?" The scene begins. Joseph is gentle, his deep voice soothing and caring. Anna seems serious and utterly desperate. On the line "I know now I'm not dying, that it isn't going to turn out to be that simple," she begins to weep. The effect is heartbreaking.

"Is it . . . impossible now?" she asks softly. And in the great speech that follows, the "topaz ring" speech in which she announces the death of her prideful former self, her voice builds in emotional intensity to the terrible conclusion, "No? Then the answer is 'no!' "

Joseph's response, that he knows now that "an immaterial something does exist in the body, is said straightforwardly, as if it were a simple truth. But she cannot be placated. "You needn't try to comfort me," she exclaims, and then proceeds to the most painful moment of the scene. "It's no longer a secret that I love you. It never was." Then come the terrible "why" questions which end the speech: "Why didn't it happen between us? Why did I fail? Why did you come almost close enough—and no closer?"

The acting of both students is full, clear, intelligent, simple and deeply felt, something like great music. On the one hand, it seems effortless; on the other, it is emotionally devastating, as if a great tragedy has just occurred. This is underscored with irony at the end of the scene. "The tables have turned with a vengeance!" Knowing that she has lost, Alma retreats with the almost casual, "Do you remember those little white tablets you gave me? I've used them all up and I'd like to have some more." "I'll write the prescription for you," Joseph says, and the scene ends.

"Is that where you end it?" Meisner asks. "It's coming very, *very* well."

"Thank you," Joseph says.

"When it's all finished I'll have a few technical things to say, but do you want to go on with it?"

They nod.

December 13

Joseph and Anna perform for the last time their scene from *Summer and Smoke*. It is well done, but her preparation is less full than the time before and the result is less heart-wrenching. Joseph has clarified his character and his feelings toward Anna, and his performance is complex and touching.

There is a long pause after the end of the scene. "Did you learn something from this?" Meisner asks finally.

"I think so," Joseph says.

"You don't want to do it anymore?"

"In one sense I would, yes, because I think it was better last time. We picked up the moments off each other"—he snaps his fingers cleanly three times—"better."

"Yes, last time was better."

"It was fuller emotionally," Joseph says.

"It's an anticlimax," Anna says.

"What?" Meisner asks.

"It feels—I don't know—unsatisfying."

"That's life," Meisner says, and the class laughs.

"Sometimes you have it and sometimes you don't," Joseph says.

"That's right. I wonder why it was better last time. Don't guess. We don't know. It's such a subtle question." Meisner pauses. "There's a scene in O'Neill's *Mourning Becomes Electra*, which starts out with the son talking to the murdered father who's in his coffin, and the sister catches him doing it. It couldn't be more different than this. Why don't you try it next time?"

"Okay," Joseph says.

"No more John and Alma?" Anna asks. "They've bit the dust?"

She seems sad, as if she were parting from someone precious to her.

"For now," Meisner says, and the class ends.

"It's time to say good-bye," Meisner says on the final day of class.

"First of all, remember that you're all young actors, and that sometimes the material you have been asked to act here was beyond you. More often, it was quite within your scope—most of it was. When that happened, you executed it well. It's when the emotional problems were deeper than you were prepared by life to realize that you were deficient. But that's not important, you know; *time* will fix that."

Ray Stanton now sits in the seat Scott Roberts once occupied. He turns up the volume on the machine that amplifies Meisner's voice.

"It's very easy to give advice, so now I'm going to tell you something that's impossible. Keep working all the time; do all kinds of plays, whether they're right for you or not, because eventually time and you will catch up with each other. One other thing: hold on to the foundation of your technique. It's *solid.*"

Meisner stands and holds up his right hand in a kind of salute. "Good-bye! I'll see you one of these days!" he says, and the students stand too, and applaud.

Acknowledgments

Basic Books, Inc., and Unwin Hyman, Ltd.: Excerpt from Sigmund Freud's essay "The Relation of the Poet to Daydreaming," published in *Collected Papers*, Vol. 4, by Sigmund Freud, authorized translation under the supervision of Joan Riviere. Published by Basic Books, Inc., by arrangement with The Hogarth Press, Ltd., and the Institute of Psychoanalysis, London. Also published in *Complete Introductory Lectures on Psychoanalysis* by Sigmund Freud, published by Unwin Hyman, Ltd. Reprinted by permission of the publishers.

Davis/Cohen Associates: A scene from *The Seagull* by Anton Chekhov, translated by Jean-Claude Van Italie. Copyright © 1974, 1977 by Jean-Claude Van Italie. First published by Harper & Row Publishers, Inc. Reprinted by permission of the author.

Grove Press, Inc., and Brandt & Brandt Literary Agents, Inc.: A scene from *Golden Boy* by Clifford Odets. Copyright 1937 by Clifford Odets. Copyright renewed 1965 by Nora Odets and Walt Whitman Odets. Reprinted by permission of Grove Press, Inc., and Brandt & Brandt Literary Agents, Inc.

Liveright Publishing Corporation and Chatto & Windus/The Hogarth Press: An excerpt from Sigmund Freud's essay "A Gen-

About the Authors

SANFORD MEISNER

As head of the acting department of The Neighborhood Playhouse for forty years, Sanford Meisner is considered one of the greatest acting teachers of our time. As a founding member of The Group Theatre, Mr. Meisner also acted in many of its stage productions, including *Awake and Sing!*, *Paradise Lost*, *An American Tragedy*, *Golden Boy* and *Crime and Punishment*. Some of the thousands of actors he has taught in his classes at The Playhouse include, among others, Elizabeth Ashley, Barbara Baxley, James Broderick, James Caan, Keir Dullea, Robert Duvall, Lee Grant, Lorne Green, Tammy Grimes, Anne Jackson, Diane Keaton, Louise Lasser, Darren McGavin, Steve McQueen, Gregory Peck, Suzanne Pleshette, Tony Randall, Jo Van Fleet, Jon Voight, Eli Wallach and Joanne Woodward.

DENNIS LONGWELL

After earning a degree in philosophy from Yale, Dennis Longwell studied acting with Sanford Meisner in the 1960s. He has also worked as an actor, teacher and museum curator. His monograph, STEICHEN: *The Master Prints, 1895–1914*, published by the Museum of Modern Art in 1978, is the definitive book on the early photographs of Edward Steichen. Mr. Longwell lives in Sag Harbor, New York, with his wife and two children, and is currently writing a biography of the American industrialist George Eastman.